As Lonely As Franz Kafka

Marthe Robert

As
Lonely
As
Franz Kafka

**Translated from the French
by Ralph Manheim**

**A Helen and Kurt Wolff Book
Harcourt Brace Jovanovich, Publishers
New York and London**

Requests for permission to make copies
of any part of the work should be mailed to:
Permissions, Harcourt Brace Jovanovich, Publishers,
757 Third Avenue, New York, N.Y. 10017

Library of Congress Cataloging in Publication Data

Robert, Marthe.
As lonely as Franz Kafka.

Translation of: Seul, comme Franz Kafka. 1979.
"A Helen and Kurt Wolff book"
Includes bibliographical references and index.
1. Kafka, Franz, 1883–1924.
2. Authors, Austrian—20th century—Biography.
I. Title.
PT2621.A26Z85313   833'.912 [B]   81-48018
ISBN 0-15-109058-0   AACR2

Printed in the United States of America

First edition

B   C   D   E

"Are you as lonely as that?" I asked.

Kafka nodded.

"Like Kaspar Hauser?"

Kafka laughed.

"Much worse than Kaspar Hauser. I'm as lonely as . . . as Franz Kafka."

Gustav Janouch,
Conversations with Kafka, p. 70.

The reason why posterity's judgment of an individual is sounder than that of his contemporaries resides in the dead man. A man does not develop in his own way until after death, when he is alone. The state of death is to an individual what Saturday night is to a chimney sweep; he washes the soot off his body. It becomes possible to see whether his contemporaries did him or he did them more harm; in the latter case, he was a great man.

Franz Kafka, "Er," in "Aufzeichnungen aus dem Jahre 1920," in *Beschreibung eines Kampfes* [Description of a Struggle], in *Gesammelte Werke*, New York: Schocken Books, 1946, p. 298. Translated for this book.

Contents

Part Two

Acknowledgments

The publishers wish to acknowledge permission to quote extensively from the following works:

The Castle
Reprinted by permission of Schocken Books Inc. from *The Castle* by Franz Kafka. Copyright © 1930, 1941, 1954 by Alfred A. Knopf, Inc. Copyright renewed © 1958 by Alfred A. Knopf, Inc.

Diaries 1910–1913
Reprinted by permission of Schocken Books Inc. from *Diaries 1910–1913* by Franz Kafka. Copyright © 1948 by Schocken Books Inc. Copyright renewed © 1975 by Schocken Books.

Diaries 1914–1923
Reprinted by permission of Schocken Books Inc. from *Diaries 1914–1923* by Franz Kafka. Copyright © 1949 by Schocken Books Inc. Copyright renewed © 1976 by Schocken Books.

Dearest Father
Reprinted by permission of Schocken Books Inc. from *Dearest Father* by Franz Kafka. Copyright © 1954 by Schocken Books.

Letters to Felice
Reprinted by permission of Schocken Books Inc. from *Letters to Felice* by Franz Kafka. Copyright © 1967, 1973 by Schocken Books.

Letters to Friends, Family and Editors
Reprinted by permission of Schocken Books Inc. from *Letters to Friends, Family and Editors* by Franz Kafka. Copyright © 1958, 1977 by Schocken Books.

Letters to Milena
Reprinted by permission of Schocken Books Inc. from *Letters to Milena* by Franz Kafka. Copyright © 1953 by Schocken Books.

Letters to Ottla
Reprinted by permission of Schocken Books Inc. Copyright © 1974, 1982 by Schocken Books.

Principal Works Cited and Abbreviations Used

(further information in acknowledgments section, pages ix–x)

WORKS BY KAFKA

Cas *The Castle*

D *Diaries 1910–1913, Diaries 1914–1923*

DF *Dearest Father*

F *Letters to Felice.* Page references are to the British (Penguin) and American (Schocken) editions, respectively.

LF *Letters to Friends, Family and Editors*

M *Letters to Milena*

O *Letters to Ottla.* The passages quoted here have been translated from the German volume *Briefe an Ottla und die Familie,* in *Gesammelte Werke* (Frankfurt, 1974)

Stories *The Complete Stories*

Tr *The Trial*

WORKS ABOUT KAFKA

B Max Brod, *Franz Kafka, A Biography*

Jan Gustav Janouch, *Conversations with Kafka,* translated by Goronwy Rees (New York: New Directions, 1971).

Symp J. Born, L. Dietz, M. Pasley, R. Rabe, and K. Wagenbach, *Kafka-Symposion,* ed. K. Wagenbach (Berlin, 1965).

W Klaus Wagenbach, *Franz Kafka: Eine Biographie seiner Jugend 1883–1912* (Bern, 1958)

(In quoting from the above translations I have occasionally made slight changes. —R.M.)

Part
One

1 · The Censored Name

One of the most striking features of Kafka's work is that though it seems to revolve around the great themes of Jewish thought and Jewish literature—exile, transgression, atonement—or, in more modern terms, guilt as associated with uprooting and persecution—not a single Jew appears in it, nor is the word "Jew" so much as uttered. True, we find occasional typically Jewish names in the novels and short stories—Raban, Blumfeld, Block, or in a pinch Samsa, though there were also Christian Samsas in Bohemia[1]—but apart from these few exceptions, the family names of Kafka's characters do not indicate their ethnic origin; some, in fact, have no name at all, a circumstance which, interpreted rather hastily as a metaphysical striving toward the impersonal, has long favored the wildest speculation. Yet Kafka's reluctance to name his characters does not follow from any set principle, and of this we find proof in certain of his early short stories whose heroes, despite their conventional German names, are as clearly characterized as those heroes of the novels most patently identified by their names (the Germanic character of Rossmann and Bendemann, for example, is indeed clearly brought out by the ending "mann," which, according to Kafka's own exegesis of the names of the characters in *The Judgment*, can connote either masculinity or humanity in the most general sense). Later on, to be sure, family names tend to give way to common nouns, sometimes designating the function performed by the main character, as in the case of the Officer, the Messenger, the Emperor, the Trapeze Artist, or the Convict; and sometimes the class of beings or things—dog, mouse, spool, or bridge—to which this character should be assigned. In the two great novels of his mature years—both posthumous and unfinished—the hero is identified only by a symbolic initial, a *K* serving as an *X*, and we do not know whether this initial is the beginning of a normal though secret name, or the last vestige of a vanished name that cannot be reconstituted. (A fact that throws ample light on the significance of his actions and of his ultimate failure is that K. is no more troubled than are the other protagonists by his lack of name and being: this anomaly reflects a state of affairs known to all, which is constantly repeated and has therefore ceased to arouse curiosity.) The two K.'s are equally deprived of the right to name themselves, but between them there is this considerable difference: the first [Joseph K.], in spite of everything, still has a first name, that is, something coming to him from his parents, which attaches him at least to his parents and the most inviolable sphere of his private life; whereas the Surveyor [in *The Castle*] no longer possesses anything making it possible to name him. (It is hard to conceive of Frieda's calling him K. at the peak of erotic ecstasy, and how would it be if he had a mother? The fact is that he has no mother.) Between *The Trial* and *The Castle*[2] the protagonist's personality disintegrated markedly; everything that in Joseph K. indicates real ties with his environment (he has an old mother, an uncle who takes an interest in his trial, a comfortable position) has been eaten away, and nothing remains but a man in the most rudimentary sense, a man truly without qualities, in whom only the ultimate essence of man survives.

The anonymity symbolized by the letter *K* does not result from any theoretical consideration. This becomes clear when we consider its variations in Kafka's work as a whole and especially its function in each particular work. Quite marked in the earliest texts—the fragments of *Description of a Struggle*

(1909), whose characters, obviously influenced by a vestige of Expressionism, are, in a manner of speaking, nothing more than agitated thoughts—the anonymity has diminished some years later in *The Judgment, The Metamorphosis,* and *Amerika,* three narratives rich in proper names—family names, or imaginary but plausible, and in any case complete, names—which would be perfectly acceptable in a conventional story. In time, to be sure, the name-sickness returns more and more alarmingly, until there remain only indefinable creatures, situated in some sort of zone between man and object, between the animate and the inanimate. But even during the time Kafka was working on *The Trial,* when anonymity seems to have become the rule for him, his notebooks show outlines in varying states of completion which surprise us not by the absence of names, but by the number and variety of names and the obvious pleasure Kafka took in creating them.[3] This profusion of proper names in texts amounting to no more than a few lines or at most a few pages makes it clear that the author of *The Trial,* far from espousing a theory of impersonal art, would have been as glad as any other novelist to "compete with the city directory," and that if he did not, it was solely because the curse attaching to his hero's birth prevented him from doing so without dishonesty.

Even in *The Trial* and *The Castle,* the two novels most often cited in this connection, the anonymity is not a legal dispensation applied to all in equal measure; it is rigorously selective, and it is just this that makes it significant: applied to some and not to others, it enables us to distinguish at a glance between the named and the unnamed. Only the hero is truly deprived of a name (and even, in the special case of the Surveyor, of a residence permit); the law to which he is subject spares the rest of the population. Since his ailment is evidently infectious, the people the action puts in contact with him—women, assistants, guards, etc.—lose their family names, but they keep their first names. Thus within the specific area of the novel, the letter *K* has primarily a functional value; it neither represents the individual aspiring to transcend his individuality, as recently contended by a metaphysical exegete; nor does it, in line with another interpretation that long enjoyed the favor of the critics, betoken the "alienation" of the individual in a modern society leveled by technology and bureaucracy; nor, finally, can it be explained in terms of any of the extraneous trends or ideas that might seem to lurk behind it. Marking by his very anonymity the inequality of condition underlying the social hierarchy constituted by the Judges and Gentlemen, K. is nothing other than the visible sign of the world's division into two conflicting spheres: the one, populous and varied, whose subjects like proper Austrians bear the names of Grubach, Huld, Titorelli, Bürgel, or Klamm; the other, consisting of just one inhabitant, where by some mysterious dispensation the most inviolable property—the *proper* name, in fact—is partly or totally done away with. Thus the discriminated name becomes the discriminator, the factor that, by acting on values and on the logical order, on series and on contents, most cogently supports the organic unity of structure and meaning.

Unlike all other known figures in novels, the typical character in Kafka—let us say K., for simplicity's sake—is without attraction of any kind, nor is he calculated to arouse interest; he is distinguished by no winning trait, by no psychological subtlety, by no faculty for inspiring passions and ideas; this denuding is deliberate. Lacking most of the characteristics that ordinarily attach to the fictitious characters of novels, without distinctive physical traits or moral qualities, he fascinates solely by the inexplicable gaps in his characterization, which makes him not an identified person but an obsessive enigma, hence a constant stimulant to thought. Who is this man so ill-equipped for the role of hero? Why does he fall from God knows where into a story situated beyond space and time? What is it that obliges him to vegetate on the lowest level of life, now as a dog, now as a mouse, a monkey, a monstrous insect, or as a broken spool named Odradek? Has he a model in reality, and if not, from what fund of experience, memory, or dream has he been drawn? Finally, how is he related to the man who created him? As closely as the initial designating him suggests? Here, of course, the text itself tells us nothing; luckily, however, Kafka broaches the question in his private writings—infrequently, to be sure, but with such precision that the genesis of his work ceases to be an object of speculation.

The most general indication of the origin of Kafka's character is provided by a note in the *Diaries* entry for 6 August 1914, a date marking the inception of a highly productive period: "My talent for portraying my dreamlike inner life has thrust all other matters into the background; my life has dwindled dreadfully. . . ."[4] Thus, according to him, his novels and short stories have their source exclusively in his inner life, in pure subjectivity; the "he" they introduce is never anyone but the "I" of a waking dream, a schematic "I," projected into an experimental space where the author's self, stripped of its social appearances and accessory qualities, is reduced to the essence of his situation. As early as 1913 Kafka noted how closely this supposedly objective "he" was bound up with his inner states and even with the dates and events of his life. In analyzing the proper names in *The Judgment*:[5] "Georg has the same number of letters as Franz. In Bendemann, 'mann' is a strengthening of 'Bende' to provide for all the as yet unforeseen possibilities of the story. But Bende has exactly the same number of letters as Kafka and the vowel occurs in the same places as does the vowel in Kafka. Frieda has as many letters as F. [Felice] and the same initial, 'Brandenfeld' has the same initial as B. [Bauer] and in the word 'Feld' a certain connection in meaning. Perhaps even the thought of Berlin was not without influence and recollection of the March of Brandenburg may have had some influence."[6]

The next day, after reading *The Judgment* to a small circle of friends and members of his family, he noted an observation of his sister's about the concordance of places: "My sister said: 'It is our house.' I was astonished at how mistaken she was in the layout and said: 'In that case, Father would have to be living in the toilet.' "[7] A few months later, at a particularly critical moment in his relations with Felice, he came back to this unsuspected tie between fiction and reality and more specifically to the sort of prophecy that the fiction suggested to him: "Conclusion for my case from *The Judgment*. I am indirectly indebted to her for the story. But Georg goes to pieces because of his fiancée."[8] Similarly, in connection with *The Metamorphosis*, he says to Janouch, who, on the strength of the obvious similarity in names, identified him rather naïvely with his gigantic bug: "Samsa is not purely and simply Kafka. *The Metamorphosis* is not a confession, though it is in a way an indiscretion." And when Janouch remained puzzled: "Do you think it's discreet and elegant to speak of bedbugs in one's own family?"[9] Naturally Joseph K. is not totally Kafka, either, but only in the essential, as an indiscreet witness to the painful family affair that constantly obliges Kafka to put himself on trial. That is why, in the famous letter he wrote to his father at the age of thirty-six—in order, as he said, "to make living and dying easier for both of us"—he cites Joseph K. in support of his demonstration: ". . . one day I wrote very correctly about someone: 'He is afraid the shame will outlive him,' "[10] as if in this case the hero were not just a figure emanating from his anxiety, but the most trustworthy part of himself, in a sense the most reliable witness in his favor.

By interpreting his work as a purely subjective view of his situation with regard to society, and by demonstrating any number of times that his heroes have no other source than himself, Kafka provides the key to the truncated name whose fate is shared by K. and all his avatars; for if in his novels he is speaking only of himself and his inability to live,[11] the missing name can only be his own, and since he was a Jew, it was his own name, his Jewish name, that he was relegating to an underground existence. Of course an attitude that at first sight seems so negative gives one food for thought, but before looking into its causes and attempting to judge it—which is precisely the aim of the present essay—we must observe that in omitting his name from these works, Kafka was first of all acknowledging a simple fact of experience, which, though sadly commonplace, gains poignancy from the fact that propriety prevented him from stating it: to wit, that in the society where his birth placed him without entitling him to call himself at home in it, the individual named Kafka was only half *presentable*, if at all.

Of this Kafka could be made aware at any time or place, whenever he emerged from his immediate family circle—at a hotel, at a boardinghouse, or among the patients at the sanatorium where he tried in vain to regain his health. Everywhere he was exposed to the same sort of snub that he suffered from the woman who sat next to him at table at the Tatranské-Matliary sanatorium; everywhere he was put in a position to cry out, as he does in a letter to his sister Ottla, "How wretched that one can never fully introduce oneself right away."[12] That is indeed the crux: he could not fully establish his identity, because he could not express all the overtones, all the social and historical implications, all the mental reservations, with which a Jewish name is charged, in the minds of others and of the bearer as well. Nor, on the other hand, was it possible to conceal this identity entirely; like it or not, he was obliged to let it *betray* itself—and that is just what K. does by revealing the one letter of his name that he wishes, or is able, to reveal. And even though this betrayal is ineluctable, even though it is imposed and not a matter of deliberate choice, it is nonetheless an ineradicable fault, the first of those which condemn K., though innocent, before his trial has even begun.

Justified by a well-defined situation of which it is a perfectly appropriate expression, the name taboo is further justified beyond space and time, since it is rooted in the most ancient tradition. Undoubtedly it harks back to the Jewish taboo against pronouncing the divine name. To be sure, the newer taboo is no longer concerned with the God of the Jews, but with the Jewish individual—which bears witness to the taboo's mysterious power of survival, yet also to the enormous historical changes that have gradually corrupted, not to say reversed, its meaning. Formerly the name of God was sacred and for that very reason taboo; but precisely by virtue of this name that was kept secret, every Jew knew who He was; today Kafka observes that in the diaspora of his time, at least as he knew it in the part of Central Europe where he was born, the divine name and the human name fell under the same interdict, so that the Jewish condition in its entirety—religion, thought, tradition, but also the daily vicissitudes of public and private life—was relegated to the twilight of clandestinity. By an unintended consequence of religious thinking, the commandment designed to draw a sharp dividing line between the earthly and the divine now hurled the Jews pell-mell into the obscure depths of language, where *what is not said* is associated with the shady and suspect. Voided of its content and radically perverted, the unsaid passed from the divine to the diabolical. No longer a sign of recognition, it leads the entire people to dissolve itself in the nameless—in other words, to deny itself. The fact is that for Kafka and for the people he saw around him in Prague, the essential was no longer to keep the name of God silent but, rather, to hide one's own, to change it, to adapt it to the linguistic environment, or at the very least not to utter it needlessly. Now misconstrued, by the faithful in whom religious scruple had given way to shame and by the indifferent or hostile who were at pains to parody it, the name taboo, which was formerly the surest pledge of Jewish existence, had lost all content.

The system of negative naming in which Kafka imitated the immemorial taboo was not, however, devised for purely satirical ends, or if it was, the satire had the unusual quality of being directed primarily against its author, who was the first to condemn himself as a gravely discredited witness. A victim, to be sure, but also co-responsible for his false position toward both his Jewish heritage and non-Jewish society, Kafka was not satisfied with observing and judging a state of affairs; he was also determined to implicate himself, to get to the bottom of his particular case, to unmask all the pitiful pretense involved in his seemingly normal attitude.

His case was typical, in that it presented, in a highly concentrated form, all the contradictions, uncertainties, and miseries of his generation.[13] The son of a prosperous self-made businessman, he grew up in a family that was half-assimilated, half-Germanized, vaguely traditionalist, and more conformist than religious. His parents wanted their children, especially their eldest son, to enjoy the middle-class security and social position that they themselves had lacked. Thus, though strongly attached to their Jewish origins, they transmitted a bloodless Judaism, devoid of substance and meaning.

Like most Jewish fathers concerned for the future of their children, Hermann Kafka, who spoke Czech in his native village, was determined to give his son a German education, for he was well aware that in Prague no social or professional advancement was possible unless one spoke the language of the ruling classes. Because of this education, customary in the Jewish bourgeoisie of Prague, most of whom looked on this sort of opportunism as a virtue, Kafka was torn from the start between diametrically contrary currents. On the one hand, the German language committed him to a foreign culture; on the other hand, his father kept trying to force him back into a mode of life known to him only through a scattering of poorly preserved vestiges. This, he believed, was what gave rise to his "infinite" sense of guilt. "As a child," he wrote to his father, "I reproached myself, in agreement with you, for not going to the synagogue often enough, for not fasting, etc. In this I thought I was doing a wrong not to myself, but to you, and I was assailed by a sense of guilt which was of course always ready at hand."[14] In his adolescence he hastened to solve the dilemma by turning his back on a "phantom of Judaism" which struck him as barbarous and useless: "I failed to see how one could do anything better with such material than get rid of it as fast as possible; indeed, getting rid of it struck me as the most pious of actions."[15] Throughout his student years and well beyond, the problem does not seem to have troubled him; at least he had sufficiently forgotten or repressed it to suppose that it was solved.

As long as he closed his eyes to the constant anti-Semitic disorders that shook Prague and the cities of Bohemia at the turn of the century[16]—and everything we know of his youth suggests that he did just this—he was able to believe that he almost resembled his fellow students and fraternity brothers at the German University of Prague.[17] And since the demon of literature already had a firm hold on him—actually, he had always written—he could also believe himself destined to become a German writer on a par with other German writers, in possession of a respected language and revered masters, if not of a soil and a history that truly belonged to him. What was Jerusalem to him? He sought the Promised Land in Weimar, and Goethe was his Bible. In the cultural sphere Judaism had nothing to offer him, for he did not speak Yiddish and knew no Hebrew. Consequently he had no difficulty in dismissing the odd scraps of Jewish lore that he had acquired at home as barbarous and unintelligible relics.

Thus until the onset of 1911, when, under the influence of various outward and subjective developments, he began to take a certain interest in his own Jewish question, Kafka did not differ essentially from the other Jews of his Prague milieu, a milieu which, however, inspired him with loathing and an intense desire to get away (it was there that he formed his picture of the Western Jew of whom he would speak so harshly later on). In his daily life he behaved pretty much like those around him; though he did not openly deny his origins or the name that bore witness to them, he preferred to pass them over in silence and mentioned them only when necessary. Regardless of whether this nondeclaration was due to shame, timidity, dread of embarrassing scenes, or simply a desire not to be bothered, he could not dispel the secret feeling that it was indeed a disavowal, and this in turn gave rise to equally secret feelings of shame and anguish, fear of other people, and guilt. Because he had made it his implicit rule to live "as if" he were not a Jew, he felt ashamed and guilty toward all: toward Christians because he was a Jew; toward his own conscience because he was not a Jew, or, what amounts to the same thing, because he was at bottom only half a Jew. Guilty toward non-Jews, whom he puzzled and deceived with his hypocritical discretion, he also sinned gravely against Judaism, which he betrayed at every moment by neglecting to profess it, though lacking the courage to break with it altogether. This twofold fault was the direct source of the guilt *without a crime* that led Joseph K. to destruction *without a judgment*. As inwardly irrefutable as it was outwardly undemonstrable, this fault functioned automatically, and automatically entailed punishment, in accordance with a mechanism upon which the arguments of law have no more effect than do those of reason.

The trial of K. would obviously be very much simplified if Kafka had had the choice between two clear-cut attitudes—between, say, total assimilation and return without reservations to the Judaism of his ancestors—but he did not have such a choice, and this he showed precisely by peopling his books with hybrid creatures that defy identification. Far from marking a purely negative decision, his censoring of the name "Jew" indicates his complex mixture of feelings; he did not know which was stronger, shame or respect, love or hate, pride in his race or humiliated self-esteem. But though not without mixed feelings, he came in time, remote as he was from the Jewish community, to realize that he was Jewish even in his way of not being Jewish, even in his eccentricity and the constant confusion of his thoughts.

By a paradox inherent in his at once commonplace and unique situation—objectively commonplace but unique in the way he experienced it—what he had in common with the Jews was incapable of bringing him closer to their mode of life, but what kept him away from them was at the same time the strongest and most authentic of ties. The common heritage of the Jews—race, history, religion—is the cause of their exile and dispersion, whereas this dispersion and an infinite diversity of interests, being the lot of the entire people, form a mysterious bond between separate individuals. Once the absolutely insurmountable nature of this contradiction was revealed to Kafka—rather late, as we shall see below—he could no longer escape the necessity of living and thinking it to the full, even at the risk of making matters worse. That is the reason for the "investigations" he carried on almost at the end of his life through the intermediary of the intellectual Dog, amateur philosopher and incorrigible questioner who, in this exceedingly complicated matter, is undoubtedly his authorized spokesman.

The date of *Investigations of a Dog*[18] and the circumstances under which it was written provide good reason for assuming that its hero was really speaking in the name of the author. Written in a quarto notebook—known as the Brown Notebook—containing texts written in 1922, this story, untitled and unfinished, or perhaps merely abandoned because Kafka could think of no way to end it, was almost certainly written in the summer of that year, when, unable to go on with *The Castle*, he feared that his inspiration was drying up.[19] At the very start of the Brown Notebook he had written: "Literary creation evades me. Hence my plan for autobiographical investigations. This is no biography, but a search for, and discovery of, the minutest elements."[20] This is soon followed by a fragmentary dog story, quite possibly a first version of *Investigations*, and then comes *Investigations* itself, the content of which corresponds exactly to the above-mentioned autobiographical investigation. Moreover, the disabused old dog whom Kafka has investigating his own life bears the mark of that painful moment in his author's life: he tells us at the very start that his investigations have had no other result than to isolate him from all and drive him to despair, and that he has therefore had to abandon them.

If the autobiographical character of this story were not proved by the documents at our disposal, we could easily infer it from Kafka's special way of treating everyday words and phrases so as to bring out their hidden implications. "Dog," as we know, is a traditional anti-Semitic epithet. Taking the insult literally, Kafka places it in a logical situation that reveals the infinite stupidity of the word and, at the same time, its bitter consequences for the insulted individual. To make matters worse, the insult is not only used by the enemy, but also has currency within the family circle. At the time of Kafka's friendship with Isak Löwy, director of the Yiddish Theater troupe that played so large a part in his development, his father, who despised and loathed Eastern Jews, said to him: "He who lies down with dogs gets up with fleas." This brutal attack on his friend drove Kafka half-mad.[21] But he took his revenge immediately—and punished himself for it: in his art of the instantaneous the two impulses are always connected—by changing the verb "get" to the verb "be," the outcome being two pseudo proverbs, variants of the popular maxim, the one saying roughly, "He who gets fleas is himself a flea," and the other, "He who sleeps with dogs is himself a dog."[22] The first is the starting point of *The Metamorphosis*, whose hero wakes up one morning transformed into an enormous insect of undefined species, but undoubtedly a parasite.[23] The other inspired first the end of *The Trial*, where Joseph K. sees himself dying "like a dog"; and then years later the story about the intellectual dog who finds himself alone in the world after his intransigence and the importunity of his endless questions have cut him off from society.

In any case, the metaphor condenses into a single image the many associations of ideas suggested by the common anti-Semitic insult and by the outrageous phrase which Kafka's father had borrowed from the enemy and which drove his son out of the family circle; taken literally and set in motion, the image instantly (in line with the "no sooner said than done" principle at the base of all enchantment in dreams and fairy tales) fulfills the wish implicit in the expression. Since in Kafka metamorphosis is always *animated metaphor*, it requires no complicated operations, but need only exploit the large selection of pseudo reasonings provided by rhetoric and grammar. If, for example, a Jew is a dog, then the Dog is a Jew; there is no grammatical objection to this second proposition, but since its absurdity is self-evident, while the first proposition passes for plausible, it glaringly exposes the absurdity of the insult.

Thus the Dog is a Jew; an inquiring intellectual, he is also the representative of his author, who by nature and necessity is also a specialist on questions that should not be asked. He is the double, denatured but recognizable by his makeup, whom Kafka created for the requirements of his "autobiographical inquiry"—the inquiry that guided his entire work, but that seemed to him more necessary than ever in the year 1922, when, to understand and if possible surmount his inability to write, he looked into his own past. Thus the Dog's reflections on his canine condition are in no sense a fable; they deal with a concrete reality, meticulously observed from within by a desperate but lucid man whose determination to know far exceeded any desire to spare himself or to display allegiance to any cause, even the cause to which he was most irrevocably bound.

From the very start the Dog sees to it that the reader knows what to make of his meditations: "When I think back and recall the time when I was still a member of the canine community, sharing in all its preoccupations, a dog among dogs, I find on closer examination that from the very beginning I sensed some discrepancy, some little maladjustment, causing a slight feeling of discomfort which not even the most decorous public functions could eliminate; more, that sometimes, no, not sometimes, but very often, the mere look of some fellow dog of my own circle that I was fond of, the mere look of him, as if I had just caught it for the first time, would fill me with helpless embarrassment and fear, even with despair."[24] Here the word "Jew" crowds in on the text so irresistibly that one has the greatest difficulty in keeping it out. *Yet it must not intrude on the text,* for it would tend to restore the situation to the realm of generalities, where all the possible solutions are already at hand, so that the Dog's investigations would be quite superfluous.[25] The word "Jew" is charged with so powerful a dynamic only because it is continually repressed: it is the implication to which the story's many meanings all relate, those one thinks one knows and the far more numerous ones to which nothing known should point. Once stated, it inevitably enters into the area of moral, philosophical, political, or religious explanations, all of which presuppose an a priori judgment—literally, a prejudice. (One such area would be Zionism, as in the H. Bergmann article previously cited; another would be Jewish self-hatred, or Jewish anti-Semitism, two possible keys in certain respects, but quite useless when it comes to explaining the mass of ideas, emotions, and anguished questions that drove Kafka to write the story.)

In suggesting but never uttering the implied word, *Investigations of a Dog* is perfectly clear but achieves a depth that would necessarily be lost in direct statement. Witness the following passage, in which the narrator invokes his observations concerning the relations between the members of his race on the one hand and the other peoples of the earth on the other. "For it should not be supposed that, for all my peculiarities, which lie open to the day, I am so very different from the rest of my species. Indeed when I reflect on it—and I have time and disposition and capacity enough for that—I see that dogdom is in every way a marvelous institution. Apart from us dogs there are all sorts of creatures in the world, wretched, limited, dumb creatures who have no language but mechanical cries; many of us dogs study them, have given them names, try to help them, educate them, uplift them, and so on. For my part I am quite indifferent to them except when they disturb me, I confuse them with one another."[26] Here again the Dog's words would be no clearer if he cast off his borrowed personality; they are indeed so clear as to become frankly *cynical* (the whole story, it might be said, is a play on the current sense of this word and its etymological sense—i.e., "doglike").

For in the Dog's opinion the canine nation is superior to those that inhabit the rest of the world; dogs alone can boast a civilization. The other peoples are only poor brutes without language, name, or history, who, left to their own resources, would be condemned to vegetate without culture or thought of any kind. On the subject of these benighted creatures the Dog, who otherwise lays great stress on his uniqueness, fully shares the presumptuous opinion of his congeners; in fact he surpasses them in egoism and pride, for many dogs, aware that their superiority implies an obligation, try to help the inferior races to become civilized, whereas he, "solitary and with-drawn, with nothing to occupy me save my hopeless, but as far as I am concerned, indispensable little investigations," feels only utter indifference toward them and cynically exempts himself from the obligation to contribute to the advancement of all living creatures. Though owing his name and condition to an ignominious insult, he transforms the insult into a claim to superiority, from which, however, he does not derive a sense of duty toward other creatures; he simply ignores these others, and though on occasion he may be troubled by the thought of their obscure existence, they are so small and he towers so high above them that it doesn't so much as occur to him that they could *persecute* him. For in this story the old question of the chosen people and the Gentiles is never raised; the Dog is interested only in dogs and in the great family quarrel that, according to him, can be understood and settled only among dogs, in this respect for once the sole masters of their fate.[27]

Excluding the Gentiles from his field of vision, the Dog is able to concentrate entirely on the functioning of his society, to which he still feels attached, though in his contemplative retreat he regards it with the cold eye of a foreigner. Thanks to this neutral interest, he discovers an aspect of things that his busy congeners, harried by work and worry, have neither the time nor the will nor the means of contemplating. His first dis-covery relates to two marked tendencies which drive them, un-beknownst to themselves, in two opposite directions: "One can safely say that we live together in a literal heap, all of us, dif-ferent as we are from one another by reason of numerous and profound modifications which have arisen in the course of time. All in one heap! We are drawn to each other and nothing can prevent us from satisfying that communal impulse; all our laws and institutions, the few that I still know and the many that I have forgotten, go back to this longing for the greatest bliss we are capable of, the warm comfort of being together. But now consider the other side of the picture. No creatures to my knowledge live in such wide dispersion as we dogs, none have so many distinctions of class, of kind, of occupation. . . ."[28] But the Dog has noticed that his fellow dogs are tacitly agreed never to speak of this fundamental contradiction in their canine life—an irrepressible need to be together and a no less irresistible tendency toward dispersion; a longing for community and boundless individualism—and since this taboo is observed by all, it further contributes to strengthen the ties between them. But how, then, does it happen that he, a normal dog in spite of everything, is alone in transgressing this taboo by molesting everyone with questions concerning just this forbidden matter? "Why," he wonders, "do I not do as the others: live in harmony with my people and accept in silence whatever troubles this harmony, ignoring it as a small error in the great account, always keeping in mind the things that bind us happily together, not those that drive us again and again, as though by sheer force, out of our social circle?"[29] The Dog doesn't know exactly why his people pass these "difficult matters" over in silence; nor does he know why he, for his part, is so intent on getting them to speak. A long life of inquiry has simply taught him that he could not have done otherwise, and he therefore has no cause for regrets, not even in the depths of the exile to which he is irrevocably relegated for having observed his people too closely.

Expelled from the group for his eccentricities and the importunity of his "hopeless little investigations," solitary by choice and necessity but in despair at having no part in the warmth of spontaneous Jewish life, Kafka, like the Dog, built his work around the "difficult matters" to which he committed himself body and soul at the risk of grieving or scandalizing his fellows; just like the Dog, he lived outside the community, yet without becoming wholly unfaithful to his race, without abjuring it; and, again like the Dog, he was able to console himself for this half-voluntary, half-forced exclusion by telling himself that in spite of everything he had never lost sight of his people: though he had gone away from them, he had not forgotten them, and had occasionally "given them reports" of himself.[30]

The Dog's ideas about his congeners and his odd relations with them are so manifestly those of Kafka himself that they might just as well have figured in his *Diaries* along with what he noted directly about himself over the years. Why then did he attribute them to a fabulous animal, why this complication of a pseudo fantasy, which merely postponed the moment when their source would be identified? The fact is that the Dog has nothing in common with a character in a fairy tale or a morality. Kafka did not use the Dog to disorient the reader and so lead him to accept statements that might otherwise shock him. The Dog was absolutely necessary to him because, thanks to the abundant images associated with his name, the Dog enabled him to explore all possible outcomes, all possible interpretations of his situation which he had not yet discovered and which, out of shame, diffidence, or pusillanimity, he preferred not to envisage. But however vast, the range of ideas opened up by a single metaphor is never vast enough to exhaust a problem. The fable is always unfinished and must always be begun anew.

Consequently the Dog's thoughts cannot simply be assimilated to those that Kafka records in his *Diaries* and personal papers. To appraise the autobiographical content of the story, one would first have to analyze the story in detail; then one would have to compare it with the many stories that obviously play on the same theme—for example, *The Great Wall of China*, where the Jews are represented as Chinese, probably because of the antiquity of their culture and the intellectual hairsplitting, the *"chinoiserie,"* for which they are often criticized; or *Josephine the Singer*, another fable in which they are changed into mice on the strength of an analogy based, no doubt, on the fecundity of these detested and mercilessly harried beasts.

Such comparison is necessary because Kafka's figures, most of them engendered by figures of speech, are interrelated, complementing or contradicting one another as though they pursued the same aim under divers masks and in a wide variety of settings and would yield their ultimate meaning only when taken together. Dog, Chinese, or mouse, not one of these images can stand by itself; not one reveals the last word; each can be rectified by the one preceding or following it; and all are needed to reveal, not of course the one truth, but the fetishist power of the truths and untruths purveyed by everyday language.

Conscious of his superiority, the Dog relegates to outer darkness the "wretched creatures" who carry on an obscure existence on the fringes of civilized society, and obviously the Chinese feels vastly superior to the Barbarians of the North, who threaten his country's civilization and against whom the Great Wall is supposed to protect him. But this tells us nothing about the author's personal attitude, for the arrogance displayed here is severely punished elsewhere, in the story of Josephine, for example, where Dog and Chinese, transformed into mice, become poor persecuted creatures, with no other title to greatness than the continuity of their historical existence and no other virtue than their collective courage. Thus each of Kafka's figures is rectified not only in his own setting, by being seen from different angles, but also through Kafka's work as a whole, which though fragmentary and unfinished derives its incomparable unity from the sum of this correction and compensation.

Since the stories are constructed in such a way that no formula can sum up their content, the Jewish question nowhere finds a *literary* solution; since it is in every case treated partially through a partial hero, one can approach it only by a painstaking inventory of all Kafka's images and their correctives; for in this organism conceived by a mind perpetually on the alert, struggling at one and the same time against collective opinions and against its own inertia, no image is true in itself; all are false, and all contribute to the truth insofar as they expose one another's share of error and illusion. But illuminating as it may be with regard to the essential, such an inventory tells us nothing about the way in which the question was experienced on the *human* plane by a man having, like all men, his passions and his tastes, his more or less rigid opinions, his enthusiasms and prejudices. Thus in the last analysis it is in Kafka's life, or, rather, in the written traces of it that have been preserved, that we must look if we wish to discover what part of his own experience Kafka put into his literary work, not in order to give us an allusive autobiography, but in order to subject his life and experience to the consuming fire of an uncompromising intelligence.

The autobiographical notations scattered through his *Diaries*, letters, and various notebooks, all of which, it should not be forgotten, he intended to burn or to have burned, are the only testimony on our question that there is no good reason to doubt. They are virtually the only evidence I shall invoke in this essay (apart, of course, from extrinsic testimony or works, which throw light on Kafka's statements and above all enable us to date them). Since Kafka's own words are the critic's only safeguard against more or less tendentious hypotheses and glosses, they can never be examined too closely; they must therefore be collated, compared with one another and sometimes with literary variations on the same theme—in short, put back into the vast complex of ideas, emotions, and experiences that under definite historical circumstances led and sometimes forced the author to note them. Then and then alone we may be able to discover why Kafka felt obliged to censor the name "Jew" in his work, and why it is precisely in Kafka that this mysteriously suppressed name finds the contemporary genius most worthy to glorify it.

2 · The Identity Crisis

If Kafka had wished to warn his future critics of the grave mistake it would be to judge him on the basis of generalizations—though, given his determination to destroy his work, he obviously had no such thought—he could have done nothing better than to copy out for them a short passage in his correspondence with Felice Bauer which, though hastily jotted on a mere postcard, was obviously the result of careful thought. On 7 October 1916 he wrote in connection with two critical essays about him: "And incidentally, won't you tell me who I really am; in the last *Neue Rundschau, The Metamorphosis* is mentioned and rejected on sensible grounds, and then the writer says: 'There is something fundamentally German about K's narrative art.' In Max's article, on the other hand: 'K's stories are among the most typically Jewish documents of our time.' A difficult case. Am I a circus rider on two horses? Alas, I am no rider. I lie prostrate on the ground."[1] Though indirect, the warning is clear, especially if we relate it to the exact content of the two articles taken as its pretext. In an essay entitled "Imagination," Robert Müller, the critic of *Die Neue Rundschau*, writes without batting an eye: "Kafka's narrative art . . . has something fundamentally German about it, something wise in a sense that does him honor, with narrative traits that recall the Meistersinger,* but it's spoiled by the hypothetical

* The Meistersinger were a fraternity of musicians and poets, largely from the artisan and trading classes, active in Germany from the fourteenth through the sixteenth century. —ED.

23

patchwork that deforms his fine objective garment."[2] As for Max Brod, he expresses himself every bit as categorically: "Though the word 'Jew' never appears in his works, they are among the most Jewish documents of our time."[3] Thus, faced with two radically opposed opinions, one emanating from a close friend, the other from a source that was in every respect alien, Kafka declares himself unable to give his own. Associated by Müller with a fundamentally German and moreover archaistic (the Meistersinger!) brand of literature, and placed by Max Brod in the forefront of militant Judaism, he could not say who he was; he knew only that, unable either to opt for one of the two mounts supposedly available to him, or to ride both horses, the German and the Jewish, properly together, he had no choice but to stay on the ground or to be continually thrown.[4]

Even if we take account of his usual strategy in dealing with Felice—once again he was trying to prove to her that she underestimated his eccentricity, which would expose her to grave dangers if they married—there is something disconcerting about this profession of neutrality; one would at least expect Kafka to draw a distinction between Brod, his long-time friend, confidant, and fervent admirer, who seems to be stating the obvious, and the German critic, whose judgment, in the eyes of any modern reader, is surely the height of absurdity.[5] It seems to us that Brod, who had the advantage over other contemporary critics of knowing most of his friend's unpublished writings—who, for example, had read *The Trial* in manuscript—was simply talking the language of common sense, whereas the idea of assimilating *The Metamorphosis* into the Gothic art of the German Middle Ages is pure extravagance. (True, we have seen worse since then, but the more recent extravagance would not reverse the direction of history; rather, it would take off from the avant-garde and simply ignore the whole German literary tradition—as manifested in Kleist, for example—of which Kafka in his way was an authentic representative.) But Kafka does not say a word to confirm or even to refute his friend's contention, and except for the reproach of "patchwork," which with his usual willingness to accept negative criticism he was only too glad to mention, he says nothing about this strange medieval *Metamorphosis* that the German critic attributed to him. Actually, despite the almost grotesque contradiction between the two writers, their judgments have one thing in common: they solve the problem before looking into it, which is one way of sidestepping it. And to these peremptory judgments which dispose of the problem with conventional formulas—"fundamentally German" and "among the most Jewish documents of our time"—Kafka offers no objection whatever; his only response, his only way of defending his truth against premature conclusions, is a perplexed question.

Already remarkable in itself, the "Who am I?" with which Kafka deflates the sublime assurance of his two critics—actually, his whole work begins and ends with this unspoken question—takes on added meaning when placed in its chronological and emotional context. In September 1916 Kafka, who had become re-engaged to Felice some months before and was writing to her almost every day, urged her to go to work as a teacher and social worker at the Jewish Home in Berlin, an institution founded by wealthy Berlin Jews to lodge and educate Jewish refugee children from the East. After turning a deaf ear for some time, Felice finally acceded, and from that moment on Kafka devoted a considerable part of his letters to her work and to the difficult problems that kept coming up. He gave her advice about her reading and about preparing her lessons, theorized about teaching methods (analyzing and criticizing at length a pedagogical work by [Friedrich Wilhelm] Foerster), sought out books for the children, and went so far as to buy and pay for certain books that he thought they should read—in short, he took so passionate an interest in this typically Jewish undertaking that Felice could hardly have suspected him of mixed feelings. She was bound to assume that his sentiments were similar to hers or perhaps even stronger.

The point is far from negligible because, after the dramatic breaking-off of their engagement in 1914 and all manner of misunderstandings and conflicts, the two young people finally decided to marry once the war was over. It was therefore essential that they agree about Judaism, but Felice, who had plenty of other things to worry about, had no doubt that she could rest easy on that score.[6] Knowing that her work with the children brought her closer to her fiancé (he told her as much: "It's the Home that brings us so close") she tended to forget his "eccentricity." Kafka sensed that this blindness was fraught with complications for their future together, and felt obliged once again to correct it. Hence his postcard of 7 October 1916 and the lesson he entrusted to it, not between the lines but made quite clear by the order in which he expressed his thoughts. First he asked eagerly for news of the Home ("the best" news, he said, that he could receive from Berlin at that time), and then without transition flung his untimely "Who am I?" designed to re-establish the old distance between them.

We do not know how Felice interpreted the question, whether she took it seriously or regarded it merely as one more eccentricity among the many to which she had to accustom herself. But that is of little importance, for the question was not really addressed to her; Kafka asked it only to put her on her guard against a misunderstanding that he was afraid he had provoked. Though it was true that he loved the little refugees in Berlin and expected a good deal from their influence on Felice; though it was true that in this matter, as in many others, he gave substantial proof of his sense of solidarity with the Jewish people, it by no means followed that he was a Jew in the sense she instinctively supposed and Brod had felt justified in proclaiming him to be. All her inferences on this score would be mistaken (just as she was gravely mistaken if from his letters she inferred "a bent for writing")[7]; nor, however (and this was perhaps even worse for the Berliner she was in part), could he claim to be a German, and she would be making a big mistake if she likened him in that respect to the Jewish writers, in Berlin or elsewhere, whose poems and novels she read. Altogether, he was none of the things she could imagine, and for that reason the question had to remain in suspense, as befitted the murky regions of the inner Diaspora, through which he wandered alone.

Strictly speaking, this "Who am I?" into which Kafka put the whole of his existential anguish is addressed not only to Max Brod, to Felice, and to other close friends, but also to all the readers and critics who, ever since readers and critics began to interpret his work, have been inclined to judge his baffling case by the norms of some particular system of thought. If one attempts to deal with him from the standpoint of a theologian, of a philosopher, or even of a literary critic, it turns out that Kafka is never where the concepts want him to be; he never quite corresponds to one's view of his interests and aims, especially not in the realm, so inadequately described, of his relations with Judaism and the Jews, where every writer tends to appropriate him, or at least to define him according to the writer's own requirements. Assimilated Jew, anti-Jewish Jew, anti-Zionist, Zionist, believer, atheist—Kafka was indeed all of these at different times in his development, sometimes all at once (he wrote *Investigations of a Dog* in 1922, at a time when he had *almost* become a militant Zionist); but none of these characterizations throws the least light on the underlying reasons for his struggle or the form it took, or explains how it was possible for the pathological indecision of a constantly torn man to give rise to the most rigorous modern art, the only art, perhaps, in which modernity and rigor have really been combined.

Condemned by an incurable wound to what in *The Trial* he calls "unlimited procrastination," but as clearsighted as any man could bear to be, Kafka undertook, not, like so many of those around him, to resolve his conflicts through an immediately available expedient, but to look these contradictions squarely in the face and think them through, so as to be sure of not misunderstanding them, evading them, annulling them by forcing an ideological choice, or, worst of all, getting used to them. And if we wish to understand this high strategy of contradiction maintained regardless of cost to his life as well as his work, there is no other way than to repeat his journey with him, to follow him in every bend and turning, without succumbing to the temptation to "save" him by locking him up, in spite of himself, in the refuge of a faith or some other established doctrine.

In the long letter he wrote to his father at the age of thirty-six about the disastrous consequences of his upbringing, Kafka devoted special attention to Judaism as the striking example of the misunderstandings that vitiated their relationship, put them into a state of permanent warfare, and in the end separated them completely. Yet on this terrain of their common origins father and son might have found ways of coming closer. ". . . it was conceivable that we might have found each other in Judaism or that we might in harmony have taken it as our starting point . . ."[8] but by the fault of an insane upbringing, at once tyrannical and blundering, Judaism, instead of bringing them together, became one more cause of conflict between them.

"As a child I reproached myself, in agreement with you, for not going to the temple often enough, for not fasting and so on. . . . Later, as a young man, I could not understand how, with the insignificant tatter of Judaism at your disposal, you could reproach me for not making an effort (at least for the sake of piety as you put it) to go through with similar meaningless motions. . . . Four days a year you went to temple, where to say the least you were closer to the indifferent than to those who took it seriously, patiently went through the formality of prayer, and occasionally amazed me by being able to show me in the prayer book the passage that was being recited at the moment. Apart from this, as long as I was present in the temple (that was the main thing) I could lounge around where I pleased. So I yawned and dozed through the many hours (I don't think I've ever been so bored since, except at dancing lessons),[9] and did my best to enjoy the few little diversions there were, such as when the Ark of the Covenant was opened, which always reminded me of the shooting galleries where a box opened in the same way whenever someone made a bull's eye, except that there something interesting always came out and here it was always the same old dolls without heads."[10]

Left to himself and his ignorance, the child regarded the time spent at the synagogue as "rehearsals staged by hell for my future office life," and it didn't take him long to realize that what went on at home was if possible even less edifying. There religious practice "was confined to the first Seder, which developed into more and more of a farce, with fits of hysterical laughter, admittedly under the influence of the growing children. (Why did you have to give in to that influence? Because you were responsible for it.) This was the religious material that was handed on to me, to which may be added the outstretched hand pointing to 'the sons of the millionaire Fuchs,' who attended the synagogue with their father on the high holidays. How one could do anything better with such material than get rid of it as quickly as possible was more than I could see; getting rid of it seemed to me the most pious thing one could do."[11] The fact is that while he was still in secondary school Kafka broke completely with this "ghost of Judaism" which he was supposed to inherit. He not only professed atheism but even—and this is surprising when we consider the extreme reserve he was later to show in matters of religious opinion—tried to convert his friends to free thinking.[12]

In the following pages of the *Letter to His Father* he makes it clear that in breaking with the Jewish religion he also turned away from "Jewish matters" in general,[13] and this is corroborated by his earliest letters. The student who wrote to Oskar Pollak, his intimate friend at the time, seems to have dismissed "Jewish matters" from his thoughts at the same time as the boring, useless, cumbersome ghost of religious Judaism. Though the extent to which he identified Judaism with its strictly religious aspect is not entirely clear, it is certain that "Jewish matters," religious or not, played no part in Kafka's letters to his first friend and confidant, and it was a long time before they were to figure in his letters to Brod or in his *Diaries.*

To his young friend Kafka spoke about his reading, his evenings out, his projects for the future, his hopes of escape (from Prague and his family), about girls, and, very diffidently, about his "scribblings"; but nothing in these letters suggests that he saw any direct tie between his inner malaise and his position as a Jew vis-à-vis his family and society. Though he must have been aware of the problem from the start, his "Who am I?" had not yet found its way into words, and expressed itself only obliquely, sometimes in odd behavior such as often occurs in adolescence, and sometimes, more seriously, in states of psychic confusion closely resembling personality loss. These states of youthful eccentricity left Kafka with a lasting fear of being regarded as a crank or a madman; but he had already begun to transpose his uncertainty about the limits of his own self and the reality of the world into his writings. For example, in one of his first long short stories, *Description of a Struggle*, a story without a story, the hero, alone in a crowd of doubles, tries to recover at least a part of his wholeness by carrying on an unremitting struggle against the excessive permeability of beings and things.[14]

The testimony of those who knew him at this time, taken together with what he himself said in *Letter to His Father*, has in general fostered the assumption that Kafka passed through a long period of "assimilation"—which indeed did not end until about his thirtieth year—before returning to his people under the influence of certain friends, and above all of his meeting with Isak Löwy and the actors of the Yiddish Theater. The hallowed term "assimilation" is certainly convenient, but what exactly does it mean in connection with the Prague of the old Austro-Hungarian empire, a city of endless social, ethnic, and linguistic complexity—officially an Austrian city, German with respect to the language of its ruling class, and Czech with respect to the majority of its population? The Jewish minority, an active, prosperous business class, were drawn between opposite poles of attraction, continually serving as pawns in the bitter struggle of the nationalities. With what could Kafka, as a German-speaking Jew, an Austrian subject, and the inhabitant of a Czech city where the mere fact that he did not speak their language made the Czechs regard him as an enemy, have "assimilated"? True, there was a Czech people, but it did not have political power, it was carrying on a struggle for its freedom, and a Jew could hope to assimilate with the Czechs only by throwing in his lot with the extreme nationalists (a faint hope, it must be said, which has grown steadily fainter since the brief euphoria born of the revolution of 1848).

Of course there was also Austria, and the Jews, by and large inclined to loyalty, were staunchly devoted to the person of its sovereign,[15] but in Prague Austria was hardly present except in the enormous bureaucratic machine and, symbolically, in the Hradčany, the imperial residence where the Emperor revered by the Jews never resided (in Kafka's time he went there only once, a fact that the author of *The Castle* obviously had in mind when he created his mythical Count West-West). As for the Germans of Bohemia, they themselves were a linguistic minority, shut up in a narrow enclave, deprived of political power or of a mother country with whose history and soil they could maintain their ties. In the midst of these heterogeneous groups, none of which had a living nation behind it, attempts at assimilation could not lead to much. And for lack of a normally constituted society in which they could hope to take root, the Prague German-speaking Jews, having to all intents and purposes only themselves to imitate, ended up taking their own Germanism as their model.

Thus, rather than being assimilated in the Berlin or Vienna sense of the word, Kafka was Germanized; that is, his language was his only substitute for everything of which destiny had deprived him: a native soil, a fatherland, a present and a past. Later, there could be no doubt, he would come to look upon this Germanization as the illusion of a foolish uprooted man, and upon his sole possession as a fraudulent acquisition—all of which would give his old sense of guilt one more thing to feed on. But for the moment his language belonged to him. If he did not yet complain in his letters of lacking "soil, air, and law," it was no doubt because the German language meant enough to him to take their place; indeed, his feeling for it may well have been as strong as an authentic blood tie.

Kafka inherited this Germanism, conceived as a substitute for an authentic social and spiritual fatherland, from a long tradition, which his parents themselves scrupulously observed. "In Bohemia," we are told, "German classical literature reached into the smallest village ghettos; the Jewish peddlers may have spoken Czech all week with their customers, but German remained their Sunday language, the medium in which one could discuss the highest of human concerns."[16] Unlike the "nationalities" around them, whose languages they regarded as vulgar dialects, the Jews possessed a language that exalted the spirit, and through this vehicle of an incomparable literature they felt truly ennobled. In addition to the sense of belonging secretly to an élite society far removed from the narrow sphere of their daily cares and occupations, the German language gave the Jews a far from negligible opportunity to rise on the social ladder (as the official language of the empire, it was indispensable to all those wishing to rise in the world for their own and their children's sakes).[17] Thus most Bohemian Jews put their trust in the German language, even when they continued to speak Czech or Yiddish in their businesses or at home. (It goes without saying that Yiddish was totally banished from the education of children; contempt for Yiddish was taken for granted in all self-respecting Jewish families, and in this, as in many other respects, the Kafka family was no exception.)

In justification of their profound attachment to the German language as a vehicle of high culture and an instrument of social progress, the Prague Jews might have cited the example of Moses Mendelssohn, the great philosopher who had not only written his books in German, but also reformed the Jewish liturgy by putting it into German. It is worth noting that in

Letter to His Father Kafka speaks more often of the "temple" than of the synagogue, an indication that the usage introduced by the Jewish reform movement was taken up in Prague. But the choice of German as the family language was above all the women's doing. The cult of German literature went so far back that it carried the force of tradition. Since the end of the eighteenth century, when Jewish ladies held a sovereign position in the salons of Berlin, and in the German Romantic movement as a whole, Jewish women had devoured everything written in German, the good and the bad: Goethe and Schiller, it goes without saying, but also serialized novels and the entire gamut of what was then, not without malice, termed *Weiberliteratur*[18] because it was the ladies' favorite fare. At the end of the last century, love of the German language was so solidly anchored in Jewish women, and so piously handed down, that according to a contemporary author this alone sufficed to assure the triumph of German over the "dialects" that the "nationalities" all around were trying to raise to the level of national languages. Consider this statement included in the *Wiener Jahrbuch für Israeliten* for 1863–64: "Anyone who knows by what subtle threads this *Weiberliteratur* attaches the emotional and religious life of the Jewish families to the spirit of the German language will harbor no illusions as to the possibility of tearing the German language from the heart of the Jews of Central Europe. . . . The imposture of the nationalities will never be able to destroy this influence. The history of woman is the history of the heart, and Jewish women have been so profoundly attached to the German language for centuries that none of the literatures that have made their appearance of late will ever replace the treasure they can find only in the realm of German. . . . The Germans had their Goethe and their Schiller long before this century's bits and pieces of nations realized that what their dialects lack is nothing less than grammar, vocabulary, and universality."[19]

In spite of his obvious prejudice, which was widespread if not general at the time (and with which Kafka later broke resolutely),[20] the writer of this passage was right in attributing to

Jewish mothers an essential role in the Germanization process that was to reduce the influence of the neighboring "dialects." Though strictly speaking they did not have a mother tongue to hand down to their children, these Jewish mothers managed at least to keep alive the flame their grandmothers had kindled at the torch of the great German classics. German-Jewish literature, so rich in forms and ideas, certainly owed them far more than its authors seem to have supposed.

In a much-quoted passage from one of his letters to Brod,[21] Kafka wrote: "Most young Jews who began to write German wanted to leave their Jewishness behind them, usually with the vague approval of their fathers (the revolting part of it is the vagueness). But their hind legs were still mired in their fathers' Jewishness and their thrashing fore legs found no new ground. The ensuing despair became their inspiration." In this analysis (we note that he already resorts to the image of the Dog), Kafka was of course essentially right; after all, he was in a position to know that in rebelling against his father he was also seeking to get rid of his origins and his thousand stubborn ties with Judaism. But on the plane of practical realities, he was disregarding the undeniable historical fact that neither Jewish fathers nor Jewish mothers regarded Germanism and Judaism as incompatible aspirations, much less as mutually hostile forces. The fathers encouraged the former and seriously wished to preserve the latter, failing to suspect that in this coexistence Judaism stood sooner or later to lose. The mothers, for their part, probably saw nothing to prevent them from admiring the great German poems and at the same time remaining good Jewish mothers, faithful to Jewish tradition. To Kafka's question "But why were they so irresistibly drawn in that direction?" they could have replied that this attraction was indeed irresistible, since, thanks to their mothers, the future writers had succumbed to it from earliest childhood, before they could even talk. Under these conditions it becomes clear that the fathers could neither disapprove of their sons for writing in German, since that is what they themselves had wanted, nor openly approve, for that would have amounted to self-repudiation. Thus they could only approve "vaguely." As soon as Kafka ceased to believe in the German language as a surrogate fatherland, it was only natural that he should rebel against this slackness of the fathers, which he held responsible for misleading the sons. His intransigence in this matter was by no means, as Brod claimed in order to soften its implications, a matter of momentary anger; it was in Kafka's eyes the only possible response to the general situation of the Jews in the West, which was "impossible in every respect."[22]

Favored on the one hand by the realism of opportunistic and ambitious fathers and on the other by the fervor of mothers piously devoted to Goethe and Schiller, Germanism was, after all, the most reliable support of Jewish petit-bourgeois society, enclosed as it was in its neighborhoods. But though in the area of the inner life it did indeed give access to a wider sphere of interests, in the realm of outward, practical life it opened out on no reality but was a mere abstract construct, an illusion which the least contact with the outside world sufficed to dispel. Kafka's irony in his *Introductory Talk on the Yiddish Language*—"We live in positively cheerful concord, understanding each other whenever necessary, getting along without each other whenever it suits us"[23]—refers to this glaring discrepancy between inside and outside. At home the young Jews of Prague lived, thought, felt, and wrote like Germans apparently resembling other Germans, but outside of their neighborhoods no one was deceived, the "others" recognized them instantly by their faces, their manners, their accent.[24] Assimilated they were beyond a doubt, but only within the restricted area of their borrowed Germanism, or better still, they were "assimilated" with their own uprootedness. Hence the odd behavior of the young men,[25] the high suicide rate among secondary-school students, the half-morbid, half-mystical sensualism which the local literature combined with a subjectivist cult of the fantastic. This is also why the most gifted dreamed constantly of escaping and why so many of them emigrated to other spiritual horizons or to countries more conducive to action. But whether they took refuge in a foreign country or in an idea, in America or in Italy with its music and religiosity, in Berlin with its unceasing intellectual ferment, in Viennese socialism or in the rather idealistic Zionist movement that sprang up in Prague,[26] the young Jews of Prague, like the monkey transformed into a man in *A Report to an Academy*, were obsessed by the search for a "way out": they fled above all for the sake of their personal salvation, and though many found it, that had no effect on the invisible bars of the Prague prison.

Kafka can be said to have devoted his whole life to this dream of escape, but the city had cast a spell on him; all his attempts to get away were doomed to failure (except at the end, when the Berlin of the years following the First World War, however tragic, gave him a feeling of freedom for the first time in his life). In 1902 he asked one of his uncles—Uncle Alfred, a director of the Spanish Railways, a resident of Madrid but then visiting in Prague, to "guide me to some place where at last I could start afresh and do something,"[27] but apparently his uncle did not understand him. The young man who in his irresolution had taken up the study of Germanic languages, from inclination no doubt but more compellingly from hatred of the study of law, thought he might escape by registering at the University of Munich, but after a few days there he returned home and abandoned his project. A few years later he thought again of his uncle in Madrid. "My uncle," he wrote to Max Brod, "would have to find us a position in Spain, or else we could go to South America or the Azores, to Madeira."[28] When he took a position with the Trieste-based Assicurazioni Generali, it was in the hope of being sent to a branch of the parent firm, or, as he wrote, of "sitting in chairs in faraway countries and looking out of the window at fields of sugar cane or Mohammedan cemeteries."[29]

None of this came to pass, but that Kafka had long foreseen: "Prague will never let us go. . . . This little mother has claws. One must submit or else. . . . We should set fire to it on both sides, at the Vyšehrad and at the Hradčany; then perhaps we could get away."[30] Though he may have remembered that he had once been called a little "Ravachol,"* it need hardly be said that he did not carry out his incendiary plans, but in *The Trial* he would revenge himself in his own way on the city the Czechs affectionately called their "little mother." Stripping it of its monumental splendor, of its legendary past and of course of its name, he preserved only the memory of a sinister, anonymous place, characterized by the ugliness of its suburbs and the squalor of its soot-encrusted buildings.[31]

Among the expedients taken by the young men of Prague to escape the city that offered them no hope for the future, writing enjoyed a surprising pre-eminence. Thus there was nothing very original about Kafka's flight into literature; it was remarkable only for its extraordinary precocity and all-engrossing character, which transformed it little by little from a quest for escape into a quest for the absolute. Kafka had been writing since childhood, and though his childhood productions have not been preserved, it is safe to assume that they already reflected a striving for liberation, or, as he said in the title he thought of giving someday to his work as a whole, "an attempt to escape from the paternal sphere."[32] Dedicated from an early age to this salvation through writing for which he was to strive all his life, he derived much less joy than suffering from the exercise of his talents. "You see," he wrote to a friend, "this misery has been on my back from early on . . ."[33] for his writing, directed essentially against his father's tyranny and the narrowness of his environment, was anything but an innocent game. It was a dangerous offensive weapon, the use of which brought with it a profound sense of guilt. Hence the conflict in which he was involved from the age of twenty on, and which he was able even then to formulate: "God does not want me to write, but I—I must. And so there is an everlasting up and down; after all, God is the stronger and there's more anguish in it than you can imagine."[34] The mysterious inner law which he here called "God"—in mockery, perhaps, be-

---

* French anarchist and convicted incendiary, 1859–92. Guillotined.

cause at the time of this letter to Oskar Pollak he called himself an atheist, or more likely through an intuition of the true nature of the commandment—only intensified its rigors as time passed, and in the end every page of his work had to be torn out of him.

For the moment, in any case, the conflict opened by Kafka's writing did not raise the question of language: Kafka naturally wrote as he spoke, in German, which he could rightly call his mother tongue since he had it from his mother and since to him it was tantamount to speech as such. German was his possession, if not from birth, then at least from the time when he uttered his first words, up to the moment when, apparently under the influence of his regular visits to the Yiddish Theater, he discovered how poorly the word *Mutter* suited a Jewish mother.[35] This possession was so self-evident to him that it never occurred to him to question his right to make use of it.

Tormented by what he felt to be the profound aggressiveness of writing in general and his own writing in particular, of whose hidden violence he was perhaps more aware than anyone else,[36] and fearing that he might be influenced by his models to the point of not always distinguishing between what he took from them and what was truly his own (he spoke ironically of his writings as a mixture of things "coming from myself and others"), the young man undoubtedly had some presentiment of the suffering that his passion for writing held in store for him. Still, his misgivings did not seriously trouble his attitude toward his work. Though at a later date he would be reluctant to discuss his writing even with his family and closest friends, at this point he had too much spontaneity to be tempted by such secrecy. Glad of any opportunity to speak of his past and present efforts, he went so far as to send his first friend a large bundle of manuscripts and to ask his opinion, in the hope, he said, that "another pair of eyes will make everything warmer and livelier."[37] He was, indeed, so eager to know his friend's verdict that he suggested enclosing an installment of a story, of which he himself had only bits and pieces, in each letter. And like every young man who dreams of publication without daring to admit it, he sent an entry to a contest organized by the Viennese newspaper *Die Zeit*, signing it with the astonishing pseudonym, characteristic of his style at the time, *Himmel in engen Gassen* (Sky in Narrow Streets).[38] During this whole period, in sum, he behaved like any budding young writer who, though quite conscious of his talents, is vaguely afraid of proving unequal to his ambitions. It is true that writing soon became the main source of his anguish. It frightened him in two ways: as a dangerous weapon against society, which not without reason he was afraid of wielding too well; and as property, created by others and belonging to others, whom he was in constant danger of robbing. But though he transferred to literature all the uncertainty, all the distrust he felt toward himself, his language at least remained above suspicion.[39] This was his soundest justification, thanks to which he could hope to take his place in German literature without cutting too foreign a figure. That was the illusion that it remained for him to unmask if he was to fulfill his destiny, for he would not achieve the definitive form of his art until the day when, realizing that in literature he could be only what he was in his country—a "visitor" or at the very most a "tolerated guest"—he resolved to leave the deceptively solid ground of the German he had learned and set up house in the world of the precarious. From then on his work would be the exact image of his situation as a radically dispossessed writer; with malicious irony concealed under a surface of impartiality, he would then say that the only language he possessed was one he had provisionally borrowed, to which he therefore had no need to claim special rights or legitimate title of ownership.

3 · The Road Back

Since our documents make no mention of the anti-Semitic riots that took place in Prague and in Bohemia at the turn of the century,[1] we do not know whether Kafka had actually forgotten them or, if not, for exactly what reasons he neglected to speak of them. He, who often complained of being "a memory come alive" and who later spoke freely on the subject in his *Diaries* and correspondence, especially in the letters he wrote to Milena Jesenska after the First World War, found nothing to say about these outbursts of rage which must, however, have wounded him deeply during his childhood and adolescence. What makes this persistent silence all the more surprising is that Kafka, inclined though he was in general toward reticence and procrastination in the expression of his ideas, never eluded the direct questions put to him by reality.

In 1893, when he was ten years old, serious disorders erupted in Kolín—a town in central Bohemia where he had relatives on his father's side—as a result of rumors, immediately taken up by a nationalist paper, to the effect that a certain Czech servant girl had been a victim of Jewish ritual murder. Though the paper was confiscated, the agitation spread to every town in Bohemia and finally got to the capital. Between 1897 and 1900—when Kafka was already at secondary school—the anti-Semitic riots provoked by the ultranationalist "Young Czechs" terrorized the Jewish population, Jewish

shopkeepers were molested, their shops were looted, their synagogues were profaned and burned.[2] In 1899 and 1900, during
the trials of Leopold Hilsner,[3] the disorders increased, and the
Hilsner case took so alarming a turn that all Europe became
aroused. (It has even been said that it did more than the
Dreyfus case to call the attention of the powers to political
anti-Semitism, then a recent and little-known phenomenon,
the danger of which they tended to underestimate.) It is hard
to believe that a young man of seventeen, even though radically de-Judaized, could have been utterly unaware of events
so sensational and so menacing to his family (the Kafkas were
indeed directly threatened, for, despite their mania for moving
house, they never moved more than a few hundred yards and
were never far from the rioters' hunting ground). Since it cannot have been delicacy that made him keep silent on these
matters—he did not have that kind of delicacy—and it is un-
thinkable that he simply forgot them, we can only suppose that
he repressed these memories, expelled them from his consciousness.

In the absence of direct sources that might help us analyze it, this troubling silence remains of course largely indecipherable; yet it becomes more understandable when we
consider the social and political situation in which Czech
anti-Semitism took on so virulent a character. As we have seen,
the Jews made up the larger part of the German-speaking population of Prague and Bohemia; thus in the eyes of the Czechs,
and especially of the extreme nationalists, the Jews belonged
to the enemy camp and were indeed its most intolerable element. They were the true enemies of the oppressed Czech nation, because, while the ethnic Germans were gradually being
won over to the advantages of Czechization, the Jews continued to defend Germanism against the encroachments of the
environing culture.[4] To these political reasons for resentment
was added bitterness due to the economic rivalries between
the Czech middle and lower classes on the one hand, and the
Jewish industrialists and businessmen on the other—all this, it
goes without saying, against a background of endemic and only

too easily activated anti-Semitism. As a consciously de-Judaized socialist and atheist, the youthful Kafka was bound to regard the bitterness of the Czechs as at least partly justified, especially if he remembered—and in those troubled times how could he have forgotten?—what he had seen as a child of his father's abuse of his own employees.

At that time Hermann Kafka's clerks were not all Jewish. Among them there were Czechs, who could not have helped regarding this crude, brutal, intolerant, and tyrannical employer as an exploiter and an enemy. Such, in any case, was the little boy's impression when his father, flying into a blind rage against his employees, presented a shameful spectacle of tyranny and injustice. Wounded in his love and pride at finding an indelible blemish on the perfection of his idol, he sadly turned against his unjust father and instinctively sided with the victims, partly to show solidarity with those persecuted by the same tyrant as himself and partly to shield himself from the terrible reprisals which an irrefutable infantile logic led him to regard as inevitable. Thus, what with his grief at finding he had a wicked father rather than a god of unalloyed goodness, what with his feeling of complicity with the maltreated employees, and the certainty that persons so gravely offended would avenge themselves sooner or later, the child handed on to the adolescent a painful and complex "Jewish question," charged with insurmountable conflicts.

It goes without saying that not all, or even most, Jewish businessmen in Prague behaved like Hermann Kafka; in this powerfully built man despotism and lack of consideration for others were more a matter of temperament than of conviction, and everyone around him, including of course his children, suffered from it. But it seems likely that in his ideas about the working class and his general view of the world he did not differ greatly from the average Jew of his milieu. Indeed, his son told him just that: "At bottom the faith that guided your life was your belief in the absolute rightness of the opinions prevailing in a particular class of Jewish society. . . ."[5] Thus it is safe to assume that his manner of treating his employees conformed to the practices current among the employers of his class. To Franz Kafka, however, it meant little that such injustice was taken for granted by a whole group. What mattered was that this father, loved, hated, adored, and feared as the repository of a mysterious authority, had shown himself to be fallible and inhumane. In this respect, to judge by the mythical figure who in his work takes on the fantastic dimensions of a god or demiurge, Kafka preserved the feelings born of his childhood love and fears. Enormously amplified by the inaccessibility that his son found in him, Hermann Kafka took on stature enough to incarnate all Jewry, so that in his son's eyes the community as a whole became guilty of his abuse of power.

We can measure the extent of Kafka's suffering by the emotion revealed years later in the long passage of his 1919 *Letter to His Father* dealing with this thorny subject: In this document, which apart from the light it sheds on the conflict between father and son is remarkable as a piece of sociological analysis, Kafka starts by describing his father's warehouse and the way in which his father exercises his gifts as businessman: the shop "was so lively, all lit up in the evening . . . I was able to help now and then, to distinguish myself, and above all to admire you for your magnificent business talents, the way you sold things, managed people, made jokes, the way you never got tired, the way in doubtful cases you always made the right decision at once, and so on; even your way of wrapping a parcel or opening a crate was a spectacle worth watching; all this was certainly not the worst school for a child."

Soon, however, the shop became hateful to him, precisely because of the revolting way people were treated: "I don't know, perhaps it was like that in most businesses . . . but in my childhood other businesses did not concern me. But you I saw shouting, cursing, and raging in the shop, in a way that as far as I knew at the time had no equal anywhere in the world. . . . For instance, the way you pushed goods you didn't want to have mixed up with others, knocking them off the counter . . . and the assistant had to pick them up. Or your constant comment about a tubercular assistant: 'The sooner he croaks the

better, the mangy dog.' You called the employees 'paid enemies,' and that is what they were, but even before they became
such you seemed to me to be their 'paying enemy.' " To judge
by these recollections, still vibrant with indignation, Kafka's
early experience of the class struggle gave him an aversion to
the shop, which added to the many already existing causes of
friction between father and son. And it was also this early experience which led him to side as long as he lived with the
"paid enemies": "But that made the business insufferable, re-
minding me as it did of my relations with you: quite apart from
your proprietary interest and from your tyranny even as a
businessman, you were so vastly superior to all those who came
to learn the business from you that nothing they did could satisfy you and I came to the conclusion that you would always be
dissatisfied with me in the same way. That is why I could only
side with the employees. And another reason was that the timidity of my nature if nothing else made it impossible for me
to understand how anyone could use such abusive language to
a stranger. And my fears also made me, for the sake of my own
safety, try somehow to reconcile the personnel, who must, I
thought, be perfectly furious with you and with our whole
family."[6] Here we see the threads of Kafka's inner tragedy
tightening: the indignant child sides with the exploited
enemy—knowing all the while that the enemy remains an
enemy and is merely waiting for an opportunity to avenge
himself. (In writing "In your battle with the world, favor the
world," the mature Kafka would only be devising a general-
ized formulation for the absurdity of the struggle into which
he was forced.) Now we begin to see why, when the long-
dreaded disaster struck—for instance, when anti-Semitic rioters pillaged the Jewish shops of Kafka's neighborhood—he
had to suffer it in silence, unable to complain or protest: in his
eyes his own father had contributed to the outrage.[7]

The *Letter to His Father*, which throws a definite though
indirect light on Kafka's silence about the happenings in the
outside world during his childhood, also accounts for the socialist ideas which he professed in secondary school and

which, as his specific interest in socialism wore off, took the more general form of a total solidarity with the insulted and injured. Our documents suggest that the owner of the whole-sale knitted-goods establishment at the sign of the jackdaw was not nearly so odious as Kafka paints him. Writing his *Letter* at a time of acute crisis, Kafka gave free rein to his resentment without stopping to think that in his mind everything con-nected with his father took on monumental proportions. But here it matters little whether the portrait was faithful or blackened; the essential is that the child experienced an emo-tional shock so violent that the adult still trembled to think of it.[8]

One might find it surprising that, with motives so deeply ingrained, Kafka's socialism never led him to join any party or movement; but quite apart from his marked tendency toward individualism and his difficulty in getting along with his fellow men, Kafka was here again reacting to the state of affairs in Prague, which made him suspicious of all political parties and formal doctrines.[9] In fact, in the days of the monarchy the Prague Jews, continually drawn as they were between the two contending nationalities, which competed for their votes at election time but otherwise made them bear the chief brunt of their hostilities, were in no position to uphold "ideas," even when they had the right to express them. At the most they could declare themselves in favor of one party or another, promise their votes in return for certain advantages or a little peace, and change camps when they felt they had been duped, or, worse, threatened in their persons or property by those they had seen fit to help. Herzl already deplored the fate of "those good middle-class shopkeepers, the most peaceful of all peaceful bourgeois . . . In Prague they were reproached for not being Czech, in Saaz and Eger for not being German. What position could they have taken? . . . The two conflicting na-tionalities in Bohemia invented a new variant to the old story of the two coachmen. . . . Two coaches meet on a narrow road. Neither coachman is willing to give the other the right of way. In each of the two coaches there is a Jew, one in this one, one in that one. Each coachman shakes his whip in the direction of the other's passenger: 'If you hit my Jew, I'll hit yours.' But in Bohemia they add: 'And mine too.' The Bohemian Jews get a double volley of blows for a single trip. It is true they try to slip through the quarrel of the nationalities like stowaways."[10] Caught between these shameless combatants, the ultimate victims of their hatred though both sides were glad to have them as allies, the "peaceful bourgeois" of Prague could not afford the luxury of opinions; they had no religion but business, and no rules of conduct but those needed to survive while preserving and if possible increasing their hard-earned prosperity. In this respect as well, Hermann Kafka must have resembled the average Jew of his class. "How easily," his son wrote in his famous *Letter*, "you let yourself be dazzled by people who were only seemingly your social superiors, how you would go on talking about them as of some imperial councilor or the like."[11] And elsewhere: "Your opinion was correct, every other was mad, wild, *meshugge*, not normal. . . . You were capable, for instance, of running down the Czechs and then the Germans and then the Jews, and that not only selectively but *en bloc*, till in the end no one was left but yourself. In my eyes you took on the enigmatic quality common to all tyrants whose rights are based not on reason but on their person."[12] Obviously this portrait shows marked individual features, and yet, allowing for differences in stature and temperament, it might have applied to a good many other fathers and Jewish businessmen. However excessive, however choleric and tyrannical Hermann Kafka may have been in his public and private life, he was probably a typical representative of Prague Jewry at the turn of the century, as molded by the history of that part of the world. The political opportunism, the lack of convictions, and the naïve snobbery that made up his outlook might in others have been blended in different proportions, but he and they were products of their untenable position between powerful antagonistic forces which they could neither overcome nor lastingly conciliate.

Just as Kafka became a socialist in secondary school out of hatred for the oppression that was revealed to him at an early age, he reacted against the opportunism and skepticism of his milieu by becoming extremely reluctant to express his own opinions: this attitude was in itself a condemnation. Whereas their situation drove the Prague Jews to change their opinions repeatedly, in accordance with what they regarded as their interest at the moment, Kafka, as befitted the "stow-away" he was conscious of being, kept his views to himself. Concerning the "administrative" sector of life, as the social sphere is termed in *The Castle*, he stated opinions only in a free, metaphorical form—his way of reserving judgment. Not that he was without clear-cut views—in the "private sector" some of his opinions were categorical and he defended them fanatically. But in the long sentences interspersed with paren-thetical clauses in which he framed his thinking, he weighed the pros and cons of the simplest matters ad infinitum, and he exhausted his faculty of judgment in examining every dossier as though the fate of the world depended on its soundness. The product of a vigorous jurist, who moreover was aware that he himself was engaged in a terrible lawsuit, Kafka's judgment was *reserved* in the twofold sense of the word; and this deliber-ate reserve by which he dissociated himself from his father's lack of principle was not only the most effective protest he could make against the ideological slipperiness of the Prague Jews; it became an essential component of his art, the stylistic principle that saved his novels from the flatness of the *roman à idées*.

If not for Kafka's way of deliberately doing and thinking the opposite of what was approved in his social milieu, it would be hard to understand the abrupt change that occurred in him virtually overnight under the influence of the Yiddish actors, or at least in connection with their appearance in his life. For according to a widespread belief it was under the in-fluence of Löwy and his strolling players that Kafka suddenly stopped regarding himself as an "assimilated" Jew, and though this explanation is supported by numerous entries in his *Diaries* for that year, it seems hardly believable that so fortui-tous an event could by itself have had so decisive an effect. After all, Kafka was twenty-eight years old and reason-

ably mature when the troupe arrived in Prague. He already
knew his main aim in life: to devote himself heart and soul to
his writing, and though his view of the world was not absolutely set, it was no longer fluid enough to be changed by the
first influence that came his way. For years the Zionist convictions of his closest friends had left him cold, and not even Max
Brod's flaming enthusiasm could convert him. Finally, there
was nothing very remarkable about Löwy and his actors except
for their craft; they had passion, talent, perhaps a certain genius, but in other respects they were poor devils, rather bewil-
dered, deserters from the *shtetl*, already far removed from
what passed as orthodoxy where they came from, in short,
none too well equipped to bring a lost Jew back to the fold.
Forever short of money, devoid of all practical sense, they
were reduced to playing wherever the opportunity offered. In
Prague they had found a refuge at the Café Savoy, a low-class
cabaret, where they suffered all sorts of humiliations at the
hands of a coarse and uneducated public. In short, the material and moral conditions they lived in left them no hope of
someday appearing on a stage worthy of their gifts. Admirable
as they were for the fervor and self-abnegation with which
they devoted themselves to the work of the great Yiddish
poets, they were assuredly a far cry from the prestigious beings
that destiny ordinarily chooses as agents of conversion. In fact,
they did not convert Kafka to a new way of living and thinking; they merely overwhelmed him by revealing to him the
warmth of a free and spontaneous Jewish life—in other words,
of the very thing that Prague had deprived him of for so long.

What may be gathered from the hundred-odd pages of his
Diaries that Kafka devoted to the Yiddish troupe during its
stay in Prague is that he was deeply moved, almost illumi-
nated, by these actors' revelation of an independent Jewish
art, an art admirably attuned to life, produced by Jews and for
Jews, and quite naturally finding its measure and its truth in
itself. On 5 October 1911 he wrote at length about the play he
had seen the night before—Lateiner's *Meshumed*, dealing with
the crime and punishment of an apostate Jew—and the emo-

tion the play had aroused in him, not only by its intrinsic qualities, but still more by the sense of communion it succeeded in
creating: "Some songs, the words *'yiddische Kinderlach,'* some
of this woman's acting (who on the stage because she is a Jew
draws us listeners to her, because we are Jews, without any
longing for or curiosity about Christians) made my cheeks
tremble."[13] Here Kafka, who, even in the stories whose heroes
are the chroniclers of a sovereign people—whether dogs, Chinese, or mice—rarely made use of the first person plural, and
even more rarely without ambiguity, responds with all his
heart to the motherly appeal of the actress, taking his place
among the *yiddische Kinderlach* of the great family he had
deserted. For a moment he ceased to be alone, for only a moment, to be sure, but for him who often accused himself of
being cold and aloof, this moment of feeling thawed by the
warmth of a community meant a hope of deliverance.

For two days, with discernible pleasure, he confided his
impression of the play to his *Diaries*: all the vicissitudes of the
action, further complicated by misunderstandings due to
transvestitism; the virtuosity of the actors, who give the action
its full meaning with their facial expressions, poses, and gestures; the direction, which seemed to run counter to the dramatic movement by highlighting the secondary characters,
while the important events occurred in the background; finally, and above all, the presence of two characters in caftans—two male parts, one played by a woman—who struck
him as out of place and fascinated him most especially because, ignorant of the tradition in which they originated, he
did not know exactly what they were supposed to signify.

"If I wanted to explain them to someone without con-
fessing my ignorance, I should say that I regard them as sex-
tons, employees of the temple, notorious lazybones with whom
the community has come to terms, *schnorrers* privileged for
some religious reason. . . . They seem to make a fool of everyone, laugh immediately after the murder of a noble Jew, sell
themselves to an apostate, dance with their hands on their ear-
locks in delight when the unmasked murderer poisons himself

and calls upon God, and yet all this only because they are as light as a feather, sink to the ground under the slightest pressure, are sensitive, cry easily with dry faces (they cry themselves out in grimaces), but as soon as the pressure is removed haven't the slightest specific gravity, but must bounce right back up in the air."[14] To these two good-for-nothings protected by some mysterious privilege which he guessed to be of religious origin, Kafka was evidently drawn by their equivocal function and extraordinary freedom. And his fascination with them was not confined to that one evening; they were to haunt him for years and turn up repeatedly in his work, with their somehow innocent immorality and all the futility, all the supernatural or inhuman capriciousness with which the tradition endowed them.

Indeed, there is no doubt that these two characters in Lateiner's *Meshumed* engendered the pairs of parasitical, wicked, lying, lecherous buffoons whom Kafka often created as companions to his heroes, to teach them to live and to cure them of their *mortal* seriousness (in Kafka's case the word "mortal" should be taken literally; that is the sense intended by the Gentleman in *The Castle*, when they use the word to accentuate the lack of frivolity that is leading K. straight to his doom). The same applies to the two tramps who try in vain to corrupt Karl Rossmann in *Amerika*; to the two bribed guards who come to arrest Joseph K. in *The Trial*; to the pair of executioners come from some unknown theater ("At what theater are you playing?"), who finally undertake to execute him "like a dog"; to the two good-for-nothing apprentices and the two celluloid balls in the story of Blumfeld, which suddenly manifest their absurd existence for the sole purpose of harassing the hardened bachelor and making him aware of his pettiness; and above all to the two assistants in *The Castle*, creatures escaped from some region beyond good and evil, whose mission it is to show K. the blessed ways of irresponsibility. All these innocent and diabolical twins show the same miraculous elasticity of body and mind as the two clowns of the Jewish popular theater. They are all reincarnations of a truth that

Kafka glimpsed one evening and continued to dream of precisely because it was beyond his reach.

It can hardly be doubted that the two buffoons are not the only element in the *Mushumed* from which Kafka drew inspiration. Though we have no direct proof concerning his other sources, it seems at least probable that certain scenes in his novels, certain movements and gestures of his characters, and even certain themes of his stories come from the same fund of experience. But in Kafka they are reworked from the perspective of the late-coming Jew, for whom the tradition was at best a cause for amazement and at worst a subject for parody. According to an author who has closely scrutinized the plays put on by Löwy in Prague in 1911 and 1912, Kafka owed them much more than his *Diaries* suggest, making use of whole scenes and episodes, and this in writings so manifestly inspired that no one would think of looking for extrinsic sources.[15] Thus the famous scene in *The Judgment* where the son takes his father in his arms to put him to bed seems to have its exact counterpart in Gordin's play *Gott, Mensch, Teufel* [God, Man, Devil],[16] where the wicked son—he has sold his soul to the Devil and, like Georg Bendemann in *The Judgment*, drives himself to suicide—likewise takes his senile old father in his arms and puts him to bed to stop his recriminations and sniveling. Evelyn Torton Beck also points out that the final scene of Scharkansky's *Kol Nidre* presents striking similarities to *The Judgment*: in both cases the father appoints himself judge over his son and condemns him to death without appeal.

There also seems to be a surprising thematic agreement between *The Metamorphosis*—the idea of which, as we have seen, is connected with Hermann Kafka's words about Löwy —and Gordin's *Der wilde Mensch* [The Wild Man], which shows an idiot (played, as it happens, by Löwy) reduced little by little to an animal, moving on all fours around the room where his family keeps him sequestered. And lastly, we might mention Kafka's predilection for theatrical attitudes, for grotesquely exaggerated mimicry, for the asides that so powerfully bring out the hero's isolation, and of course his abundant use of music and song as indicators of an ill-defined, equivocal, but essential atmosphere. From all these features, which indeed give his narrative prose an exceptionally theatrical quality, it may be inferred that Löwy's influence on his work was far greater both in depth and duration than most critics have supposed; though with the reservation that in Kafka these borrowed elements, removed from their original religious setting, function very differently than in his models and manifest not their eternal nature but the absurdity of their survival and the degeneration of their original meaning into incongruity.

True, the author just cited, in attributing certain stories to an outside influence, disregards the core—that is, the psychic "superdetermination" which, in Kafka's inner life as well as his dreams, governed the organization of his images. Still, she deserves credit for pointing out how receptive Kafka was, despite his fanatical striving for purity, to the humblest popular art, even when presented in an impure and rather degenerate form. For the Yiddish theater that touched such a profound chord in him was on the decline. In it tradition had frozen into convention; aiming solely to entertain and to edify, it bore little relation to art. Along with serious dramas of Biblical or profane inspiration, the repertory, heterogeneous and on the whole rather mediocre, almost always included hackneyed tear-jerkers, so-called family plays, combining elements of melodrama, operetta, and vaudeville.[17] Löwy's 1911 repertory in Prague was on a higher plane; it included plays by Goldfaden and Gordin, two authors with sufficient dramatic talent to breathe new life into the tradition; and works of Lateiner, Scharkansky, and Feimann, admirable writers, closer to popular art and less marked by literary refinement.[18] None of this, however, rose above the level of a purely provincial theater, and at the Café Savoy, the productions suffered from the small size of the stage, the absence of sets, insufficient rehearsals, and the mediocrity of some of the actors, who failed to learn their lines and who clowned shamelessly. Under these conditions it is hard to understand Kafka's enthusiasm and the sudden change, not so durable as has sometimes been claimed, but undoubtedly real and important for his development, which association with this troupe made in his life. It is hard to believe that these plays could carry him out of himself to the point of making him cry out after seeing Feimann's *Sejdernacht*, "At times, if we did not enter into the action, it was only because we were too moved, not because we were only spectators."[19] But we are made to believe it by the conviction with which Kafka identifies himself with the transported audience, infected by their naïveté and ceasing to feel the slightest, discrepancy between fiction and reality.

The Yiddish theater may well have been a minor and impure genre, yet it achieved what the highest art cannot always boast of achieving: a total opening up of the body and soul, an almost physical unity between audience and stage, a moment of self-forgetfulness in which the individual merges with the crowd. The disdain of the aesthetes and Hebraists was powerless to inhibit the surge of emotions and ideas which the little troupe had the gift of inspiring and which, effacing all distinctions of age, sex, and rank, broke through the narrow limits of individual existence. Kafka, in any case, did not join in their criticism, though he deplored the poor conditions under which the actors were obliged to perform. Not only was he stimulated by what a good many people found revolting, but, alone perhaps among Jews of the intellectual élite, he also sincerely looked up to Löwy and would, so he said, have been glad to worship him "on his knees in the dust," because in him he found what he considered the essence of genius, the rare combination of creative passion with profound humility.

For months, as Kafka tells us in his *Diaries*, he devoted many of his evenings to the performances at the Café Savoy. He soon made friends with the actors. After the play he often joined them at their table, where he heard them speak of their affairs, discuss their plans, and occasionally quarrel, for their relations were not always harmonious. As if to partake more fully of the intimate life of the little clan—Löwy was a bache-

lor, but most of the others were married—Kafka went so far as
to fall in love with the "leading lady," Madame Tschissik, evidently a highly dedicated actress whom the attentions of this
distinguished gentleman, a "doctor, as she imagined," says
Kafka, who had few illusions, seems to have embarrassed
somewhat.[20] But among these new friends, at once so close to
him and so alien, he was doubtless most attracted to Löwy,
who both as a man and as an actor aroused his amazement and
respect, for his ability to breathe fire into things and ideas.
Tormented by all manner of real or imaginary ailments, conspicuously ill-equipped for the practical tasks of life, Löwy was
exemplary in Kafka's eyes because of the way the artist in him
strengthened rather than weakened the Jew. Embracing art as
one might embrace a religion, he had been obliged to break
with the rigid Hasidism of his family, in whose eyes he had
"gone wrong." And yet he remained one of those indefectible
Jews, in whom "Christians inspired neither desire nor curiosity," whose entire being was in the image of their people and
its culture.

During long walks through the streets of Prague, Löwy
told Kafka his own story and other stories as well; he depicted
life in the Jewish quarter of Warsaw, the harsh existence of
the yeshiva students at the turn of the century, the young people's struggles for emancipation, the rites, the holidays, the
sayings and legends of the wonder-working rabbis—in short,
everything that Kafka had not known and was now eager to
learn about the "Russian Jews." Afterward Kafka would fill
his *Diaries* with bits and pieces of stories and traditions that to
him seemed to come from the cradle of time. The meticulous
care with which he took these things down shows the depth of
his interest, but also the astonishment, the bewilderment of
the neophyte eager to be initiated into a new mode of thought.
For Kafka had only the most indirect acquaintance with the
Jewish life that Löwy was trying to communicate through his
stories, and the more intensely he longed for knowledge, the
more conscious he became of the remoteness of its object. He
was somewhat in the situation of an explorer or anthropologist
studying the customs of a primitive people "in the field" who,

as long as he lacks the key, is baffled by everything he sees, incapable of perceiving the simple everyday nature of perplexing facts. Kafka certainly did not have the key, and his almost scientific pursuit of his observations did not suffice to procure it—especially since in his case the ethnologist could not forget that the tribe in question, exotic as it might look to him, was his own.

Be that as it may, Kafka carried on his investigations vigorously, and though at bottom he was more interested in people than in ideas, what he learned through Löwy and the Yiddish theater made him want to fill in the gaps by reading at least those Jewish writings to which he had direct access. Comparison of dates points beyond a doubt to a direct connection between his encounter with the troupe and the beginning of this reading. He attended his first performance on 5 October 1911, and on 1 November he wrote in his *Diaries*: "Today, eagerly and happily began to read the *History of the Jews* by Graetz.[21] Because my desire for it had far outrun my reading, it was at first stranger to me than I thought, and I had to stop here and there in order by resting to allow my Jewishness to collect itself. Toward the end, however, I was already gripped by the imperfection of the first settlements in the newly acquired Canaan and the faithful handing down of the imperfections of the popular heroes (Joshua, the Judges, Elijah)."[22] In January 1912 he cites his reading and his efforts to help the actors as being among the reasons for a lapse in his *Diaries*: ". . . read, and indeed read greedily Pines's *L'Histoire de la Littérature Judéo-Allemande*, 500 pages with such thoroughness, haste and joy as I have never shown in reading a book of this kind; now I am rereading Fromer, *Organismus des Judentums*; finally I spent a lot of time with the Jewish actors, wrote letters for them, prevailed on the Zionist society to inquire of the Zionist societies of Bohemia whether they would like to have guest appearances of the troupe; I wrote the circular that was required and had it reproduced; saw *Sulamith* once more and Richter's *Herzele Mejiches* for the first time, attended the folksong evening of the Bar Kochba society. . . ."[23]

Two days after drawing up this list of his Jewish activities, with which he was visibly pleased, he copied certain passages from Pines's book into his *Diaries*, either because they contained useful information—on the Haskalah movement, for instance, which he obviously knew very little about—or because they fell in with his own preoccupations.[24] Throughout this period he steeped himself in Jewish literature, and though he could hardly expect books to give him the clear consciousness of his identity that life had denied him, they helped him to discover within himself untapped resources that gave him hopes of becoming a new, almost self-confident, almost happy man, almost delivered of the constant need to disparage himself. After writing a letter designed to procure help for Löwy, he thought it "good": "Each fresh rereading of the letter calmed and strengthened me, there was in it so much unspoken indication of everything good in me."[25] It was most unusual in him to speak so confidently of anything he thought or did. Such an entry marks a respite in his bitter struggle with himself.

Not that he was freed from his anguish and sense of guilt—he was not, and what little illusion he had on that score was dissipated at the start of his relations with Felice. Still, the Jewish feeling instilled in him by people and books made him feel stronger, more resolute, more inclined to accept himself as he was, and by the same token more capable of devoting himself to a common cause, even if it meant cutting down on the enormous amount of time and energy he was beginning even then to devote to his writing (throughout this period he wrote nothing, but contrary to his habit he noted the fact with hardly a word of complaint or self-recrimination). The fact is that his *Diaries* nowhere else show him so confident of his talent, so proud of his ease of movement and action, as on the day when, in delivering an introductory address at a benefit performance he had arranged to raise money for Löwy, he succeeded in overcoming his inhibitions and holding his audience.

For two weeks, it is true, the fear of failure had tormented him day and night; he had been racked by "uncontrollable feverish spasms," the blood flowing in his veins stabbed him like "little tongues of flame"; and yet, no sooner had he set to work than his enthusiasm got the better of his fears. "Cold and heat alternate in me with the successive words of the sentence; I dream melodic rises and falls, I read sentences of Goethe's as though my whole body were running down the stresses."[26] And a few days after brilliantly withstanding the test, he recorded what he had got out of it in spite of his morbid terrors and doubts: "Joy in Löwy and confidence in him, divine self-confidence during my lecture (coolness in the presence of the audience, only the lack of practice kept me from using enthusiastic gestures freely), strong voice, effortless memory, but above all the power with which I loudly, decisively, resolutely, faultlessly, irresistibly, with shining eyes, almost casually, put down the impudence of the three town hall porters and gave them, instead of the twelve kronen they demanded, only six kronen, and even these with a grand air. In all this there are revealed powers to which I would gladly entrust myself if they would remain. (My parents were not there.)"[27] Divine self-confidence, coolness, strong voice, shining eyes—all this, to be sure, badly weakened by the parenthesis that marred his dream: his parents had not come, and because of them, or, rather, because of the conflict betokened by this eloquent absence, the powers here revealed to him would not last. But regardless of what was to become of these powers, he would never again speak of them in words so simple and so enthusiastic, never would he feel so free in the presence of the terrible inner judge—or, in Freudian terms, his superego—who condemned all his actions in advance and in advance prevented him from living. Nor would he ever again speak so clearly of the exorbitant value he attached to those purely social qualities—energy, self-confidence, vitality—that were, as it happened, most incompatible with his personal hierarchy of values. Even if the *Introductory Talk on the Yiddish Language*[28] were not the admirable literary work we know it to be, it would have been enormously valuable for the harmony it created between Kafka and himself, between Kafka and the

Jews, between the Western Jew and the Yiddish language, but also between him and the German language, which Goethe in person, Goethe his god, had granted him the right to use.

In composing this talk, designed primarily to ensure the success of Löwy and his theatrical evening, Kafka obviously drew inspiration from Pines's book, and especially from the preface by Charles Andler, which provided ample material with which to refresh his knowledge of philology. But this specialized knowledge did not interest him as such; he made use of it solely to prove to his audience—consisting chiefly of prosperous businessmen inordinately proud of their German culture—that the performance would not seem so foreign to them as they visibly feared; that they would find no difficulty in understanding Yiddish, provided, of course, that they did not resist it. For Yiddish was not so far removed from the modern High German they held in such high esteem; it was made of the same substance. In a way, it was even nobler and purer, since it was in Yiddish that the authentic forms of Middle High German are best preserved.

What, Kafka asked, was the reason for the fear of Yiddish that he thought he could read on the faces of his listeners? For that fear which, "mingled with a certain fundamental distaste, is, after all, understandable"? He personally had no difficulty in explaining it, for he knew from his own experience that it was the counterpart of a false sense of security. And this he stated quite bluntly, the harshness of his tone hardly attenuated by irony: "Our Western European conditions, if we glance at them only in a deliberately superficial way, appear so well ordered; everything takes its quiet course. We live in positively joyful harmony, understanding each other whenever necessary, getting along without each other whenever it suits us, and understanding each other even then. From within such an order of things who could possibly understand the tangle of Yiddish—indeed, who would care to do so?" If Yiddish was feared as a troublemaker, it was for one reason only, because it shattered the linguistic illusion on which the Prague Jews based all their social relations. It frightened them because it

instantly unmasked the "positively joyful harmony" created
by the use of German, a use that was out of place and above all
ineffectual, providing no more than a travesty of communication: "getting along without each other whenever it suits us,
and understanding each other even then."[29] But, said Kafka,
to reassure his audience—or, rather, to awaken the real fear
concealed beneath their surface calm—you can come closer to
Yiddish in spite of everything: you "need only bear in mind
that apart from what you know there are active in yourselves
forces and associations with forces that enable you to understand Yiddish intuitively . . . and once Yiddish has taken hold
of you and moved you—and Yiddish is everything, the words,
the Hasidic melody, and the essential character of this East
European Jewish actor himself—you will have forgotten your
former reserve. Then you will come to feel the true unity of
Yiddish, and so strongly that it will frighten you, yet it will no
longer be fear of Yiddish, but of yourselves."[30]

  Thus the fear of Yiddish and of all the thoughts and feelings with which it vibrates should lead the Western Jew to a
far more justified fear, the fear he would experience in looking
at himself, if he were not blind to his repudiation of his people. That fear was intolerable; you would not be able to bear it,
said Kafka with the authority born of experience, "if Yiddish
did not instantly give you, besides, a self-confidence that can
stand up to this fear and is even stronger than it is. Enjoy this
self-confidence as much as you can! But then, when it fades
out, tomorrow and later—for how can it last, fed only on the
memory of a single evening's recitations!—then my wish for
you is that you may also have forgotten the fear. For we did
not set out to punish you."[31] Flouting the conventions pertain-
ing to entertainments of this sort, Kafka deliberately created a
scandal by citing his listeners before the tribunal of their own
conscience. But though in this trial he for once held the role of
prosecutor, he surely did not forget that he had always figured
conspicuously among the accused. The fear he wished to
arouse in the audience was the very fear that he had recently
come to recognize as his own. In promising strength and self-

confidence to the Jew who became reconciled with Yiddish, he knew whereof he spoke, for it was to just this strength and self-confidence that he owed the inspiration for his address and his sense of freedom in the face of his audience. As for his skepticism concerning the durability of the forces thus activated, he expressed it as much for himself as for his listeners; he already suspected that they would be short-lived, and his suspicion was to be confirmed only too soon.

Not long after the memorable night when he had this intimation of an almost miraculous metamorphosis, Kafka met Felice and resolved to marry her. His decision plunged him more deeply than ever into the hell of his inner conflicts, at the same time thrusting him back into the wretched situation of the Westernized Jew, from which for a moment he had thought he might escape. In the test that he then faced—for it was a test, and he was convinced that his whole life depended on it—the Eastern Jews were of no help to him; they had nothing to teach him except what they were, and that was something that could not be communicated. For all the admiration and respect he felt for them, he had no share in their existence, and they, for their part, with all their friendship, could not help regarding him as an upper-class foreigner, which is just what he was by virtue of his language, his upbringing, his education, his writing, and above all his social position. But the unbridgeable gap he was forced to recognize between these people and himself did not by any means lead him to modify his judgment; on the contrary, it durably reinforced his certainty that he stood to gain by association with them, and he continued to the end of his life to regard the Eastern Jews as the repositories of the only form of Jewish life that was still worthy of being defended and loved.

His discovery of Yiddish culture led Kafka to draw a radical distinction between the Eastern Jew and the Western Jew that he himself so eminently exemplified. Humble and proud, endowed with an exuberant life that did not contaminate his purity, the Eastern Jew, in Kafka's eyes, was everything the Western Jew lost by trying to become civilized. The former was noble and authentic without making any particular effort in that direction; the latter was a mutilated creature, a psychological cripple incapable of living and not even worthy of having children.[32] Obviously this distinction was not a product of rational argument; in Kafka it was based on a highly complex mixture of feelings and ideas, the dominant factor in which was the longing for an existence in harmony with the forces of life, forming an indestructible unity with a soil, a language, and a law.[33] This, in a manner of speaking, was an article of faith which, by cutting the Jewish world in two, added an insurmountable obstacle to his own quest for identity. But regardless of anything Max Brod could say to minimize the significance of this attitude of Kafka's,[34] Kafka never departed from it; the antinomy between East and West remained the foundation of his thinking on the Jewish question, and here for once he did not concern himself with subtleties or shadings. This attitude, however, proved fatal to him, for in consigning himself to the category of condemned Jew, he forfeited all hope of salvation—to the end of his days, as he saw it, he would be useless, incomplete, socially and spiritually sterile.[35] And so, instead of stimulating him, the vital forces in which he thought he would share by opening his heart to authentic Jewishness turned against him in the end, merely convincing him, to all intents and purposes, that he could never be anything but an exile.

4 · The Thornbush

In spite of his initial enthusiasm and the metamorphosis whose positive signs he had observed (the negative signs, as manifested in his written *Metamorphosis*, would be all the more terrible), Kafka could no more assimilate to Eastern Jewry (if it is permissible to reverse the sense of the hallowed term) than his Surveyor could become like the Gerstäckers and Lasemanns at the opposite pole, in the extreme Occident whose civilization was incarnated by Count West-West. Though at the start this sort of reverse assimilation did not strike him as inconceivable, he soon began to doubt that the Yiddish theater could give him the right kind of help with it, and as early as January 1912—a month before he delivered his address—he wrote in his *Diaries*: "My receptivity to the Jewishness in these plays is deserting me. . . . When I saw the first plays, it was possible for me to think that I had come upon a Judaism on which the beginnings of my own rested, a Judaism that was developing in my direction and so would enlighten me and carry me further along in my own clumsy Judaism; instead it moves further away from me the more I hear of it. The people remain, of course, and I hold fast to them."[1]

In hoping that Löwy's theater would give him an impulsion powerful enough to awaken and direct his "clumsy" Judaism, Kafka was obviously risking grave disappointment. And he was indeed disappointed. But though the strictly Jewish

(i.e., religious) element remained beyond his grasp, he preserved his devotion to individuals—whom, on the other hand,
he thought worthy of admiration only because in them this
strictly Jewish element remained unadulterated. It is true that
in general—and here we encounter the paradox that punctures
most religious interpretations of his work—people meant infinitely more to him than beliefs or ideas, or more accurately,
beliefs and ideas meant a great deal to him in living beings and
very little in the abstract. He loved believers without sharing
their reasons for believing or their need for prayer, and without drawing any value distinction between the various doctrines their piety invoked.[2]

Thus, regardless of the vicissitudes or eclipses of his Jewish feeling, he never lost his personal predilection for those
men, women, and especially children, whom he would never
see in their own native surroundings but only as refugees; he
would always regard them as justified in advance, as being
saved and even as saviors, and all for one reason—that their
life was at all times cut from the cloth of their truth. That is
why he thought that Felice, in her eagerness to educate the
little Galician refugees at the Berlin Home, mistook the nature
of her task. He was convinced that neither she nor the teachers had anything of value to teach them; on the contrary, the
teachers had everything to learn from the children: "Beware
of the arrogance of believing the opposite, this is most important. What form will the help in the Home take? Since people
are sewn into their skins for life and cannot alter any of the
seams, at least not with their own hands and not directly, one
will try to imbue the children—at best respecting their individual characters—with the spirit and more indirectly the
mode of life of their helpers. In other words, one will try to
raise them to the standard of the contemporary, educated
Western European Jew, Berlin version, which admittedly may
be the best type of its kind. With that, not much would be
achieved. If, for instance, I had to choose between the Berlin
Home and another where the pupils were the Berlin helpers
(dearest, even with you among them, and with me, no doubt,

at the head) and the helpers simple East European Jews from
Kolomyja or Stanislawow, I would give unconditional prefer-
ence to the latter Home—with a great sigh of relief and without a moment's hesitation."[3] At the very start of her work at
the Home, when Felice worried that the question of faith and
religious observances might create difficulties for her as a non-
practicing Jew, he tried to relieve her misgivings. "The main
thing," he wrote, "is the human element,"[4] a view which, incidentally, minimized the importance of the theological and political arguments that the Eastern Jews were then raising on all
sides.[5]

And yet these people whom Kafka idealized without
shading or reservation—he had never seen them on their native soil; he knew them only in Prague or Berlin, where they
were in every respect "displaced persons." But wherever he
had occasion to become acquainted with them—at the meetings that the Prague Zionists organized during the war, at the
courses in literature given by Max Brod and Felix Weltsch for
young Galician girls, or in institutions—it was always to people
that he became attached, regardless of ideology; he expected
nothing more of them than what—in the serenity of their unadulterated traditions—they were. In 1923, for instance, while
staying at Müritz on the Baltic for his health, he spent a good
part of his time in the summer camp of the same Berlin Home,
and there, among the children of plain Jews from "Kolomyja
or Stanislawow" he experienced "moments of intense happiness" that almost made him forget his sorrows. True, his happiness assumed, more and more, the features of Dora Dymant,
whose love was soon to reconcile him with women and life.
This young Polish woman, recently emancipated from the
rigors of her Hasidic family,[6] was able to do something that
neither Felice, the Berlin petite bourgeoise, nor Milena, the
passionate intellectual, could. And this beyond a doubt was
because, imbued as she was with the authentic spirit of the
shtetl, she was brimful of the pure and passionate Jewish life
that he himself could only dream of.

In saying "The human element . . . always the human element" and "The essential is people, people and nothing else," Kafka surprises us by disjoining two things that are ordinarily held to be inseparable: the Eastern Jews and the religious sphere in which from generation to generation their modes of being and thinking were formed. These people attracted him and moved him with the qualities they owed to their fidelity, including, of course, the many specific traits determined by their religious tradition. But though their religion as such did not leave him entirely indifferent, it touched him very little. Despite all his efforts to penetrate it, it remained largely alien to him; by and large, he was able to view it from a distance, as one views some strange relic that has lost all meaning except for history or archaeology.

True, he never saw this religion as observed in the East, where it was more or less taken for granted, and it was not in the synagogues of Prague that he could have convinced himself of its living reality. The few services he attended struck him as no less absurd than those that had so bored him as a child; they merely confirmed his conviction that the Jewish religion was nothing more than an unintelligible archaism, and for that very reason interesting to observe. Observe it he did, for want of being able to participate, and this observation—on the occasion, for instance, of the circumcision of a nephew— led him to some rather disabused reflections. "Today, when I heard the *moule*'s [*mohel*, circumciser] assistant say the grace after meals and those present, aside from the two grandfathers, spent the time in dreams or boredom with a complete lack of understanding of the prayer, I saw Western European Jewry before me in a transition whose end is clearly unpredictable and about which those most closely affected are not concerned, but, like all people truly in transition, bear what is imposed on them. It is so indisputable that these religious forms which have reached their final end have merely a historical character, even as they are practiced today, that only a short time was needed this morning to interest the people present in the obsolete custom of circumcision and its half-sung prayers by describing it to them as something out of history."[7]

In judging Western Judaism so severely, Kafka seems to imply that Judaism of the East was less flawed with unreality, but he knew this Eastern Judaism only from hearsay, and when he did manage to come closer to it—in 1915, for example, when numerous Polish Jews, driven from their homes by the Russians, arrived in Prague—he observed it with the passion of an anthropologist studying a remote tribe. When, with Brod and other friends, he went to see the wonderworking rabbi of Žižkov, he noted that along with a "strongly paternal nature," this holy man, in spite of his extreme uncleanliness, had the gift of remaining absolutely pure, which instantly reminded Kafka of "the world of childhood imaginings," where one's parents were miraculously preserved from the unclean things of life.[8] This father, to whom everything was permitted, even sin—obsessed as he was with cleanliness in daily life, Kafka undoubtedly regarded any association with dirt as heinous sin—this father figure exalted above the law certainly fascinated him, but less through the content of his teachings than through the extraordinary whiteness of his hands—with which he had just wiped his nose.[9]

But that day Kafka was accompanied by an initiate, who offered to explain the deeper meaning of what went on in the stifling room into which the miracle-hungry faithful had crowded. Like Kafka a native of Prague and the son of a prosperous businessman, this Georg Mordechai (Jiri) Langer had chosen, to escape from the evils of Prague, a path as original as it was scandalous to his family and social group. At the age of nineteen he had converted to Hasidism and gone to study with the rabbi of Belz, the most famous and certainly the most revered of living *zaddikim*. To his thoroughly Europeanized though still-practicing family, this had come as a fearful shock, comparable to what a rich and respected family of our day must feel when one of their children runs off to join the Moonies or the followers of some equally disreputable prophet.[10] In the eyes of a Prague middle-class family in 1913, such a conversion was more than an affront to common sense and the laws of historic development; it was absolutely indecent. This of course was not Kafka's opinion; he had very different reasons for rejecting this sort of solution. Believing as he did in the individual's indissoluble bond with his social roots—soil, language, family, upbringing—he could not help regarding a deliberate choice of allegiance as an illusion, worthy of respect in Langer's case, but every bit as futile and dangerous as the illusion of assimilation. Still—and here again what counted was the human being—despite his skepticism he was drawn to this man who had been brave or insane enough to live up to his convictions in defiance of public opinion.

Kafka enjoyed listening to Langer, who for a time became his friend. At their frequent meetings, Langer told him the legends of the Baal Shem and of the great *zaddikim,* which Kafka noted in his *Diaries* and even treated as a source of inspiration, attempting a new version of the legendary Golem theme. This sketch, consisting of two short fragments, was soon abandoned; we see the rabbi, "his sleeves rolled up like a washerwoman's,"[11] kneading a lump of clay in a basin, trying to give it a human face, and that's all; the rabbi remains featureless, and one cannot help wondering whether Langer, if he had known of this version of the legend, would have thought it worthy of his efforts to initiate Kafka into his beliefs.

He also failed in his attempts to enlighten Kafka about the rabbi of Belz, his own teacher, whom Kafka came across by chance at Marienbad, surrounded by his court. Kafka watched the rabbi's strange perambulations with skepticism, though also with delight. To judge by the account of this memorable episode that Kafka wrote to Brod,[12] Langer's explanations were unrelated to what Kafka himself eagerly observed: the minutely regulated ceremonial governing the rabbi's walk to his usual thermal spring; the rain, which cruelly belied Langer's belief that it never rained when the rabbi went out; the retinue of the faithful, who escorted him at a respectful distance in accordance with an extremely complicated etiquette; the suspect zeal of the *gabim* (more properly *gabaim,* the rabbi's retinue of close friends and assistants), who vied for the honor of serving him; the extraordinary concentration

with which the old man scrutinized every detail of his surroundings; his inexplicable interest in the hideous architec-
ture of the thermal establishment, and the trance into which
he was plunged by the sight of common water pipes—Kafka
reported all this to Brod in a tone of half-real, half-affected admiration, his fervor tempered by a healthy dose of the irony
that always came over him when he spoke of certain father figures who were slightly senile, slightly feeble-minded, and yet
endowed with a certain unquestionable authority. For even
more than the rabbi of Žižkov, the rabbi of Belz was a father
raised to incredible heights: "He looks like the Sultan in a
Doré illustration of the Münchhausen stories, which I often
looked at in my childhood. But not like someone masquerad-
ing as the Sultan, really the Sultan. And not only Sultan but
also father, grammar-school teacher, gymnasium professor,
etc."[13] Nevertheless—and to an adept such an observation was
undoubtedly the beginning of blasphemy—this incontestable
sovereignty resided entirely in itself, following neither from
the rabbi's words nor from his actions, all of which were perfectly commonplace: "He inspects everything, but especially
buildings, the most obscure trivialities interest him. He asks
questions, points out all sorts of things. His whole demeanor is
marked by admiration and curiosity. All in all, what comes
from him are the inconsequential comments and questions of
itinerant royalty, perhaps somewhat more childlike and more
joyous. At any rate they reduce all thinking on the part of his
escort to the same level. Langer tries to find or thinks he finds
a deeper meaning in all this; I think that the deeper meaning is
that there is none, and in my opinion this is quite enough."[14]
Coming from a writer whose work has too often been regarded
as a romanced transposition of metaphysical and religious
problems, this categorical subordination of "deeper meaning"
to immediately visible human meaning is undoubtedly disturbing; but though it by no means disposes of the spiritual
concerns with which Kafka's life is permeated, it plays so essential a role in his relations with Judaism and Jewry that its
importance cannot be overlooked.

Here again, as we see, living people—and preferably the humblest, most obscure, literally, the most *insignificant*—count far more than the body of beliefs and traditions in which, however, their truth is rooted. The rabbi of Belz may have been a father and sultan, but in the presence of so much majesty Kafka's feelings were merely those of a curious spectator, certainly not comparable to the poignant regrets aroused in him by the sight of a simple Polish Jew taking his little boy to the temple on a holiday. When he wrote in his *Diaries,* "The Polish Jews going to Kol Nidre. The little boy with prayer shawls under both arms, running along at his father's side. Suicidal not to go to temple"[15]—he was having painful thoughts about himself, due not to regret for piety in itself, but, as shown by the close association of his concluding exclamation with the image immediately preceding it, to his nostalgia for piety as, for a true Jewish family, the strongest of bonds, the pledge of love and unity. Some years later, in a letter to Milena which deserves to be quoted at length if only for its beauty, he says once again that he would have liked to be that probably lice-infested little boy walking by the side of that probably poverty-stricken father.

Time and again Kafka told this non-Jewish young woman, accustomed to associate with Jews in the literary cafés of Vienna and moreover married to a Jew, how mistaken she was in denying that his Jewishness could seriously affect their already difficult relations. From the start of their relationship, he spoke to her of his destiny as a Western Jew, as he experienced it in every moment. Evidently she did not understand him,[16] so, without troubling himself over the fright that he would be almost sure to provoke, he tried to enlighten her by describing the Eastern environment in which he would have liked to be born. "If I'd been given the choice last night (it was 8 P.M. when I looked from the street into the banqueting room of the Jewish Town Hall, where far more than 100 Russian Jewish refugees—they're waiting here for their American visas—are housed, the room is packed full, as during a public meeting, and later at 12:30 I saw them all asleep there, one next to the other, they were even sleeping stretched out on chairs, here and there someone coughed or turned over or groped his way carefully through the lines, the electric light burns all night long)—if I'd been given the choice to be what I wanted, then I'd have chosen to be a small Eastern Jewish boy in the corner of the room, without a trace of worry, the father in the center discussing with other men, the mother, heavily wrapped, is rummaging in the traveling bundles, the sister chatters with the girls, scratching in her beautiful hair—and in a few weeks they will be in America. It isn't as simple as that, of course, there have been cases of dysentery, there are people standing in the street, shouting threats through the windows, there's even quarreling among the Jews themselves, two have already attacked each other with knives. But if one is small, if one takes in and judges everything quickly, what can happen to one? And there were enough boys like this running around, clambering over the mattresses, creeping under chairs and lying in wait for the bread which someone—they are *one* people—was spreading—with something—everything is edible."[17]

These Eastern Jews, of whom Kafka longed to have been one, were filthy, quarrelsome, quick to draw their knives. Always hungry, they would eat anything at all: for them there were no forbidden foods. Wicked in every way, they were a far cry from the idolized image Western intellectuals projected upon them in the rare instances when they did not prefer to banish them from their memory and their lives. They were not the pure beings in whom great philosophers seek mystical wisdom; not Hasidim haloed in the wisdom of their legendary masters, but the very dregs of Jewry, those generally known at the time as Polacks, whom no cultured Jew could help feeling ashamed of, even if he denied it. Harried, so depraved by poverty that they knew neither law nor religion, and yet *one people*—all in a heap, as the Dog says, possibly in recollection of a refugee camp—*one people,* whom Kafka loved and wholly accepted, with all their violence, their dubious morality, their deformed mothers and lice-infested children. And nothing

could console Franz Kafka, the most Western of all Western
Jews, the most clearly conscious of his uprootedness, for being
the lost son of this people gifted with indestructible unity.

Written under the impact of a profound emotion, and not
without ulterior motives in regard to the addressee (such motives were seldom absent from his communications with
women), but free from all polemical intention, this admirable
page should suffice to demolish the sophisticated Kafka whom
the theological or metaphysical exegetes so love to project
upon the heavens. It should also temper very considerably the
image, which critics who ought to know better have not hesi-
tated to promulgate, of a Jew sick with self-hatred, because
contaminated with the deadly virus of the anti-Semitism
around him. Drawing on his incomparable knowledge of
Kafka's writings and of the historical material to which he had
access, Heinz Politzer had good reasons for writing: "Franz
Kafka's self-hatred was the source of all the sufferings that
made up his life. . . . The fact that he attributed his psychic
disorder to his Jewish origin and to his surroundings only
proves that he succumbed to the anti-Semitic atmosphere of
old Austria and young Czechoslovakia; he seized the poisoned
arrows, which a rapidly deteriorating tolerance barely diverted
from him, and plunged them into his heart."[18] Few assimilated
Jews were immune to this Jewish self-hatred, which Kafka
carried to positively suicidal lengths. It dominated even their
relations with one another, so much so that in 1910 the following comment appeared in *Die Selbstwehr* (Self-Defense), the
Zionist organ of Bohemia: "To hear them speaking among
themselves of their coreligionaries, one would think one had
strayed into the best anti-Semitic society."[19]

Arthur Schnitzler described another aspect of contemporary Jewish life as he found it on emerging from the ghetto, at
a time when his situation forced him to see himself no longer
through his own eyes, but through those of his enemies: ". . . no
Jew really respects another. Never. No more than prisoners
of war in enemy territory can respect one another, especially
when they have no hope. There may be envy, hatred, some-

times admiration and, come to think of it, even love, but respect, never. Because all their emotional relations develop in an atmosphere where respect is bound to stifle."[20] Of this lack of respect among Jews, Hermann Kafka himself provides the prime example. He was forever fuming, not only against Jews in general, but against members of his own family as well: ". . . one is a crook, another makes you want to spit (Phooey!). . . ."[21] He called Max Brod a *meshuggener Ritoch* and Löwy a "dog," which shows a certain gradation in contempt, but also the total dependence of his judgment on that of non-Jews, which unbeknownst to him determined even his choice of insults.

When Kafka expressed his desire to exchange his lot for that of a starved and lice-ridden little Polack—an unseemly wish, absolutely incomprehensible to the people of his milieu and even no doubt to the Viennese intellectual to whom his letter was addressed—it was obviously not from his Jewish origin that he wished to be freed, but from the ruinous assimilation which condemned a Jew to see his fellow Jews through the hostile, contemptuous, threatening, or merely foreign eyes of a Christian, which by the mere fact of judging and appraising him reduced him to an object. Kafka imagined that if he had been born in some small town in Poland or Galicia, he would have had a direct, independent, pure view of himself—pure in the sense that it would have taken on none of the hateful coloration of the anti-Semitic view, which had become a part of him and never ceased to cloud his gaze. Under such conditions, the poverty, the promiscuous overcrowding, even the absence of culture in which he would have had to live mattered little; the sacrifice of everything he had and everything he was seemed a small price to pay for deliverance from this Jewish gaze compelled to refract the hatred of non-Jews.

Unlike his numerous contemporaries whom Jewish self-hatred led to renounce themselves, Kafka complained not so much of having come into the world as a Jew as of having become by the accident of his birth a kind of ape in love with his aping; a hybrid impossible to classify, unviable and sterile; the product of a cross between two species, neither of which recognized itself in him—a condition that condemned him, not to die, but to wander eternally in a zone intermediate between death and life.[22] Fundamentally hostile to the section of contemporary Jewry that is ordinarily regarded as the most advanced, he was radically opposed to all those who, taking on the attitudes of the Gentiles among whom they lived, including their anti-Jewish prejudice, believed they had merely rejected obsolete beliefs and customs condemned by progress. Inevitably the assimilated Jew, who had become an anti-Semite through identification with his tacitly hostile or rabidly anti-Jewish neighbors, turned against all things Jewish; for him there was nothing worth saving; the whole was repellent to him and he did everything in his power to get away from it. Kafka, on the contrary, distinguished between the Jews denatured by their contact with the West and the other, true, Jews, whom he regarded as exemplary, if only because they cared nothing for the impression they made on foreigners and measured themselves by their own law. In this question, where the pros and cons must be carefully weighed, especially since for Kafka all life depended on the balance between them, the difference cannot be regarded as negligible; on the contrary it must be stressed, for it would be difficult to conceive of a Karl Kraus, to cite only one of the most notorious of Jewish anti-Semites, in despair because he was what he was rather than a little Yiddish-speaking Jew in some remote Galician town. Still less can one see him forgoing the privilege of writing in German, getting down on his knees to Löwy, or championing the Yiddish language in public. Undoubtedly there was Jewish self-hatred on both sides—with the difference, however, that Kafka's introverted anti-Semitism did not impel him to exterminate the Jews in his writings, but lodged within him like a foreign body that destroys its host and kills him in the end. And, moreover, unlike the pure violence manifested, for example, in the work of Weininger, who thought he could put an end to Jewry by killing himself, Kafka's hatred was so closely bound up with an unhappy love, with sympathy for the entire

Jewish people, that, far from debasing the Jews, it singularly exalted them.

Even while hating the Jew that he was by the accident of birth—in consequence, he says, "of my origins, my education, disposition and environment"[23]—Kafka felt surges of tenderness for his people, an active solidarity, a sympathy in the fullest sense of the word, which do not by any means square with the sentiments of a confessed or prudently camouflaged anti-Semitic Jew. Irritated, perplexed, often even scandalized at the spectacle of Jews in whom his own sort of vacillation seemed to him only too discernible, he was nevertheless moved by the way in which each one of them bore the destiny of the community. Thus he "wept over the report of the trial of twenty-three-year-old Marie Abraham, who because of poverty and hunger strangled her not quite nine-month-old child with a man's tie she used as a garter,"[24] and beyond a doubt he was more effectively reconciled with himself because he wept over this Jewish Margarethe seduced by some suburban Faust, than because of any of the extraordinary triumphs registered by the Jewish intellectual élite of the time. But his Jewish self-hatred was not only disarmed by Jewish misfortune, it also melted away in the presence of Jewish children and young people, who, wherever they came from and wherever he came across them, filled him with vague hope of salvation and almost consoled him for his personal failure. The younger generation was as dear to him as his own generation was suspect; he loved those girls and boys wholeheartedly and indiscriminately; he loved even their ignorance, their bad taste, and their lack of originality.

That such faults, which he would have detested in anyone else, held a certain charm for him in young Jews is made apparent by the portrait he drew of the young girl he chanced to meet in the course of one of his cures and soon considered marrying: "The Jewish element [at Olga Stüdl's pension at Schelesen, where he went for his health in 1919] is a young woman, only, it is to be hoped, slightly ill. A common and yet astounding phenomenon. Not Jewish and yet not not-Jewish, not German and yet not not-German, crazy about the movies, about operettas and comedies, wears face powder and veils, possesses an inexhaustible and nonstop store of the brashest Yiddish expressions, in general very ignorant, more cheerful than sad—that is about what she is like."[25] This description makes it clear enough that the "Jewish element" that appealed to Kafka was not necessarily very refined; its members could be shockingly crude and commonplace, provided they resisted outside influences and preserved at least a nucleus of Jewishness intact: "Not Jewish and yet not not-Jewish, not German and yet not not-German." Julie Wohryzek seems to have been the least likely person to attract someone as fastidious as Kafka was in every respect. To judge by the many negations in his portrait of her, she was hardly a model of Jewishness, or even the strong, healthy person who might have been a support to him. And yet it was she he chose to make a home with, to the horror of Hermann Kafka, who, not entirely without justification, it must be admitted, regarded this latest marriage project as the worst sort of provocation.[26]

But Kafka did not envisage marriage—the great trial of his life, which accelerated his flight into illness—as a means of escaping from the clan. To judge by his choice of fiancées, exogamy was not one of the solutions he spent his life looking for; or, if the idea did sometimes come to him, he seems to have had little difficulty in rejecting it. Not that he was opposed to mixed marriage in principle. Unlike his parents and even Max Brod, who seems to have been stricter on this point than Kafka, he reacted rather sympathetically to his sister Ottla's marriage to a Christian Czech, as can be seen in the letter to Ottla in which he explains Max Brod's indirect reservations: "He [Brod] simply thinks (apart from deploring a loss for Judaism and a loss of Judaism for you and the future, but on this score I do not see clearly) that you are doing something extraordinarily difficult, which of course is easy for you on the one side, the heart side, so that you overlook the extraordinary part of the other side. But this I do not believe, so I have no particular ground for complaint."[27]

Some days earlier he had given her the same argument: "I am really surprised that Max's remark has troubled you for so long. . . . You know you are doing something extraordinary, and that it is extraordinarily difficult to do the extraordinary well. But if you never forget the responsibility incurred by so grave an action, and remain aware of the fact that you are stepping out of the ranks as self-reliantly as when David for example leaves the army, and if despite this awareness you preserve your faith in your power to carry the matter to a good conclusion, then—to conclude with a bad joke—you will have accomplished more than if you had married ten Jews."[28] And later on, Kafka's relations with Joseph David became warm and almost playful, in any case freer than his relations with his Jewish brothers-in-law.

Though, as we see, he had no objection in principle to mixed marriage for others, even his closest relations, for himself he seems to have objected strenuously.

The two women to whom he contemplated marriage were Jewish. Milena was not, and the insistence with which he harped on the fact—telling her, for instance, that to come to him she would need nothing less than the heroism of a Joan of Arc—makes it amply clear that he felt seriously guilty. As for the one Christian girl whom he knew intimately and loved,[29] we do not know why he was so ready to obey when she forbade him to try to see her again, to write to her, or even to pronounce her name again. There is reason, however, to suppose that the question of background and religion had something to do with this mysterious interdiction—at least in Kafka's mind, since all we know of the girl is that she was young and inexperienced.[30]

Still, a comparison of the circumstances attending Kafka's adventure in Riva with what happened when he became interested in Milena throws some light on the mystery. G.W., the Swiss girl, appeared in his life at a time when the prospect of marriage with Felice had put him in a state of extreme anguish, and Milena turned up seven years later to enable him to leave Julie, to whom he was officially engaged—

actually, she obliged him to. In both cases Kafka's passion for a Christian girl seems to have served the purpose of saving him from a Jewish fiancée, and in both cases it achieved its end—at its own expense, it is true, because, by taking on the excess burden of guilt connected with this unconscious duplicity, the forbidden passion became doomed to sterility.

Unable to marry a woman who would become a Jewish mother to him or to escape the horror of this equivalent of incest by resorting to exogamy, Kafka could no more marry than he could leave Prague and the cramped Jewish environment that held him captive. Others traveled, emigrated, looked elsewhere for more solid ground and freer air, hoped, like Brod, to find it in Berlin, or, like Werfel, in the richly sensuous Italy of music and the Church, or, like the few Prague Zionists who put their ideas into practice, in Tel Aviv. Because of his special neurotic make-up, but also because of the aims he deliberately set himself, Kafka could resort to none of these solutions, convinced as he was that for him they would never be anything but pathetic expedients. In 1912 his dream of Berlin took on just enough consistency to aggravate his torment, and one of his main grievances against Felice was that she insisted on coming to Prague to live with him instead of helping or even forcing him to emigrate. It was not until eleven years later that he found a haven in Berlin, when his illness was too far advanced to leave him much hope of starting a new life. If "little mother" Prague, in secret alliance with his own mother, finally consented to let him go, it was no doubt only because he had made up his mind too late.

Nor, indecisive by nature and in a sense by choice, was Kafka able to escape his destiny by conversion, though there, too, he was extremely tolerant toward others, if not toward himself. Just as his sister's mixed marriage found him benevolently inclined, he felt only affection for his maternal uncle Rudolf Löwy, who had been converted in his youth and whom the whole family, with the exception of Franz, regarded as an eccentric if not a madman. His father had often told him that he resembled this uncle—a soft-spoken man devoid of ambition, easygoing and obstinate in his eccentricity—and he himself was so close to believing as much that he sought to reassure, or possibly to frighten, himself by drawing up an inventory of the qualities that made him another Rudolf in the unflattering mirror of the family tradition: ". . . both of us quiet (I less so), both dependent on our parents (I less so), at odds with our fathers, loved by our mothers (he in addition condemned to the horror of living with his father, though of course his father was likewise condemned to live with him), both of us shy, excessively modest (he more so), both regarded as noble, good men—there is nothing of these qualities in me and, so far as I know, very little in him (shyness, modesty, timidity are accounted good because they offer little resistance to other people's aggressive impulses)—both hypochondriacal at first, then really ill, both, for do-nothings, fairly well treated by society (he, because he was less of a do-nothing, treated a lot more poorly, as far as a comparison is possible at this point), both civil servants (he a better one), both living the most monotonous lives without a trace of development, young to the end of our days ('well-preserved' is a better word for it), both on the verge of insanity; he, far removed from Jews, with tremendous courage, with tremendous vitality (by which one can measure the danger of insanity) escaped into the church where, so far as one could tell, his tendencies to madness were somewhat held in check, apparently he had not been able to hold himself in check for years. One difference in his favor or disfavor was that he had less artistic talent than I, he could therefore have chosen a better career when he was young, he was not inwardly torn, not even by ambition . . . he was infinitely more innocent than I, there is no comparison. In the details he was a caricature of me; in the essential I am one of him."[31] In this significant passage Kafka does not say that he himself is "far removed from Jews"; but he has no word of reproof or regret at the fact that his uncle was; on the contrary, in associating apostasy with "tremendous courage" and "tremendous vitality," he sees it in an almost heroic light.

Whereas Kafka fought desperately for years to escape celibacy, it cost him no great struggle to resist conversion, though the idea seems to have suggested itself to him at least once. In the summer of 1912, while he was staying at the naturist colony of Jungborn in the Harz Mountains, he made friends with a certain H., a surveyor. This H. was an adept of the "Christian Community" and gave Kafka "four tracts for my Sunday reading," because, misled no doubt by Kafka's strange interest in religions of every kind, he thought him fit to be touched by grace. Kafka tells the story in detail in his travel notes, in the half-mocking, half-affectionate tone he always takes in speaking of religious cranks. The titles of the pamphlets—*The Prodigal Son, Redeemed, or You Are No Longer Mine (for Unbelieving Believers)*, etc.—give an adequate idea of the apostle's literary gifts. No matter; Kafka read the pamphlets and, as he wrote in a letter to Felice, "made hesitant by the respect he inspires in me, I try to explain to him why at the present time there is no prospect of grace for me,"[32] which of course the adept of the "Christian Community" felt free to doubt. Some months later, when he was making no progress with his "American novel" and Felice's silence plunged him into despair, he confessed to her that that same evening, "I decided that my one chance of salvation was to write to a man in Silesia with whom I had made friends this summer and who spent long afternoons trying to convert me to Christ."[33] Kafka's resolution was short-lived: a wire from Felice sufficed to cheer him up. His letter, he wrote, could "wait a while," and indeed he seems never to have sent it. For, aware that "horrid Jewish energies live on close to the bursting point in a baptized Jew,"[34] and knowing that he would never as long as he lived "be able to change his skin," he not only felt an instinctive horror of conversion but was also well aware that it would do no good.

Kafka seems never to have abandoned the hope of consolidating his existence by making a change of scene, by falling in love with foreign women, or by freeing himself from his ethnic and religious ties. But, what with his perpetually divided nature, he never tried to fulfill this hope except in thought—that is, in his writing, for in him thought and writing were virtually identified. There were so many situations that he could have experienced if he had decided to act, but in the chaos of his irreconcilable desires every decision struck him as premature, so he contented himself with testing them all in his books, with examining them in every detail, so as to evaluate the possibilities and dangers that each might hold for him. Caught up in this systematic experimentation with possibilities, which consumed the greater part of his time and energy, he was quite well able to remain what he was and where he was, a Kafka among Kafkas, a Jew among Jews, with them yet in exile, unapproachably remote from them yet, in the complicated system of his human relationships, in some sense close to them. Far as he may have been from the Jews in his thinking, he remained near them physically; from 1911 on, at any rate, he never ceased to associate with them and sought them out wherever they might be gathered together—in their synagogues, at their reception centers and meetings. He sometimes attended their religious services, more often their social gatherings, lectures, classes for refugee children—all this in silence, taking refuge in a zone halfway between presence and absence. Now moved to tears, now violently irritated, almost always a prey to the distress that the "mere sight of my dear fellows" causes the Dog in his story, he notes what he observes from his isolated post, not in order to derive from it a valid reason for staying or leaving—he would stay in any case—but to put himself to the test vis-à-vis the people that, beyond all question of right and wrong, wholly determined his human status. And what was important to him in this constant activity of bringing his judgment up to date was far less to formulate a coherent verdict than to keep a meticulous record of the variations in his Jewish feeling, with a view to finding out whether he was moving a little further out into the desert or whether in spite of everything—"in spite of everything" was always his last word—he was not coming closer to the land of Canaan.

It need not surprise us that Kafka, profoundly committed as he was to the Eastern Jews, could write after attending a meeting organized for them by the Jews of Prague, "I, as if made of wood—a clothesrack pushed into the middle of the room," though adding, it is true, "and yet hope";[35] or that he admired "the good strong way in which Judaism separates things. There is room there for a person. One sees oneself better, one judges oneself better";[36] that he had just written, about his friend Bergmann's lecture on "Moses and the Present," "In any event, I have nothing to do with all that";[37] and again, in 1914, "What have I in common with Jews? I have hardly anything in common with myself and should stand very quietly, in a corner, content that I can breathe";[38] that this confession, so easy to cite as proof of his Jewish anti-Semitism, is constantly belied not only by other statements, but also by the orientation of his whole life; that he could urge Felice to learn spiritually from her little Polish pupils, but at the same time urge her to follow the example of the German pietist Erdmuthe von Zinzendorf, whose life in the sect of the Moravian Brethren, founded by her husband, he thought especially edifying. Nor, finally, should one be astonished at his writing to Milena, "Sometimes I'd like to cram them all (including myself) into the laundry chest, then wait, then open the drawer a little to see if they have all suffocated, and if not to close the drawer again and go on like that to the end."[39] This fiendish desire to exterminate the Jewish family does not prevent him from expressing, in a letter written soon afterward, also to Milena, a wish for rebirth inspired by his vision of the true family that the emigrants from the East had taught him to long for. It was possible for him to say, be, and do all those things by turns, and sometimes almost simultaneously, because, capable of living only in a contradiction imposed by his transitional Jewishness, he knew no other truth than that of his own inner incoherence and no other task more urgent, no other mission more imperative, than, for want of a higher aim, to manifest this contradiction to the full.

Thanks to his inability to create order within himself, but also to his absolute insistence on honesty, Kafka was an unimpeachable witness to chaos, and this he remained even in his attitude toward Zionism, which was then widely regarded as the only possible remedy for the innumerable evils facing the Jews of the diaspora. His two closest friends were staunch Zionists. Max Brod devoted articles and lectures to Zionist propaganda, while Felix Weltsch directed the Zionist organ *Die Selbstwehr* from 1918 on and was active in the movement. But, far from rallying to their ideas, Kafka long viewed them with hostility and distrust. It seemed to him that the people he saw leaving for Palestine were none too sure they had made the right decision. They "have downcast eyes, feel blinded by their listeners, fumble around on the table with the tips of their extended fingers, their voices quiver, they smile feebly and prop up their smiles with a little irony. Dr. K. told us that his students are chauvinists, are forever talking about the Maccabees and want to take after them."[40] Evidently the Prague Zionists were too much like him to fool him; like him they were looking for a way out. To them Zionism seemed to be an instrument of personal salvation, and this in itself sufficed to make him suspicious of their project. Much as he admired their courage, they lacked, as he saw it, the immediate truth which the Eastern Jews possessed without effort. To the Prague Jews, he thought, Palestine was a mere hypothesis, an expression of the desire to be elsewhere which even at home made them miserable. It was an expedient of whose absurdity and dreariness they themselves were aware; hence their lack of assurance, their shifty eyes, and the irony with which they tried to keep up their courage. They were not authentic pioneers any more than the assimilated Prague Jews were authentic Czechs or Germans; like everyone else they were victims of the city's curse, which weighed on them even in their efforts to escape it.

Of course we cannot expect Kafka's writings of the period to provide a theoretical formulation of the more general reasons for his hostility to Zionism: Kafka was not a theoretician. Besides, his anti-Zionism did not take the form of any public action; he argued the question only with himself, in the restricted area of inner struggle, to which his absence of contact with the outside world confined him. But it may be possible, by examining the concept of "the people" emerging from his personal writings and some of his stories—*The Great Wall of China*, for example, where the people is seen as the source and pledge of all truth—to see why for a long time he looked askance at Jewish nationalism, whereas the nationalism of other peoples struck him as a natural phenomenon, as inaccessible to proof or refutation as is a tree solidly planted in its soil.

It is indeed one of his most constant ideas that a true people must have its roots in a community grounded as much on language and history as on land and blood, and that where this biological, linguistic, territorial, and historic unity has been preserved, the individual requires no special effort to justify his existence; he is, as it were, saved in advance, his people holds him fast, and he need have no fear of falling. Joseph David, the proud leader of the Sokol [a gymnastic society founded in Prague in 1802], was cheerful, healthy, pleased with himself for good reason, and for equally good reason displeased with others—all this because he "lives in the midst of his people"[41] and partook naturally of the people's strength. He had precisely "the tremendous advantage of Christians who always have and enjoy such feelings of closeness in general intercourse, for instance a Christian Czech among Christian Czechs."[42] The advantage was no doubt less for Eastern Jews, who lived in exile, enclaved in an enormous universe of distrust and prejudice; still, it undoubtedly existed, thanks to the concrete soul of the *shtetl*, which in the course of time enabled the Eastern Jews to refashion a unity. Despite the exiguity of the territory into which they had plunged their deep roots, their existence required no other legitimation; it was sovereign within its limits, and those who were fully conscious of it "do their work so thoroughly within their sphere that one believes they could succeed in anything on earth—yet it is part of their perfection that they don't reach out for anything beyond their sphere."[43] Thus it matters little whether or not the people is a duly established nation or even whether it is the legal owner of its soil; it is a source of happiness and perfection as long as it unites in one and the same place all the forces for cohesion created by biology and everything that, thanks to a common language and history, it has had the power to endure.

Zionism was born of the desire to reunite in one country the Jews who had been dispersed for centuries, and in this sense at least Kafka should have recognized that it was not alien to him; but in 1912—five years before the Balfour Declaration: the date is not without its importance—Jewish nationalism, seen from Kafka's special point of view, was no better than a ludicrous imitation of various European nationalisms, exalting as a *reality* a purely hypothetical national homeland, a Promised Land, a land of dreams; to his mind, it had all the shortcomings of the European nationalisms but—and this is what condemned it out of hand—could not lay claim to their reality. Dr. K.'s students, forever talking about the Maccabees, were ridiculous and exasperating; they were going to war against an imaginary enemy to defend a land that was not their own, failing to suspect that they were merely aping what was most suspect in their real enemies, who at least had an actual soil under their feet. Whatever may have been Kafka's reasons for rejecting the Zionism of 1912, it seems likely that this naïve and aggressive imitation of Christians, in which, paradoxically, the Zionists resembled the assimilated Jews, sufficed to make the movement suspect in his eyes. (By a coincidence that may not be without significance, Kafka moved definitely closer to Zionism in 1917, when the Balfour Declaration for the first time gave the idea of a national homecoming a possibility of fulfillment.)

Though the explanation here suggested must remain hypothetical, what lends it probability is that it fits in perfectly with Kafka's tendency to base his judgments more on people than on ideas.[44] To him ideas had no value in themselves; they had value only insofar as they gave people the strength, not to do the impossible, but to realize the possibilities that life put in their way. Kafka did not know what faith or philosophy Chaim Nagel professed, whether he was a Zionist, an anti-

Zionist, or a partisan of *Yiddishkeit*. Clearly, the question did
not interest him; he was content to know that Chaim Nagel was
fully adequate to his personal sphere and looked for nothing
outside it. What connection was there between Zionism and
Felice's work at the Berlin Home? From the standpoint of
doctrine, none. The only connection is that "the work in the
Home derives from Zionism a youthful, vigorous method,
youthful vigor in general, and that where other means might
fail, it kindles national aspirations. . . ."[45] Considering Zionism
as a vehicle for forces that could benefit the children directly,
Kafka accepted it as an active pedagogical principle without
regard for his own opinions, which at that time had not greatly
changed. In his eyes opinions were never the essential, only
the catalyst that helps some people discover their true aim and
pursue it unswervingly.

If it were not for this general orientation of his thinking,
it would be easy to misjudge the seemingly eclectic attitude
shown by Kafka in his choice of spiritual models. Indeed, what
similarity was there between the two women he continually
held up as examples to Felice—the socialist Lily Braun, a revolutionary who had turned against her social class, whose
memoirs he thought so admirable that he passed them on to
everyone he knew, and the pietist Erdmuthe von Zinzendorf,
who out of passion for humanity had renounced the privileges
of her caste? Between the Prague anarchists whose meetings
he attended and the adept of the "Christian Community" who
had once tried to convert him to Christ?[46] Between the obscure faith healer from Warnsdorf whose advice he was ready
to follow when his illness took a turn for the worse, and Pyotr
Kropotkin, the revolutionary Prince who meant so much to
him at one time that he adjured himself not to forget him (the
phrase is heavily underlined in the *Diaries*)? Obviously these
objects of his admiration form an extremely heterogeneous
group, but if we consider them from above, outside our usual
intellectual frame of reference, we see what enabled Kafka
to have for them the same exalted admiration (and the same
envy as well, for he was painfully aware that he lacked what

he most valued in them): all incarnated to an exceptional degree the perfect harmony between an individual and his spiritual choice, and in this harmony all found the strength to act in the world against the established order, undeterred by doubts and conflicts.

Another consequence of Kafka's attitude toward ideas is a contradiction which during his lifetime already exposed him to repeated misunderstandings, even on the part of those friends, both men and women, who were most lastingly close to him. Since ideas meant infinitely less to him than the individual metamorphoses they were capable of provoking, they themselves, he held, were not the source of their own truth or untruth; one was as good as another, inasmuch as their formal content gave us no inkling of what they did to help an individual to become absolutely himself, in harmony with himself and his chosen aim in life. Accordingly, Kafka welcomed all ideas provisionally, with infinite tolerance, as befits a neutral observer who must see for himself before he judges. On the other hand, while ideas count only insofar as they affect the concrete organization of life, this last cannot be left to chance, but must be constantly prepared for a possible change and to that end meticulously regulated. The nature of the work to which one wishes to devote oneself, the degree to which one satisfies one's needs, the way in which one drinks, eats, dresses, and cares for one's health, the use one makes of one's money and property—on all these questions of hygiene and discipline Kafka was absolutely intransigent; he was as intolerant, as insistent on the scrupulous observance of certain rules, as he was neutral, though attentive, in regard to conflicts of ideas in which neither the body nor the soul was directly involved. Felice, for instance, could think what she wished of Zionism ("That is your affair,"[47] he told her bluntly); but eat meat, have a comfortable apartment that was heated in the winter, or travel first class—these were things she would have to forgo if she decided to marry him. Before committing herself, she would have to realize that in these matters he would never give in (indeed, his unwillingness to make concessions was largely responsible for the breakdown of their marriage plans). He was the same with his sisters; with regard to their opinions he allowed them perfect freedom, but when it came to the rearing of their children, he meddled actively in their family life, undismayed by the disturbance he was creating. He went so far as to ask his elder sister to send her ten-year-old son away, for no other reason than to spare him the "spiritual incest" to which every child brought up by his parents is condemned, especially if he has the misfortune to be born "among well-to-do Prague Jews."[48] This authoritarian attitude in private matters—which from the standpoint of bourgeois morality were purely a matter of personal taste, hence not open to discussion—stands in the sharpest contrast with Kafka's excessive reserve in matters of public concern, and those close to him must have found it quite disturbing if not frankly shocking: even Max Brod owns that sometimes when they lived together he was exasperated by his friend's obstinacy. It might not have been so bad if Kafka had justified his intransigence by clearly defined metaphysical or religious beliefs; but not at all, he was a vegetarian without holding doctrinaire vegetarianism in particularly high esteem; an ascetic without the faith from which asceticism draws its chief justification and without any particular affinity with the mystics of self-abnegation, whom he often ridicules in his stories and aphorisms; a zealous propagandist for practices advocated by the most divergent sects, but far from blind to the sectarian, more or less unbalanced mentality of the adepts whose part he seems to take. Clearly it is no easy matter to classify Kafka, and if only for that reason he was quite right in saying that there was no one in his intimate circle who understood him "in his entirety." In his entirety, this man, an extreme liberal when it came to ideas and an equally extreme fanatic in practice, was indeed as indecipherable, as bewildering for his most understanding friends as his writings would be for posterity.

Ideas conceived as agents of inner purification obviously have no place in politics, and in this sense politics did not interest Kafka, except in the case of men who took political

movements as the privileged instrument of an ascetic vocation—a qualification that political movements in general and
Zionism in particular certainly had no interest in testing. And
true enough, political Zionism, with its doctrine, its factions,
and its internal struggles, takes up so little space in Kafka's
private writings that, if it were not for what one can infer here
and there from his conversations with his friends, one would
be tempted to remove it entirely from the list of his preoccupations. As it is, one wonders: What exactly did he know about
it, and from whom had he learned what he knew? His library
offers no certainty; the inventory, which was not drawn up
until ten years after his death, is incomplete. Still, it may be
significant to note that the only one of Herzl's works cited is
his *Diaries*,[49] one more indication that Kafka was less curious
about the ideas of the founder of Zionism than about the extraordinary adventure of his life and especially his private
tragedy. Of course, Kafka may have read *The Jewish State*
without personally owning a copy. Be that as it may, the meager representation of works dealing with Zionist history and
politics makes it plain that they were not Kafka's favorite
reading matter; he preferred the history of religions, Jewish
folklore, and works dealing with the "great old days" of historic Judaism. (On the other hand, he read a good many periodicals.)

Kafka hardly ever mentioned the Zionist movement as
such in his *Diaries* or his letters. We know only that in 1913,
more by chance than by design, he attended a Zionist congress
in Vienna (he happened to be in Vienna with his employer for
a congress on work accidents). This brief stay in the Austrian
capital made such an unpleasant impression on him that he
would have liked, he said, to obliterate it from his memory,
and the Zionist congress itself gave him nothing but boredom,
as can be seen from the hasty notes he took for Felice: "The
worker delegate from Palestine, perpetual screeching. Herzl's
daughter. The former head of the college in Jaffa. Bolt upright
on one of the steps, meager beard, flying coattails. Speeches in
German, ineffectual, lots of Hebrew, the main work is done at

small meetings, Lise W. [Weltsch] just sits around through all this, without being really present, throws spitballs around the hall. Discouraging."[50] As he confided to Brod, he was "so depressed that for two cents he would have machine-gunned the delegates."[51] Kafka did not get over his anti-Zionism until the First World War with its disastrous effect on the condition of the Jews of Central Europe, and in particular of Czechoslovakia. Undoubtedly his concern over the recrudescence of anti-Semitism during and after the war had a good deal to do with his change of attitude, which occurred only gradually, by fits and starts. In any case, what most of his biographers call his "Zionist phase" did not begin until 1914; witness his often quoted letter to Felice, in which he bids her face up to her responsibilities: "How you come to terms with Zionism is your affair; any coming to terms with it (indifference is out of the question) will give me pleasure. It is too soon to discuss it now, but should you one day feel yourself to be a Zionist (you flirted with it once, but that was a mere flirtation, not a coming to terms), and subsequently realize that I am not a Zionist— which would probably emerge from an examination—it wouldn't worry me, nor need it worry you; Zionism is not something that separates well-meaning people."[52] As we see, Kafka did not wish to interfere in Felice's confrontation with Zionism. She must manage without knowing his opinion; at the very most she could guess his opinion from his "probably" and the series of conditionals with which he veiled the truth that he himself was not a Zionist and would "probably" not have become one even when she herself had made up her mind.

Thus we see that by the end of 1916 Kafka had not yet rallied to the Zionist cause; yet a few months later he began to learn Hebrew, which at least denotes a serious desire to come closer to it. By 1917 he may have contemplated going to Palestine, as he definitely wished to do six years later, when the worsening of his health had made the long journey impossible. He did not speak of it, but beyond a doubt 1917 marked a turning point—not only in his life, which from then on was dominated, both physically and morally, by his illness, but also in the destiny of Zionism itself, which the Balfour Declaration provided with the solid foundation needed for its development. Ill and obliged to leave Prague for his health, Kafka took his first step toward a Return at the very moment when the Return ceased to be a vague idea and became a justified hope. This seems to substantiate our explanation of his antipathy for the vague Zionism that had hitherto prevailed in Prague and elsewhere. And he assuredly attached the utmost importance to his first cautious steps, though it is impossible to say whether, under different circumstances and with unimpaired strength, he could have reached or even glimpsed the Promised Land.

Kafka did not become a militant Zionist; his state of health would not have allowed it, and in any case militancy was not in his character. His main activity in that direction was the study of Hebrew, which he carried on assiduously for years, sometimes alone, sometimes with the help of private lessons. He filled whole notebooks with letters and grammatical exercises (his notebooks for 1918 contain more Hebrew exercises than literary notes), and studied so industriously that in the end he was able to converse in Hebrew with a young Palestinian woman who gave him lessons.[53] He was even capable of reading a work about the Cabala in Hebrew, or so one can reasonably suppose, since he asked Brod to bring him one—any one, he said, adding, "I suppose it is in Hebrew,"[54] which shows how little he knew of such matters and how little credence is to be given to the cabalistic interpretations of his work.[55]

But his interest in Zionism went beyond his study of Hebrew; at Zürau he subscribed to *Die Selbstwehr*, the Zionist organ of which his friend Felix Weltsch became editor in chief in 1918; he read Jewish periodicals and the Bible, especially the Pentateuch; while in Prague he often attended lectures by Brod and others, though never taking part in the discussion; and in Berlin he attended courses at the School for Scientific Judaism, a place that offered him "a haven of peace in this wild and woolly Berlin and in the wild and woolly regions of the mind ..." and where the teaching appealed to him because of "the liberal reformist tone and scholarly aspects of the whole thing."[56] It was then that he first spoke openly of the possibility of a move to Palestine. He spoke of it often to Dora Dymant: they would work together, she as a cook, he as a waiter in the same establishment. When his childhood friend Hugo Bergmann invited him to join him in Jerusalem, he claimed to have tested his "transportability" by going first to Müritz on the Baltic, but implied that the experiment had not been conclusive enough for him to risk going farther. "I had actually meant," he wrote to Milena, "to go to Palestine in October. I think we talked about it, of course it would never have come off, it was a fantasy, the kind of fantasy someone has who is convinced that he will never again leave his bed. If I'm never going to leave my bed again, why shouldn't I travel as far as Palestine?"[57] But his weakness was not the only, and perhaps not the real, reason for this failure, as he explained to Else Bergmann, who was actually preparing to come and take him back to Jerusalem: "I know now I shall certainly not sail—how could I? ... even assuming I could carry out anything of the sort, it would not have turned out to be a real voyage to Palestine at this time ... but in the spiritual sense something like a voyage to America by a cashier who has embezzled a large sum of money. And by traveling with you I would have aggravated the spiritual criminality of the case. No, I could not go that way, even if I had been able to...."[58] Here again Kafka does not ask whether what impelled Jews to set out for Palestine was in keeping with his ideal; it mattered little in the end whether they were right or wrong; what mattered was whether he had enough strength, rectitude, and purity to feel justified in accompanying them.

The answer was not long in coming. Torn as he still was, doubting in Zionism and in himself, Kafka would have been guilty of a pitiful imposture in going to Palestine. Even if he had been physically able to make the trip, his chronic state of moral misery would have prevented him, though that same state had prompted his attempt to escape. In this respect his

Zionism was no better than all the other unsuccessful expedients to which he had resorted over the years and which he listed one day in 1922: ". . . piano, violin, languages, Germanic studies, anti-Zionism, Zionism, Hebrew, gardening, carpentry, literature, attempts at marriage, an apartment of my own . . ."[59] In this inventory of setbacks, the order of whose importance is reflected by their chronology—the last being obviously the gravest—anti-Zionism and Zionism are put more or less on a level. They seem to count a little more than violin or piano and about as much as gardening and carpentry. Even writing, the madness to which Kafka had sacrificed everything, figures here only as one of the items on his negative balance sheet.

So Kafka would not go to Jerusalem; this he knew long before planning the trip in his feverish dreams. He knew he would finally have to content himself with "running his finger over the map of Palestine" and resign himself to remaining to the end the solitary poet, the prophet without law, people, or soil, the savior powerless to save himself, whom he depicts with so much humor and so much sadness in all his stories. Imprisoned forever in the desert of his inner imagery, the only place to which, unluckily for him but luckily for his work, he really had access, he wished to be nothing more than a "trifling episode in the eternal history of our people" and condemned himself to oblivion, without suspecting that in this will to self-effacement other generations would someday find the authentic seal of prophecy.

5 · Before the Law

Despite the changes his feeling of Jewishness may have incurred over the years, Kafka never at any time considered returning to the congregation. That for him was impossible
because, lacking faith in the very strict sense understood in
Judaism, he could not "approach the temple by stealth." But
though this mixture of unbelief and scruple obliged him to
stand aside even at times when his isolation struck him as a
form of suicide, he drew no advantage from the freedom that,
for so many Jews who have broken away from their religion, is
the immediate consequence of their break. Incapable as he
was of giving the little refugees from the East as much as a
"sad answer" to questions of faith and piety, he was not free to
organize his life—in the material order which to him was only
the visible aspect of the spirit—as if the old law had never
concerned him. Having lost the law, but not his passionate desire to possess it, which on the contrary became dangerously
exacerbated as the law receded from his grasp, he was infinitely more enslaved to his absence of law than any believer
could be to the stringent rules of orthodoxy.

Where assimilated Jews are at pains to free themselves
from ritual constraints conflicting with their desire to merge
with the society around them, Kafka missed the constraints.
They had not come to him with his upbringing, and if he had
been tempted to try them out, he would not have known how,

why, or to what extent to incline to them. For to his mind the commandment was not nullified by the disappearance of the commander who had uttered it long ago. In a sense, it outlived its own necessity; and not only did it remain isolated, but also, having wholly become emancipated from the divine order whose agent it was in the "great old times," it became more constrictive than ever and so tyrannical that there was neither measure nor limit to its demands. Thus it is not surprising that in *In the Penal Colony*, in which Kafka imprisons his demon of justification, the commandment without a commander is at the service of nothing but a malfunctioning mechanism, which in the end will tear it to pieces. Deprived by its monstrous autonomy of the power to regulate life, which was the essential part of its mission, it reduces the law to a disproportionate coercive power with no other function than the automatic application of punishment.

Himself irreligious, yet held fast by one essential vestige of his Jewish faith—namely, the compelling need for a law-governed life protected within from outbursts of passion and without from the absurdity of time experienced from day to day in the emptiness of pure flux—Kafka tried to remedy this untenable situation by creating out of whole cloth a code for his own use. In other words, he created something that, emanating as it did from the subjective depths in which his anguish was rooted, was by nature powerless to relieve him. For the "strong and beautiful distinctions" that Judaism had practiced, and that he was now obliged to reinvent, were no part of his birthright; the ability to distinguish just and unjust, pure and impure, licit and illicit was precisely what he most lacked, and his personal code could not remedy this inherent flaw except by enlarging the sphere of impure things and prohibited acts ad infinitum.

Because of this paradoxical position before the law, which, as we shall see, concealed a profound conflict, Kafka was unable to derive the least advantage from his Jewish heritage. He suffered from the part of it that he preserved, unbeknownst to himself, as an inalienable possession, and from the rest he derived only strictly negative effects. In a development whose logic would have been very close to Freud, it was in his attitude toward food that Kafka was most at pains to provide himself with a substitute law, and it was in this respect that his condition became most dangerously pathological.

Heir to a tradition that forbids indiscriminate eating,[1] but ignorant of—and rejecting—the code of prescriptions and prohibitions which permits one to eat after all, Kafka rejected the dietary habits adopted by his family, no member of which, incidentally, seems to have observed the dietary laws very scrupulously. On the pretext of choosing a diet better suited to the needs of a nervous stomach, he adopted other habits, which actually constituted a new system of strict prohibitions. In 1912—at the time when Löwy and the actors aroused his longing to lead a Jewish life, in full consciousness of its worth and its legitimacy—he turned vegetarian and began to abstain not only from meat, fish, eggs, and alcoholic beverages, but also from tea, coffee, chocolate, and as far as possible from all foods possessing the slightest nutritive value ("nothing," he said one day only half in jest, "is more nourishing than a slice of lemon"). Obliged to regulate himself by a purely restrictive principle which nothing, either inside or outside himself, enabled him to moderate, he took the strictest abstinence as a sort of makeshift solution, pending the day when he would be able to go without eating altogether.

Naturally Kafka never mentions this secret thought in his letters or in his *Diaries*, but the emphasis on fasting in his stories suggests that the idea was profoundly anchored in his mind, especially since it is treated with a precision and abundance of detail born of long practice. Two of his most important characters die of starvation—Gregor Samsa because his metamorphosis has destroyed his taste for the human food that his family insists on offering him, and the other—the Hunger Artist—because starvation has become both the substance of his work and his one means of creating. As for the Dog, who also staged a memorable hunger strike in his youth, he regards fasting as the activity most conducive to his investigations, though well aware that his early experiments, from which he never fully recovered, resulted only in his near-death. Less disembodied than Samsa and not so insane as the Hunger Artist, he has the enormous advantage over these two suicidal heroes of having by the skin of his teeth survived his dangerous experiments, so that now, in his advanced age, he can meditate on the causes of his failure and take account of them in framing his projects for the future (for he is not cured of the temptation, and his only thought is to try again). Indeed, he knows these causes well; in his opinion they consist chiefly in the naïveté and presumption of youth, but another important factor is the unforeseen obstacle which the canine law has suddenly put in the way of his dangerous challenge.

Informed of Kafka's intentions by his largely autobiographical function, the Dog is certainly the person best qualified to open the discussion of the complex relationship between fasting and law. Endowed as he is with a powerful intellect and a level of intelligence equal to that of his author, he is in a position to explain the motives that impelled him to undertake a purely experimental fast and the unspoken objections with which the forgotten canine law, though acting without his knowledge, was able to frustrate his design. And what makes this all the easier for him is that in addition to his intellectual qualities and the gift of self-analysis, he has at his command a science of exegesis that the most consummate Talmudist might envy.

Having undertaken to investigate the origin of food, the Dog comes to the conclusion that his findings are unsatisfactory because he cannot at one and the same time eat his food and observe it scientifically. Science is to him what art is to the Hunger Artist: it relates to the very substance that maintains life and therefore cannot be consumed, because if it were, it could no longer be *observed.* (This was Kafka's own positively disastrous reasoning: he failed to see how one could both write and eat.) To solve this dilemma, the Dog decides to undertake an almost total fast, "as long as I could stand it, and at the same time avoid all sight of food, all temptation."[2] Actually, his de-

cision was not free from calculation: he hoped that if he abstained from food as long as possible, food would be obliged to
knock at his jaws and force him to open up; in this way he
would at last capture the secret of food and, thanks to this
amazing discovery, demolish at one stroke both the supersti-
tions of the common people and the useless knowledge of the
scientist.

The first days of the experiment pass without incident;
the Dog is proud to say that he feels perfectly calm. "Although
in reality I was laboring to annul the findings of science, I felt
within me a deep reassurance, indeed, almost the proverbial
serenity of the scientific worker." During this period of euphoria, he has exalting dreams of glory, sees himself reconciled
with his family, "accepted with great honor, bathed in the long
yearned-for warmth of assembled canine bodies . . . I would
ride uplifted on the shoulders of my fellows. Remarkable effects of my first hunger." Remarkable indeed and unfortunately ephemeral, for in a short while the beautiful images
fade, and the Dog, left alone with the hunger that is devouring
his entrails, knows such terrible torment that he hardly dares
recall it to mind: "A bad, bad time! I still shudder to think of
it, and not merely on account of the suffering I endured then,
but mainly because I was unable to complete my tasks and
consequently shall have to live through that suffering once
more if I am ever to achieve anything; for I still hold fasting to
be the final and most potent instrument of my investigations."[3]
Here Kafka gently sets aside the fictitious character who
serves as his interpreter and, speaking for himself, reveals
what indeed set the seal to his fate: he would never cease to
regard fasting as the supreme instrument of his investigation
and achievement, not even when tuberculosis warned him of
its danger. By one of those hideous ironies of fate which he so
well knew how to exploit in his work, he would really die of
undernourishment, but without having wanted to and without
being able to tell himself that he had attained his goal.[4]

The Dog recognized that he had failed, first of all no
doubt because of his weakness, but also because the thought of

his ancestors had again taken hold of him and almost immediately he had lost "the unspoiled ardor of youth." His decision to fast implied in itself a challenge that, if he had been able to maintain it, might have enabled him to continue his experiment to the end. But that did not happen; his naïve combativeness ceded only too quickly to the onslaughts of the law and its terrible guardians: "It vanished in the great privations of that first fast. All sorts of thoughts tormented me. Our forefathers appeared threateningly before me. True, I held them responsible for everything, even if I dared not say so openly; it was they who involved our dog life in guilt, and so I could have easily responded to their menaces with countermenaces, but I bow before their knowledge; it came from sources of which we know no longer, and for that reason, much as I may feel impelled to oppose them, I shall never actually overstep their laws, but shall content myself with wriggling out through the gaps, for which I have a particularly good nose."[5] Once again the Dog states aloud—and with what wisdom, what dialectical skill!—what Kafka does not dare say openly or even own to himself in private (his *Diaries* and notebooks contain nothing anywhere near so decisive on this subject). He wants to combat his forebears because he holds them entirely responsible for the "dog's life" to which the Jews are condemned. On the other hand, he respects them as the repositories of a knowledge made all the more imposing by the fact that its remote origins are shrouded in oblivion, that his bellicose plans have no chance of being carried out, and that, petrified with respect, he cannot even resolve to declare war. And indeed, Kafka's war against his venerable and guilty forebears was never to be fought on the battlefields of life; it would be fought only within himself, where, for lack of actual combatants, it would degenerate into a permanent conflict and finally into illness.

Loath to transgress the law, which he regards as disastrous—for after all, what is it but the law that continues to determine the "dog's life" centuries and centuries after the forebears promulgated it?—the candidate for total fasting does

not fling himself into the adventure without taking a maximum of precautions, and this, because the texts dealing with
this point are equivocal, raises new obstacles in his path. On
the subject of fasting, the law is not so explicit that one can
dispense with interpretation, and since every sage puts
forward his own opinion, the Dog, who, without renouncing
his intention of fasting, really wants to remain within the
bounds of legality, naturally adopts the interpretation most favorable to his project. To cover himself, he invokes a famous
colloquium on the subject of fasting: ". . . one of our sages expressed the intention of forbidding fasting, but was dissuaded
by a second with the words: 'But who would ever think of fasting?' whereupon the first allowed himself to be persuaded and
withdrew the prohibition. But now arises the question: 'Is not
fasting really forbidden after all?' The great majority of commentators deny this and regard fasting as freely permitted, and
holding as they think with the second sage do not worry in the
least about the evil consequences that may result from errone-
ous interpretations. I had naturally assured myself on this
point before I began my fast."[6] Extreme in his scrupulousness,
the Dog thus wishes to show respect for the law even when
running the risk of violating it. For a risk there is, and he
knows it; and that is why he protests his good faith so vigorously. Whatever happens, he will not have sinned voluntar-
ily, and he sees to it that the mysterious powers whose
vengeance he fears are duly informed of this.

Unfortunately for him, however, the powers are not so
easily circumvented; this he notices just as his hunger begins
to torment him in earnest. It looks as if hunger and the law
were in connivance—or, more precisely, as if the law made its
will known only by forcing the faster to experience in all its
unspeakable horror the hunger he had wished for. As long as
his belly was full, the Dog could play with the meaning of the
law and serenely engage in exegesis: "But now that I was
twisted with the pangs of hunger and in my distress of mind
sought relief in my own hind legs, despairingly licking and
gnawing at them up to the very buttocks, the universal inter-

pretation of this dialogue seemed to me entirely and completely false, I cursed the science of the exegetes, I cursed myself for having been led astray by it; for as any child could see the colloquium had presented much more than one prohibition of fasting; the first sage wished to forbid fasting; what a sage wishes is already done, so fasting was forbidden; as for the second sage, he not only agreed with the first, but actually considered fasting impossible, thus piling on the first prohibition a second, that of dog nature itself; the first sage saw this and thereupon withdrew the explicit prohibition, that is, he imposed upon all dogs, the matter now being settled, the obligation to know themselves and to make their own prohibitions regarding fasting. So here was a threefold prohibition instead of merely one, and I had violated it."[7] Superlatively versed as he was in exegetic science, his study of the law did not advance by virtue of his subtlety, but solely thanks to the law, which is the supreme test of reality. Like all Kafka's characters and like Kafka himself, he learns the law only through the sentence it pronounces against him deep in his flesh long before he grasps it in spirit.

If it is permissible to take the author at the word of his philosophical dog—and the striking concordance between the story and numerous passages in the *Diaries* leave no doubt in the matter[8]—Kafka was well aware that his ascetic striving put him on the one hand in opposition to ancestral law, the rigors of which, it is true, could be attenuated or its ambiguities exploited by exegesis, and on the other hand to natural law, which, rooted in immanent justice, is totally insensible to quibbles and glosses, however subtle. Though thus doubly at fault and aware of it, he did not resolve to "obey better late than never" and to break off his fast, but succumbed on the contrary to the temptation to go on with it, which of course added a little to his guilt. Unlike the ascetic sustained by a solid theological foundation, who, if he suffers, is at least convinced of being in the truth, Kafka, to his misfortune, was compelled to regard the only sort of life he thought worth living as illegal. He regarded as a crime what in other ideological

spheres is looked upon without question as a striving for sanc-
tity, and since it was not within his power to change, this
crime, from which he could not refrain and of which he could
not repent, was at least as responsible as his most excessive ascetic practices for undermining his health.

Since the commandment without a commander which he
felt obliged to obey was never satisfied, Kafka did not confine
himself to consuming as little nourishment as possible; he also
developed all manner of food-related eccentricities, as though
to compensate with an elaborate ceremonial for the lack of
substance in his meals. One of these ritual procedures was inspired by a certain Fletcher, an American thaumaturge, who
encouraged his followers to chew every mouthful a hundred
times, something the most elementary good manners forbids
one to do in public. And so, thanks to a starvation diet painful
for those about him to behold[9] and to the Fletcherism that his
good breeding prevented him from exhibiting, he managed to
re-create the conditions for an alimentary segregation similar
to that imposed by the Jewish law, with the difference, however, that his personal rules, springing from the depths of his
anguish and not from a shared view of the world, had the opposite effect of that aimed at by the Torah. Instead of separating him from non-Jews, the better to unite him with his
coreligionists, his rules separated him from Jews no less than
from Christians, and ultimately excluded him from all meals
taken in common, even with his closest friends. Because of the
law whose yoke he still bore, but which, denatured by ignorance and semiforgetfulness, spoke to him only through the
imperatives of his own cruelty, Kafka was never able to take
his meals in company; both at home and in public places he ate
by himself. This lends the story of the colonel and the general
a note of particular sadness: to oblige these people, whom at
first sight he liked, he managed with great difficulty to overcome his eccentricity—and was severely punished for it. Considering the importance for human relations of eating and
drinking together, his having to take his meals alone amounted
to a forced withdrawal from mankind.

Similarly, in all the important affairs of life Kafka based his conduct on an authentic Jewish idea which, since for him it had lost all social and religious content, he was able to pervert, as it were, by carrying it to excess, and which in the end led him far away from the law he was stubbornly seeking. Just as in adopting a personal system of dietary rules he manifested both his nostalgia for the law of his forebears and his desire to abolish it, in regard to marriage he so exaggerated the traditional Jewish conception as to turn it into its opposite. From this exaggeration he gained nothing; it merely made it impossible for him to marry. Here again his contradictory efforts to provide himself with a substitute law merely led him astray: his conception of marriage became the main obstacle to his marrying and condemned him to celibacy, which for every pious Jew and for him as well was a state of dreary unfulfillment.

Kafka lived at a time and in a society where the only valid motives for marriage were generally held to be love or social convenience, but he had ideas that brought him much closer to the rabbis of olden days than to the Jews of his generation (or even to his elders; his father, for instance, was frankly disgusted with them). To Kafka's mind, marriage not only fulfilled the natural right of every adult to satisfy his sexual needs and establish a home, but was also, in the strictest sense, an obligation of so high an order that to evade it was to exclude oneself from the human race. In his *Diaries* he noted a sentence from the Talmud that he had heard quoted in a play by Gordin: "A man without a woman is not a human being";[10] and it almost looks as if these words were graven on his heart—to his misfortune, for when he could not help realizing that all life with others was forbidden him, first by the religion he made of writing and then by his other "singularities," it was this Talmudic adage that pronounced his condemnation.

By a coincidence that gives one food for thought, Kafka began to suffer from his bachelorhood and to worry about his future at the very time when his association with the Eastern Jews made him discover a Jewishness in every way different from his own, as essentially pure as that of Prague seemed to him adulterated. Up until then—he was twenty-eight—his bachelor life does not seem to have weighed on him very heavily, to judge at least by his *Diaries* and letters to his intimates. But no sooner had he made friends with the actors than the specter of celibacy began to haunt him, and he tried to conjure it—as usual, in writing, since writing was his only real means of action. Whatever one may think of this chronological coincidence, it was in November and December 1911 that the Bachelor made his appearance in his writing,[11] treated in a plaintive and even somewhat tearful tone which offers no intimation of the extraordinary role he was to play later on. In the first passage, this wretched creature is only an unfortunate man—"It seems so dreadful to be a bachelor, to become an old man struggling to keep his dignity while begging for an invitation. . . ."[12] In the second,[13] he is already half-dead and half-alive, the frozen, repellent ghost who, from *The Judgment* to *The Castle*, undermines the hero's strength from within and helps to lead him astray (sometimes the ghost and the hero are one, as in the case of the Hunter Gracchus, who wanders eternally in a zone halfway between death and life). Kafka was already haunted by this figure, and that is why he suddenly decided to marry Felice at the end of a single evening with her, during which he had hardly spoken.[14]

The contrast between this extraordinary haste and the "endless procrastination" that made him drag out his engagement for five years suggests that though Kafka was really taken with Felice, his only reason for being in such a hurry just then—later on he would make up for it by taking his time—was that he needed her to exorcise the demon of celibacy, to which he feared he was already enslaved for good (the memory of Uncle Rudolf had suggested as much to him only a short time before). Undoubtedly he loved her for her own sake, but also for the help she could give him against his own will to isolate himself; Felice became—obviously unbeknownst to her and almost before she knew she was being courted—the innocent object of a well-prepared bargain: she would serve as compensation for Kafka's shame at not being a married man. And it was in part because of this self-interested speculation that he would not be able to possess her. For Kafka's calculation was half-conscious, as he more than implies by attributing the same calculation to two of his heroes who also wished to "get through with the help of women"—Joseph K. to his judges, and K. the Surveyor to the "Gentlemen"—and who, like him, were severely punished for it.

Though desired chiefly as a protection against the shameful misfortune of celibacy, marriage was not reduced to a purely negative function, or, rather, it was this negative aspect that heightened its value, making it capable of appreciably raising the level of existence. Marriage saves a man simply by removing him from the narrow sphere in which his coldness and his petty calculations have hitherto held him captive. It ennobles the individual and so performs a truly religious function, which raises it far above any practical value it can have for any one couple. A particular marriage may be happy or unhappy, successful or unsuccessful; marriage in general is nevertheless a state that enables the individual to redeem himself. All the adventures of K. the Surveyor revolve around this redeeming virtue which he attributes to his union with Frieda and which (this is his gravest mistake) he wishes in addition to make official (Frieda, as we recall, is a young waitress in a café, and her name is more or less a German translation of the Italian Felice). When Kafka notes in his *Diaries*, "The broadening and heightening of existence through marriage. Sermon text. But I have almost an intimation of it,"[15] he is conscious of thinking like a theologian—almost, that is, and the restriction is vital, because it corresponds exactly to the falseness of his position; and although his doctrine is based on a mere intimation, it puts him in the direct line of the Talmudic master who, when asked, "What must one do to fit oneself for the study of the Torah?," replied, "First marry."[16]

First marry—over and over again Kafka repeated this precept of Jewish wisdom. He became positively obsessed with it, but never succeeded in fulfilling it—and for this very reason the inherited wisdom turned to madness in him. For here again he was deprived of the law, since he was totally without the sense of proportion it implied; all he could find to replace it was an absolute idea of purity. Whereupon this absolute—tied to a living object quite incapable of adjusting to it, arrived at by a perversion of the law—cut off all vision of human marriage and sent him in pursuit of an ideally pure marriage which, absolute only in its impossibility, doomed him to the condition he most dreaded, giving him nothing but a sense of his own helplessness and unworthiness.

Felice was notified almost at the start that the union desired by Kafka had only its name in common with marriage, but in terms so veiled that she hardly knew what to think (or if she vaguely guessed the truth, she chose not to worry too much about it). First Kafka told her about his dietary habits, though neglecting to tell her how much importance he attached to them or what an inconvenience they could be to others in daily life. He spoke a little more freely of his feelings about heating and clothing, admitting quite frankly that his special resistance to the cold was not his real reason for "not wearing an overcoat, neither a light nor a heavy one [in mid-November, in Prague!], and walking around like a lunatic in a summer suit and a little summer hat."[17] After this purposely exaggerated self-portrait—intended at once to frighten Felice and to temper her alarm with amusement—Kafka gradually approached the essential, or rather adumbrated it, for it was not merely difficult but quite impossible to acquaint the young woman with the essential. And so he approached the matter indirectly, by way of his poor health: ". . . my health is only just good enough for myself alone, not good enough for marriage, let alone fatherhood."[18] And then, when Felice thought she detected a desire to break off—she didn't know him very well yet—Kafka hastened to undeceive her and approached the difficult question by another tack, which he conveniently found in one of his favorite Chinese poets. After introducing the author, Yan-Tse-Tsai, he went to the length of copying out the whole poem, entitled "In the Heart of the Night." The hero is the man ordinarily called "the scholar" or the "stay-at-home," as opposed to "the warrior." This scholar has worked all through the night by the light of his lamp while his mistress was waiting patiently for him in bed. Immersed in his studies, he has let the fire go out. The room is cold and the perfumes sprinkled on the bed have long evaporated when, with the coming of dawn, his infuriated mistress snatches the lamp out of his hands and cries, "Do you know what time it is?"[19] That is all. Kafka simply asks Felice to savor the poem, without for the moment commenting on it. But a few weeks later, as he is writing to her at night and notices the late hour, the Chinese scholar comes to his mind: "Alas, it is not my mistress who calls me, it's only the letter I want to write to her. You once said you would like to sit beside me while I write; listen, in that case I could not write (I can't do much anyway), but in that case I could not write at all."[20] What now follows goes far beyond the situation in the poem, for the Chinese scholar at least endures the presence of a woman beside him. Not Kafka. No, for writing he requires absolute solitude, a night blacker than all other nights, the silence of the tomb where he dreams of burying himself: "I have often thought that the best mode of life for me would be to sit in the innermost room of a spacious locked cellar with my writing things and a lamp. Food would be brought and always put down far away from my room, outside the cellar's outermost door. The walk to my food, in my dressing gown, would be my only exercise. I would then return to my table, eat slowly and with deliberation, then start writing again at once. And how I would write! From what depths I would drag it up! Without effort! For extreme concentration knows no effort. The trouble is that I might not be able to keep it up for long, and at the first failure—which perhaps even under these conditions could not be avoided—would be bound to end in a grandiose fit of madness. *What do you think, dearest? Don't be reticent with your cellar-dweller!*"[21] For the moment Kafka holds back the main point, contenting himself with warning Felice—but very clearly—that if she decides to marry him, they will each be getting married separately, she to an absent husband and he to his writing, which has all the rights over his life.

One easily imagines Felice's revolt against such a picture of her married life. To appease her Kafka calls once again on his Chinese, who, well defended as he is against seduction, finally lets the woman triumph over his will: "But finally, able to contain herself no longer, she did take the lamp away from him, which was after all quite right, beneficial to his health, not, it is to be hoped, harmful to his studies, conducive to love, which inspired a beautiful poem, and yet, all things considered, was mere self-deception on the woman's part."[22] Horrified by the reaction of Felice, who seems to have been overwhelmed by the business of the cellar, Kafka tried to present the situation in a less terrifying light. Perhaps, he said, he wouldn't spend all day and all night in the cellar after all, perhaps he would come up now and then, letting the lamp be taken from his hands as did the Chinese scholar, and join his woman in bed. Perhaps, but two days later this fragile hope was destroyed, still thanks to Yan-Tse-Tsai's poem, which Kafka plays on like a virtuoso, blowing hot and blowing cold at will: "Didn't you notice that it was specifically about the scholar's mistress, and not his wife, although the scholar is undoubtedly an elderly man, and the combination of scholarship and age would seem to argue against the presence of a mistress." Should one suppose that the poet preferred "an improbability to an impossibility"? Or that he feared "that such a confrontation of the scholar with his wife might rob the poem of all its gaiety . . . The mistress in the poem is not too badly off; this time the lamp really does go out, it was not too much trouble, and there was still plenty of fun left in her. But how would it be if it had been his wife, and that night not just any night, but a sample of all nights, and then of course not only of nights, but of their whole life together, a life that would be a battle for the lamp."[23] Felice is duly warned: what a mistress would obtain from him with little difficulty his wife would have to fight for day after day, and he would not be able to give it to her, "even though he may be only pretending to look at the books, while for days and nights on end he thinks of nothing but his wife, whom he loves above all else, but loves with his inherent inadequacy."[24]

Here Kafka almost stops dissembling. Even if he were not devoted body and soul to his work and were only pretending to be, he would still be incapable of union with his wife except in *thought*. Thus it was not because of his writing, or not solely or mainly because of it, that he prepared Felice for a marriage closer to the life of a convent than to that of a true home. Indeed, he brought in the scholar only to conceal the other aspect of his person, the "bookworm," who was in every respect the opposite of the warrior: "It is a wife who awaits his return, no doubt anxiously, but overjoyed at the sight of him; they look into each other's eyes like a devoted couple who love each other and have the right to love each other; there are no sidelong glances like those of the mistress when, from the goodness and the bidding of her heart, she is watching the scholar. Moreover, there are children who wait and skip around the returning father, while the 'bookworm's' house is empty; there are no children there." After this transparent allusion to what he had previously called his "innate incapacity," Kafka adds ironically, and not without a suggestion of duplicity, "Dearest, what a dreadful poem that is; I hadn't realized it."[25] Dreadful indeed, but the dreadfulness comes mostly from Kafka, who puts into the poem everything he needs to enable him to touch on the essential without frankly admitting it.

Felice would no doubt have understood the "dreadful" poem about the scholar a good deal better if she had had access to her fiancé's *Diaries* (only Milena would have that privilege; since Kafka gave her all his notebooks, she was not misled for too long), for there, in that same year of 1913, she might have read: "Coitus as punishment for the happiness of being together. Live as ascetically as possible, more ascetically than a bachelor, that is the only possible way for me to endure marriage. But she?"[26] There she would have found out what Kafka expected of her without saying it in so many words: a marriage of love, to be sure, but consummated as little as possible, hence hardly any marriage at all. A marriage effectively protected against what Kafka one day described to Milena as the black magic of sex: "Here is the world that I possess, and I'm expected to leap across for the sake of a sinister black magic, a hocus-pocus, a philosopher's stone, an alchemy, a wishing ring. Away with it, I'm terribly afraid of it."[27] But Felice did not yet know of this fear or why Kafka refused to "try and catch in one night by black magic, hastily, breathing heavily, helpless, obsessed, to try and obtain by black magic what every day offers to open eyes."[28] Otherwise it would be hard to see how she could have persevered for so many years and consented to renew her engagement after its dramatic rupture in 1914. It is true that at that time Kafka still regarded the sexual act as "a bond that sunders," but in spite of everything a bond, whereas in the Milena period it would become what prevented union: "a wall or a mountain, or rather a tomb."[29] (Kafka's second fiancée, Julie Wohryzek, seems to have more or less resigned herself to the sort of unconsummated marriage that he did not dare propose to Felice; according to him, she accepted as fact "that marriage and children were in a sense my highest goal on earth but that it was impossible for me to marry."[30])

Among the reasons he cited publicly to explain why he could have neither wife nor children, Kafka obviously gave first place to his writing, but in private he insisted chiefly on his imperative need for purity. In the list he drew up in 1913 of "all the arguments for and against my marriage," he first noted that he was "incapable, alone, of bearing the assaults of my own life, the attacks of time and old age, the vague pressure of the desire to write, sleeplessness, the nearness of insanity . . ." but that nevertheless everything remotely connected with sex immediately gave him pause: "Every joke in the comic paper, what I remember about Flaubert and Grillparzer, the sight of nightshirts on my parents' bed, Max [Brod]'s marriage"[31]—all this brought him back to his old anxiety, in which fear of tying himself down combined with the fear of defiling himself. In another "balance sheet," drawn up in 1916, marriage is entered in the "impurity" column, but since that did not prevent it from being the highest goal on earth, the perpetually balanced pros and cons deprived him of all possibility of self-fulfillment. Thus torn between two irreconcilable laws, the Jewish law which commanded him to marry if he wished to become a man in the full sense of the word, and the other, foreign, law, which compelled him to sterilize the marriage bond by dissociating it from sex, Kafka derived from each law nothing but the torment of not being able to fulfill it completely, and an intolerable feeling of being outlawed whatever he did.

Kafka was too well aware of the root of his trouble to deny that this sense of being torn between two incompatible laws was only the visible manifestation of a much deeper psychological condition; he knew that the primary cause of his difficulty was to be sought in a profound sexual disorder, which condemned him to desire almost every woman and remain cold in the presence of the woman he loved. After he had left the truth in the twilight of metaphor and allusion for a long time, the day came when he finally had to admit it to Felice: "My own fear—surely nothing worse can be either said or heard—is that I shall never be able to possess you. At best I would be confined, like an unthinkingly faithful dog, to kissing your casually proffered hand. . . . I would sit beside you and, as has happened, feel the breath and life of your body at my side, yet in reality be farther from you than now, here in my room. . . . You and I would ride past the entire world, hand in hand, seemingly united, and none of it would be true. In short, though you might lean toward me far enough for you to be in danger, I would be excluded from you forever."[32]

Some years after his "great confession" he tried to explain to Brod, who did not fully understand the reason for his despair, the exact nature of this form of impotence, which had just made him lose Milena: ". . . but later it came about that the body of every other girl tempted me, but the body of the girl in whom I had placed my hopes (for that reason?) not at all. As long as she withheld herself from me (F) or as long as we were one (M), it was only a distant threat, or perhaps not so very distant, but as soon as the slightest little thing happened, everything collapsed. Evidently because of my dignity, because of my pride (humble as the devious Western Jew may seem!), I can love only what I can place so high above me that I cannot reach it."[33] This clinical description could not be clearer, except that the pride of the Western Jew was only a screen behind which Kafka hid the main cause of his infirmity.

The impotence from which he suffered, which some observers term psychological, meaning that it is not absolute, is one of the mysteries that Freud made it possible to decipher by revealing its infantile origin and its close ties with the "Oedipal" dream. Identified with the mother, toward whom the child's first desires were directed, and placed on the same level in the internal hierarchy of the neurotic adult, the beloved woman thus becomes a sacred idol: she is the object of the incest taboo, just as the little boy's true mother was for him, and this makes her a perpetual source of anxiety and a perpetual temptation. Diverted from its true object, desire then attaches itself to the women excluded from this circle of passionate images—that is, those devaluated by their low social condition or bad reputation. In the last century, the women sexually available to the young men of the bourgeoisie were chiefly governesses, servants, and above all prostitutes, who, situated as they were at an infinite distance from the idealized mother, had the advantage of sparing the neurotic young man the incestuous phantoms that would otherwise have given rise to anguish and feelings of guilt. A doubtful advantage, it is true, for, since the infant's mother had appropriated his entire potential for desire and love, it was still she who was possessed through the servant girl or prostitute, the consequence being that incest-related guilt feelings were by no means extinguished and that the mother exalted above all other women was abased to the level of the most degraded among them.

From the standpoint of psychoanalytic theory, Kafka's

case is so typical that it might well serve as a textbook example. We find, if not directly then at least by inference, hatred of the all-powerful father; passionate attachment to the mother, who was all the more desired in the child's infancy because she was often away from home; initiation by a governess during adolescence; later on, a sex life limited almost entirely to prostitutes[34] and the Jossies and Effies who waited on table at cafés and restaurants; and finally, the lapse of desire in the presence of every woman who incarnated the mother-wife.

Kafka, who called Milena "mother" and his younger sister, Ottla, "big mother," seemed almost to suspect the incestuous character of his attachments and consequently the true nature of his incapacity (one recalls the sight of nightshirts on his parents' bed and the thoughts of incest that came to him continually at the sight of marriage chambers and nurseries). He also suspected that if he tended to idealize the woman he loved, it was precisely to situate her at such a height that it would not be permissible to touch her. Moreover, the Freudian theory that would have explained his case was not unknown to him. He accepted it up to a point when he said, "all these so-called illnesses . . . are efforts to find . . . moorings in some maternal soil";[35] but he categorically rejected the therapy in which psychoanalysis finds its principal raison d'être, no doubt because deep down he felt that any attempt at a cure would be as insane as trying to change one's vital organs. Rightly regarding his trouble as "an illness of instinct,"[36] and convinced, possibly not without reason in his own case, that such a disorder could not respond to any treatment, he decided to live *in opposition* to his enfeebled instinct by shutting himself up in a world of purity where everything relating to sex was violently repressed.

An illness of instinct which was also an illness of the times—Kafka was not mistaken; but he observed that though many others were afflicted with it, there were ways to deal with it, depending on the vitality of the individual concerned. "But in accord with my lack of vitality I cannot find such ways . . . at the most I can run away, though I am in a condition that makes it impossible for an outsider (and even more so for me) to see what there is left to save. . . ."[37] Accept celibacy; take those women one feels to be permissible and reject those forbidden by one's psychic disorder; build a life on this forced restriction, taking advantage of all the joy and freedom it allows; avoid making it intolerable by constantly comparing it with supposed normality—most men afflicted with such a disorder resign themselves to it without too much suffering, and even when they are conscious of a deficiency, they do not feel damned. Kafka, however, could not console himself so easily (his uncle from Madrid, whom he questioned one day on the subject, surprised him no doubt by replying that though he sometimes regretted not having married, he could say that on the whole he felt quite satisfied with his lot);[38] the expedients to which most men resorted in such cases were not within his reach, and what prevented him from making use of them was not only his diminished "vitality" but also the two laws that were at war within him, each dictating its most imperative commandments, and working together to destroy him.

In terming coitus a "punishment for the happiness of being together" or a "dangerous breach of bounds," Kafka cut himself off doubly from the Jewish law, first because he condemned what it regards as a sacred obligation, second because he did so in agreement with a very different, Christian, or, better still, Pauline tradition, for which the flesh is in itself a curse. If the Kafka who wished above all to marry to broaden the meaning of his life was indeed a descendant of Moses, the one who rejected the sexual act was, rather, a descendant of Saint Paul, a great renegade, as we know, who, as a latecomer to Judaism and a typical representative of a transitional period, likewise took upon himself the task of correcting the ancestral law and finally decreed its abrogation (this achievement, it is true, marks the limits of the analogy). Still, we have no reason for supposing that Kafka rallied consciously to this theology of the sinful, despised flesh; he never mentions Saint Paul in his letters or notebooks (though the figure of Christ appears now and then) and gives no evidence of familiarity with the apostle;[39] but though the church attracted him at certain times in his life—and we know that it did—it could only have done so through the current of thought most apt to support his need for asceticism and purity.[40] But it matters little whether Kafka was consciously attracted by certain points in the Pauline doctrine or whether he shared these beliefs without knowing it, on the strength of his need for self-abnegation. The essential remains the irreducible antagonism between the two laws to which he heedlessly tried to conform and which, keeping him at a distance from marriage as well as celibacy, left only the terrible issue of illness open to him.[41]

Independently of the dietary or ideological value they later acquired for his internal economy, the coercive measures Kafka decided on to ensure his return to a *legalized* world all presented one particularity: whether they applied to food, to sex, or to social relations, all originated in an essential principle of Jewish legalism, and all culminated in its reversal, since in this domain doing too much was equivalent to not doing what was necessary, hence to transgressing the law in the very point where he most wanted to remain within it.

True, Kafka's practice of radical vegetarianism gave him the assurance of not violating the blood taboo, but by extending the taboo to all meat he abolished the distinction between licit and illicit, which it is the law's function to maintain; in other words, he killed the living law in the name of an absolute moral exigency (particularly since his vegetarianism was merely the socially acceptable form he gave to his refusal to eat). Similarly, his desire for a marriage without sex protected him effectively against the transgressions to which his ignorance of the law still threatened to expose him; but the preventive measure so far exceeded its purpose that it destroyed both the inherent raison d'être of marriage and the basis of his own need for it. From the standpoint of Jewish legalism, this constant exaggeration, all of which betrayed the fear of not doing enough and the no less imperious need to do too much, was not only suspect as a borrowing from a foreign ideology, but also positively sacrilegious, in that, by abetting only the de-

structive forces of life, it culminated in the most inexpiable of
sins, namely, a barely deferred suicide.

Apart from its secret masochism, Kafka's disciplinary
system is also remarkable in that, wholly negative as it may
appear at first sight, it resulted from a real effort to reconcile
the irreconcilable, or, as Freud said with regard to dreams and
neurotic symptoms, to arrive at a more or less tenable compromise between two violently antagonistic tendencies. In Freud's
view, the dream image and the neurotic symptom always represent the disguised expression of a repressed desire, but they
function in such a way that, beneath the disguise, they reveal
both the hidden desire and the censorship that prevents it
from expressing itself. Thus on both sides the operation re-
solves into a half-failure and half-success: though forced to
compromise through repression, the latent desire nevertheless
makes a way for itself, even if at the cost of a displacement and
deformation that blur it in large part; on the other hand, the
censorship thus circumvented nevertheless does the greater
part of its work, since it compels desire to speak not in its own
name but only indirectly, through an incongruous message,
the illicit or improper content of which is dissolved in absurdity. In short, the symptomatic acts Kafka imposed on himself to express his love and hatred for the lost law also had
the value of an expressive language, created with a view to
compromise: concentrating the two absolutely contradictory desires that determined his system in one and the same re-
pressive measure—sexual abstinence and continence—he let
them betray themselves together and affirm themselves one
with the other and one against the other.

In letting himself be attracted by small marginal sects
outside all official religions and doctrines, Kafka may, unbeknownst to himself, have been submitting to his need for a
compromise between the impossibility of not being a Jew and
the impossibility of remaining one or becoming one again in
an authentic sense. Coming, as he did, of a people which in its
day also formed a distinct sect among the nations, his interest
in sectarianism in general expressed on the one hand a nostal-

gic homage to his distant origins and on the other hand a quest
for a faith freed from hereditary constraints, regenerated by a
small group or an individual inspiration—in other words,
something that itself bears witness to his need to break
through the narrow circle in which ties of blood and history
confined him. He made use of sects in accordance with the
same irrational logic as that governing his relations with food
and sex—his purpose being to get back to his people as it had
been in the "great old times" and to escape it in the present by
substituting other, present-day, minorities, based on a law of
their own in opposition to the world.

In view of the half-passionate, half-ironic curiosity that
Kafka displayed throughout his life for the most divergent
movements of thought—for the anarchist circles of Prague,
for libertarian puritanism, for the Hussite heresy, the anthro-
posophy of Rudolf Steiner, the Moravian Brothers, or even a
certain Moritz Schnitzer,[42] the inventor of a new method of
natural medicine—it seems evident that what fascinated him
in these doctrines was far less their ideological content than
the sectarian spirit itself, which offered an original solution to
certain of his own problems, especially those concerning his
paradoxical relations with faith and tradition.

For all sects, whether political or religious, represent an
attempt at compromise between two actions that it is very difficult to perform at the same time: on the one hand to isolate
oneself, on the other to unite; on the one hand to break away
from the majority, and on the other to unite with other isolated individuals within a new brotherhood, cemented by the
very fact that dooms it to remain a minority, outside of all established institutions. What with his personal quest for a solution that would free him from collective constraints and at the
same time enable him to sink into the warmth of a community,
Kafka was bound to be tempted by the way sects solve the
problem for their adepts. But strongly as a Schnitzer or as an
apostle of the "Christian Community" may have attracted him
in a moment of distress, the seduction, as we have seen, was
never so great as to blind him to the stupidity and absurdity of

these self-styled saviors; he never took the step from curiosity or admiration to the total devotion which, up to a certain point, would have met his emotional needs. In his dealings with the sects, as with the Judaism of Eastern Europe, in which he so much regretted not being at home, he could only stand aloof, "as lonely as Franz Kafka," at the observation post to which he was relegated by the uniqueness of his case.

He himself was well aware that he could derive nothing from the example of the fanatical ascetics, the puritan anarchists, the sectarians, whom he admired as much for the radicalism of their faith as for their living sense of community. For if they were able to stand apart and oppose the conformism of their surroundings, it was because they possessed by birth exactly what he lacked—a soil, a law, an uncontested place in the world made for them. If they were able and entitled to reject what they had, it was precisely because they had it, and when their passion for reform made them revolt against the prevailing state of affairs, they were able to act because in spite of everything they belonged to a great and living social body. Any attempt to follow in their footsteps would amount to acting "as if," to deceiving himself and others; it would be relapsing into the impotent imitation typical of assimilated Jews, and into the morass of guilt which already threatened to engulf him. From this point of view, the gap between these people and Kafka remained unbridgeable; all he gained by his association with them was one more indictment of the hybrid, perpetually displaced existence that drove him at every turn to justify himself.

Thus the apostles and adepts whom he admired from afar for the courage with which they pursued their road had nothing to teach him; they helped him only negatively by supplying him with proof *a contrario* of the absurdity of his attempts to escape and by sending him back to the original source of his anguish. This he undoubtedly knew before even taking the first step in their direction, on the rare occasions when he got that far (in the case of Rudolf Steiner, for example, whom he once went to see, knowing in advance that his venture would be fruitless; as always in such cases, his account of his visit quickly turns to comedy[43]). And yet they continued to fascinate him—or, rather, he continued to use them as an expression for his own ambiguities, something to which they lent themselves very well, since, insofar as they all regarded themselves as rebels, they all resembled him. And thanks to these romantic figures situated on the periphery of organized societies, Kafka was finally able to unify the contradictory themes of his "family romance," to pride himself on belonging by birth to an eternal people, and console—or avenge—himself for all the humiliations attaching from the start to that fatality.

The law left Kafka no peace—precisely because it eluded him and because, unable to live without it or to reinvent it, he was forever pursuing it in an attempt to make it deliver its secrets. It is this law—incomprehensible, indecipherable, absurd, revealed only by sentences that are always without appeal—which speaks in *The Judgment* through the terrible voice of the grandiose yet senile judge-father; which Joseph K. pursues (and not the contrary: it is correctly stated that the justice he is dealing with receives the accused when he goes to it but makes no attempt to come to him) down corridors and through attics in the tenements of a working-class suburb; which, inscribed in the books of the Old Commander in *In the Penal Colony* and rendered illegible by underscorings and flourishes, makes the sentence known only by imprinting it directly in the living flesh of the convict. It was this immanent law, which manifests itself in automatic punishment and in which all notions of justice are equally flouted, that killed Kafka, if it was true, as he firmly believed, that the lesion in his lungs was merely a symbol of another, invisible, wound provoked by the fury of his constant attempts at self-justification.

Not knowing for what crime, to what end, before whom he should justify himself, and unable to dispense with justification, Kafka never wearied of seeking a remedy for his law mania. Sometimes he seemed on the point of finding one: witness the famous "Legend" in *The Trial*, from which, if he had been able to understand it, Joseph K. would have derived a decisive lesson. A countryman, hence an ignoramus, an *am ha-arets* (literally a "man of the earth," i.e., an illiterate) appears at the gate of the Law and asks leave to enter. The gate is open, but the terrible gatekeeper posted at the threshold forbids him to enter "now." The man decides to wait for the authorization which is sure to be granted him sooner or later. He spends his whole life in this hopeless wait, for the gatekeeper has promised nothing. In the end he dies of exhaustion, having just learned that this gate was made expressly for him. If only he had ignored the threats of the blustering, childish gatekeeper, he would have gained access to the one right way, his way, which, since it was made expressly for him, would have led him to his goal, and which no arbitrary authority could have either forbidden him, or suggested to him, or imposed upon him.

The countryman is lost, because he does not dare put his individual law above the collective taboos, whose tyranny is personified by the gatekeeper. And like him Kafka was lost—but with the difference that the sovereignty of decision, which he so cruelly lacked in reality, was amply restored to him in the realm of literary creation, where, finally free to think for himself and to manifest his truth, he was subject only to the supreme tribunal of his writings.

Part
Two

6 · Escape

According to a conversation recorded by Brod,[1] Kafka would
have liked to call his work as a whole "An Attempt to Escape
from the Paternal Sphere," assuredly a most significant title—
not just because it refers to the old conflict between father and
son, but especially because it throws a bright light on what
Kafka expected of literature in general and the conclusions he
derived from it, both for his creative activity and for the conduct of his life. He could not have expected his stories to provide a means of severing the ties that in spite of everything
attached him to the "paternal sphere" unless he had faith in
the liberating power of literature, if not of his own writings; he
had to believe in a transcendent literature, exalted above the
confusion and disorder of temporal life, yet capable of restoring the world's lost plenitude and purity. He had to believe in
salvation by the written word as such, even if he foresaw what
enormous sacrifices this salvation would exact of him (and he
foresaw it so clearly that he did not speak of a successful escape, but only of an attempt, an experiment, with little chance
of succeeding).

Capable as it was of fostering hope, this belief in the
name of which he organized his daily life and work—without
it neither his biography nor his work would be intelligible—
did indeed involve unforeseen complications. Chief among
these was that his writing did its redemptive work not in

heaven but, by the nature of things, in the depths of a psyche that was prey to doubt, to revolt, and to the most anarchic, obscure, and murderous desires. To write as a means of escaping from the paternal sphere was to exploit literature for a deliberately impious end, and consequently to burden it with the full measure of guilt, from which a writer aspiring to salvation wishes precisely to be delivered. Since in this case the paternal sphere was also the Jewish sphere, the desire to escape from it further presupposed a disavowal similar to that of the German Jewish writers, whom Kafka condemned because, drawing their main inspiration from their desire to "forsake the Judaism of their fathers," they were, as he saw it, working as renegades and falsifiers.[2] And to complicate things further: he could not escape through writing without introducing the sworn enemy—the father, with all the murky violence, obscure feelings, and half-avowed resentment that his son had injected into him—into the very tissue of the work written for the express purpose of eliminating him. Thus, as punishment for his twofold impiety, his writing was gravely compromised in the shady transactions of reality and could save no one before extricating itself from this morass.

To harness his work to a mission of salvation when the sick reality it purported to eliminate was lodged in the very heart of its subject matter, and therefore contaminated all his writing, was indeed a mad undertaking, the difficulty of which seems at the start to have escaped Kafka. The tone and content of his early stories suggest that, like any young man conscious of the power of his imagination, he wrote for pleasure, as a game, to give form to his dreams of emancipation and also no doubt to make a name for himself. His words to the contrary when he first saw his name in print[3] are not proof of modesty, but seem, rather, to indicate an unbridled ambition whose very excessiveness forced him to repress it. Writing already occupied an enormous place in his life, but he was not yet possessed by it; he became so only with the overwhelming experience of *The Judgment*, the story made of his flesh and blood, which came out of him "like a real birth, covered with filth and mucus"[4] and finally taught him on what condition writing could become an act of liberation. Convinced that thus far, even and especially when working on his first novel [*Amerika*], he had dwelt "in the shameful lowlands of writing," he now wrote no longer in order to gain on paper a moment of freedom, but like a true believer in order to be reborn by submitting body and soul to the true literature that had been revealed to him.

Still vibrant with exaltation on the day after the memorable night on which *The Judgment* came into being, Kafka described this mutation: "This story, *The Judgment*, I wrote at one sitting during the night of the 22nd, from ten o'clock at night to six in the morning. . . . The fearful strain and joy, how the story developed before me as if I were walking on water. Several times during the night I hoisted the weight of my own body onto my back. How everything can be said, how for everything, for the strangest fancies, there waits a great fire in which they perish and rise up again." All earthly heaviness left behind him, the author in ecstasy seemed to be carrying his own body on his back as Saint Christopher carried Christ; he walked on water, his story had performed this miracle for him, supernatural grace had touched him, and from then on nothing he did without it would ever satisfy him: "The conviction verified that with my novel-writing I am in the shameful lowlands of writing. Only *in this way* can writing be done, only with such coherence, with such a complete opening out of the body and soul."[5] And to be sure, Kafka would never again attempt to write except in this state of illumination where the self bursts its bounds and where words set fire to things, to destroy and resuscitate them. For now he knew that deliverance was possible—on condition, however, that he prepare for it in advance by devoting a constant and exclusive cult to the god Literature, a cruel cult demanding the sacrifice not only of all his other interests, but also of his own life and those involved in it. Now it was a question of writing or living—writing like one who has died to himself, like a mystic, or living like a living corpse, drifting as most men do with the monotonous flow of time. To write without living and thus to gain eternity, or to live without writing, resigned to transience without meaning—this was the dilemma which seized him and in which he remained caught to the very end, even when, seeing his creation prematurely interrupted, in large part because of the fatal alternative to which he had confined himself, he would despair at having lost at once his work and his life.

Once *The Judgment* had revealed to him the true nature of his vocation, Kafka devoted himself to writing as one devotes oneself to a religion, or, rather, as one did in the days of faith—such faith as his own day did not impart to him, except perhaps in a ludicrous image, rendered insipid by bigotry. He served his art with the jealous passion but also with the humility, the self-abnegation, the intransigence of a believer, and just as the religious adept obsessed with salvation trades a life of asceticism and purification for a promise of grace, so he fled the distractions and temptations of the world in order to concentrate his forces in the silence of the night. There is no doubt that this cult of art, which the "cellar-dweller" wished to celebrate in the blackest night, like a Saint John of the Cross praying in the blinding light of his darkness,[6] benefited greatly from the cast of mind that led Kafka to seek solitude, continence, and privation, but of course the predisposition preceded its application, and it would doubtless have served for some other form of piety if this one had been lacking. Sometimes work exalted him, sometimes it drove him to despair, sometimes a perfect sentence brought him fulfillment, sometimes words eluded him, and then he knew the agony of a mystic forsaken by his God, and tumbled without transition from ecstasy to utter wretchedness, from heavenly hope to the last circle of hell. With this difference—a difference so weighty that the analogy would almost have to be abandoned, were it not for Kafka's own language and images, which never ceased to impose it—that the mystic in him never clouded the piercing eye of the critic and that, far from singing the praises of his madness, he denounced its ravages with cold irony even in the seemingly fantastic stories it had the gift of inspiring.[7]

Cruelly lucid as he was vis-à-vis his passion, writing remained, in spite of the torments it made him endure, Kafka's sole desire and aspiration, the ultimate goal in whose name he gradually renounced all normal life among men, and for which in the end he died, not knowing, any more than did his Hunger Artist, whether the strange perfection of his unfinished work was worth the price he had paid for it, or whether he had really lost his wager. Indeed, intransigent as he was in everything, but especially when he thought essentials were at stake, Kafka could accept no compromise between the sacred, i.e., literature, and the profane, i.e., reality; for him there could be no question of reducing his work to the reasonable proportions that would make it compatible with a normal human existence, filled with a variety of occupations and interests. The sacred was entitled to all his time and energy, but since he could not profane it by drawing profit from it,[8] he found his road barred once again. This commonplace conflict between art and livelihood, which others somehow resolve, providing their works are salable, became tragic in his case, because of the fatal alternative that paralyzed him in every respect: since he saw no possible accommodation between the writer he knew himself to be and the functionary he had become out of necessity, one had to eliminate the other and make himself sole master of the field; if neither was able to do so, he preferred to be crushed between them rather than make some accommodation that would enable them to share his strength and creative powers.[9]

This he explained frankly to Felice's father in a letter that, in the light of the circumstances under which it was written, would seem to be the most provocative profession of faith ever inspired by the phantasm of literature: "My job is unbearable to me because it conflicts with my only desire and my only calling, which is writing. Since I am nothing but my writing and neither can, nor wish to be, anything else, my job will never take possession of me, but it may shatter me completely. And this is by no means a remote possibility." Thus before they were engaged, he held out to Felice the prospect of either working alone to support them or destroying her husband in spite of herself. In any case, her life would be one of loneliness, thanks to an impalpable rival, all the more dangerous in that, far from helping Kafka to become more human, it intensified and exploited to the full the very qualities that made him impossible to live with. "Not only because of my outward circumstances, but far more so because of my essential nature, I am a reserved, silent, unsocial, dissatisfied person, and yet I cannot regard this as a misfortune, for it is only the reflection of my aim in life. Conclusions can at least be drawn from the sort of life I lead at home. Well, I live in my family, among the best and most lovable of people, more strange than a stranger. . . . The reason is simply this, that I have not the slightest thing to talk to them about. Everything that is not writing bores me and I hate it, for it distracts me or delays me, if only because I think it does."[10] This last sentence does not appear in the letter that was sent (nor, for that matter, does the "I am nothing but my writing" of the start[11]), but Kafka retained it in his *Diaries* as the most appropriate expression of the postulate to which his religion led him. For him writing came before life, and anything outside or inside him that threatened this primacy became his enemy.

Writing came before life—this can be read between the lines even when it is not explicitly stated in the many pages of his correspondence and his *Diaries* in which, from day to day, he recorded his complaints, aspirations, enthusiasms, depressions, and finally his despair at the unpredictability of his inspiration. When inspired, he felt capable of anything: "and not only of what is directed to a definite piece of work. When I arbitrarily write a single sentence, for instance, 'He looked out of the window,' it already has perfection."[12] Only writing would decide his fate, determine whether he was to be saved or lost; in accordance with laws that had no currency elsewhere, it would transform what was bad in him ("the reflection of my goal") into good, and what the world regarded as good qualities into bad ones; it would shelter him as a mother shelters a child, and anything that took him away from it

would destroy him; at the office, for instance, he was seized
with "the great fear that everything in me is ready for a poetic
work and such a work would be a heavenly enlightenment and
a real coming-alive for me, while here, in the office, because of
so wretched an official document, I must rob a body capable of
such happiness of a piece of its flesh."[13]

Not only did writing conceived "as a form of prayer"[14]
give him spiritual joys; it was also an incomparable source of
physical pleasure, and anyone depriving him of this pleasure
was flaying him alive. "The joy of renouncing the greatest
human happiness for the sake of writing keeps cutting every
muscle in my body";[15] it far surpassed any joy that love could
offer, and that is why he would not marry Felice, for if he did
he would make her lead *"a monastic life at the side of a man
who is peevish, miserable, silent, discontented and sickly,* a
man who, and this will strike you as akin to madness, is
chained to invisible literature by invisible chains, and screams
when approached because, so he claims, someone is touching
those chains."[16]

For this madness he had no reasonable explanation; he
could only cite, like a believer, the examples of his venerated
saints—Grillparzer, Dostoyevsky, Kleist, and Flaubert—for of
these four men, who were his "true blood-relations," "Dostoyevsky was the only one to get married, and perhaps Kleist,
when compelled by outer and inner necessity to shoot himself
on the Wannsee, was the only one to find the right solution."[17]
Invisible, all-powerful in the uppermost heavens where it is
hidden, like all religions sustained by the dead and itself carrying death in its innermost core, literature is in every respect
fatal, and Kafka knew it; indeed, he was one of the first writers
to know this aspect of literature that is so easy to disregard.
However, he saw nothing frightening in it, but, rather, a compelling reason to persevere in his worship. For persevere he
did, even in the cruel satire he made of his own madness,
which is surely the height of quixotism, since he portrayed
himself as the madman he was in his own eyes, without for one
moment wavering in his resolve to pursue his madness. Never

since the appearance of Don Quixote in our cultural sphere
has the sacralization of literature had a champion so logical
and so fanatical (not even Flaubert carried it to such an extreme), and never has it been reflected in a work so pure and
so worthy to celebrate it.

Yet Kafka was not alone in investing writing with the
properties of religion; in this he was merely following a general trend of his time, when, like him, though more vaguely
and for less pressing reasons, many were looking for a way out,
for a spiritual opening, for some form of salvation. Throughout
nineteenth-century Europe, and not only in Prague, where
every moderately gifted young man, especially if he was a
German Jew, resorted to creative writing as an escape from his
cramped surroundings (in Kafka's circle it was taken for
granted that everyone wrote), literature benefited from a remarkable transfer of values, to which just about all the artistic
movements of the century contributed. Begun by the Romantics in perfect accordance with their ideology, this operation
was continued with varying degrees of determination by all
those who, without necessarily subscribing to the Romantic
doctrine, and sometimes even opposing it, nevertheless shared
the Romantics' dissatisfaction with the world and, correla-
tively, their unlimited faith in the power of dreams and the
work of the imagination. The various schools that followed one
another up to the turn of the century—Romantics, realists,
symbolists, naturalists, and, in an area closer to Kafka, Expres-
sionists—might argue with one another and sometimes even
regard one another as enemies, but they had one thing in common: they all overestimated the power of the written word to a
degree that would have been inconceivable in earlier periods.
Striving obscurely to restore the realm of the spiritual, threatened by the modern world, they exalted all writing to the level
of Scripture.

Diverse as it was in different times and places, and complex as were its effects, this phenomenon can be seen as West-
erners' instinctive reaction to Western progress, which while

attacking traditional values on every side, could neither replace them, destroy them radically, nor cast them into oblivion. The withering of religious thinking and of the system of relationships that formed its concrete foundation; the increasingly visible discrepancy between the teaching of the revealed religions and the irreversible secularization of life; the moral and intellectual consequences of the great economic and social upheavals resulting from the enormous advances of science and technology; the headlong development of heavy industry and concomitant growth of the big cities, which, as was aptly said at the time, were becoming "tentacular"—the entire picture that Nietzsche summed up when he said that God was dead—made Western civilization a gaping void, which its most conscious spokesmen tried to fill in different ways. Science, philosophy, social and political utopias, nascent sociology—all tried to compensate for this breakdown of the ideal world; each hoped to contribute, if not a revolution, at least a truth in keeping with the spirit of the times, and so help to absorb some part of the diffuse religious feeling, which for want of occupation had turned to vague yearnings and *"mal du siècle."* But for reasons that go far back in the history of our myths, no activity of the spirit is better equipped to serve as a substitute for the ideal than writing, especially writing in the noble form of poetry, to which at all times the highest dignity has been accorded.

This merging of roles has its roots in antiquity, when it was thought that poetry provided communication between the human and the divine worlds, and when it consequently enjoyed special rights in the realm of the sacred. Homer was not a man, he was a god, the father of all knowledge, the infallible guide who purified his readers and led them in the traces of his sacred truth. Of course not every poet is Homer, and few after him were deified by posterity, but poetry itself retained the gift of connecting the things of earth with heaven, or with the mystery that took the place of heaven when the gods forsook it. And soon poetry transmitted this gift—which seems to have been recognized at all times, certainly long after there was any justification for it—to prose, which became its historic successor. After that it was no longer the poetic art but the art of writing in general that opened the way to the marvels, mysteries, or terrors of some realm beyond experience, inaccessible to the common mortal.

The concept of literature had scarcely been born when it began to benefit from the superstitious belief that had endowed poetry with its exclusive privilege. In this it was singularly helped by the vocabulary with which it defined its techniques and its aims: claiming the right to be considered on a par with religion, which was no longer legitimated by any vision of the world, it spoke of inspiration, election, mission, vocation, and even, to complete the analogy, of a curse. It had its chapels, its prophets, its saints and martyrs, and, quite naturally in the diabolical order which theology opposes to the divine order, its alchemy, its black magic, its hermeticism, and its heretics. Finally, it had its canons and dogmas, not to mention the multitude of commentators, who interpreted it endlessly and authoritatively determined what was authentic and what was not. The entire nineteenth century used and misused this confusion of words and feelings so strongly favored by our habits of speech; in this, indeed, it went further than any preceding period, since the cult of literature flattered the century's megalomania as well as its nostalgia for religion. Toward the end of the century, literature came to take its self-appointed role of substitute for faith very seriously; emancipated by its own efforts, it gave itself the sacred investiture and became, in Flaubert's profound phrase, the mysticism of those who believe in nothing.

Given the local conditions under which Kafka was destined to be educated and to spend his life, he offered this surrogate mystique a receptive soil, in which it had no difficulty in taking root. In his youth, as we know, he was a positivist, Darwinist, socialist, and atheist. All this satisfied the needs of his mind, but could not absorb the full emotional fervor underlying even his intellectual interests. In a manner of speaking, he had always written, and whereas in confronting life he felt irresolute, incompetent, incapable of human relations, nearly speechless with timidity, at his writing desk, at least, he was fully conscious of his talent. Accordingly, he had good reason to value what he regarded as his only gift, and in this Prague helped him in its way by offering only the most limited prospects, and also because in that city, where religious indifference was everywhere discernible under a surface of conventional piety, and where even Judaism was only a shadow of its glorious past, faith in literature was perhaps the only faith still considered worthy of recognition and love. It should not surprise us that Kafka—admiring those who held religious beliefs though he himself could not; radically skeptical but endowed with a core of religious feeling which, cut off from every sort of institutional religion, expressed itself only in vague regrets—should at an early age have looked to literature to satisfy the two conflicting tendencies within him: the spirit of "enlightenment" which governed his intellectual life and the need to believe in something beyond himself, two tendencies which neither the religious material available in his milieu nor his own individual cast of mind allowed him to conciliate. In view of his precocity, it seems no more than natural that he succumbed to the magic of the written word long before he knew what he would do with his work and his life.

In keeping with this religion without a church, to which he was already devoted, the pre-*Judgment* Kafka found the main source of his inspiration in the conventional opposition between art and reality—corresponding to the theological opposition between this world and the kingdom of heaven—by which Romantics had always justified their revolt or simply their boredom. The real world is heavy, opaque, impure, and cold; it is the pitiless age of iron against which the eternal Don Quixote mobilized his chimerical weapons, and which is reborn for each new generation of poets. Art, on the contrary, restores to things and beings all the transparence, all the readability they have lost by existing; situated outside of space and time, immutable though endowed with divine mobility, it is an inexhaustible source of warmth and light, and not just for its adepts but for the entire human and animal world. This is how Kafka as a boy felt about his new art, as he was later to write in his *Diaries*, while meditating as he did so often on the good and bad motives for his need to create: "Once I projected a novel in which two brothers fought each other, after which one went to America while the other remained in a European prison. . . . I wrote something about my prison one Sunday afternoon when we were visiting my grandparents and had eaten an especially soft kind of bread, spread with butter, that was customary in their house. Of course it is possible that I did this out of vanity, and that by moving the paper about on the tablecloth, tapping with my pencil, looking around under the lamp, I was trying to tempt someone to take what I had written from me, look at it and admire me. . . . An uncle who liked to make fun of people finally took the page that I was holding only weakly, looked at it for a moment, handed it back to me without even laughing, and only said to the others who were following him with their eyes: 'The usual rubbish'; to me he said nothing. To be sure, I remained seated and bent as before over my by now useless page, but with one thrust I had been banished from society, my uncle's judgment was repeated inside me with something bordering on real meaning, and right there, despite the feeling of belonging to a family, I caught a glimpse of the cold spaces in our world, which I would have to warm with a fire that I would first seek out."[18]

Here the young Romantic saw without understanding them —understanding them would be the work of the adult writer— all the contradictory implications of his pre-established convictions: he complained bitterly of being banished from society, though it was he who had isolated himself by heedlessly starting to write in the midst of a peaceful family gathering. He savored the intimate warmth of that Sunday afternoon as much as his grandparents' excellent bread, but he had broken the spell for the mere pleasure of distinguishing himself from the family and being admired; since this pleasure was refused him, the affectionate family warmth was changed for him into an inhuman world, which he would have to warm with the charisma of his art—once he had found it.

The child-poet was confronted with an untenable paradox—the notion of an unearthly art, destined despite or precisely because of its unearthliness to cure the earth of all its evils, a notion that would weigh heavily on Kafka's creative powers until the moment when he resolved, in judging his work as a whole, to hale it into court and make it confess to the puerile lies, the tendentious superstition and overweening ambition that lay concealed beneath its ostensible sublimity. Unjustifiable yet impossible to eliminate, this paradox is a fatal poison to one who is its prisoner, and becomes creative only when it can be *figured* in all its grandeur, along with its irresistible seduction and pitiful illusions. As a child Kafka was overwhelmed by it, and he would never throw it off completely, but it was to this paradox that he owed his incomparable stories about messengers without messages, about artists destroyed by the absolute, or the Country Doctor, cursed for making the "mistake" of following his vocation as a healer, which was symbolized by the "night bell," and condemned to wander eternally in an "earthly carriage, drawn by unearthly horses," and to remain naked, "exposed to the cold of this unfortunate age,"[19] forsaken even by the patients he tried to save.

We do not know how many more or less serious attempts to escape followed the story of the two enemy brothers,[20] but in *Description of a Struggle*, the oldest story to have been preserved—an unfinished work, posthumous apart from a few fragments that Kafka published in his lifetime—we find the same sort of Romantic attack on reality, exacerbated by the accumulated grievances of the adolescent and the radical Expressionism then (1904–05) in fashion. Judging the life he had led up until then to be "most monotonous," the narrator, as unsure of his own existence as he is all-powerful in his narrative, fashions a world that suits him by calling into being, one by one, the elements of a landscape that can be transformed at will. This enables him to stage fantastic changes of scene—which he calls "Diversions, or Proofs That It Is Impossible to Live"—and thanks to the power of the word, of which he is then absolute master, he amuses himself by positioning the things of heaven and earth according to the exclusive dictates of his momentary desire, in a space that has been previously thrown out of joint.

Thus he was able on a winter night to walk the streets of Prague (this is the only one of Kafka's stories in which the streets and monuments of Prague are named; for the moment the author avenges himself on them merely by putting them down haphazardly wherever he pleases) and at the same time to take a very different stroll in a landscape whose features he invents as he goes along. There he orders the stones to disappear, "flattens" the path on which he is walking, brings forth "an enormously high mountain, overgrown with brushwood, bordering on the sky"; "because he loved pinewoods" he passed through woods of that kind, and because he liked to "gaze silently up at the stars, the stars appeared slowly in the sky."

This is the world of all-powerful thought, where desires are fulfilled more magically than in magic, before they have been formulated; but it is also a purely linguistic realm, where a well-constructed sentence instantly makes its content a reality and, anticipating the desire that dictated it, *provokes* the event instead of representing it. In this realm the weakest, most disarmed of persons is endowed with fantastic strength by reason of his weakness, which forces him to be pure spirit. Totally confounded, as is his author, he can, like him, not only move rivers and mountains but also, thanks to his verbal charisma, produce, one by one, hitherto unthought-of happenings.

Armed with the sovereign word, the prerogative of which Kafka has passed on to him, the "I" of the story exploits his power to the full as soon as his own phantasmagorias begin to lose interest for him; then he wishes to "turn and leave this region," which he had at first found so amusing. For this he needs no great sorcery; a single sentence suffices: " 'How strange it is that even in our time distinguished people are transported across a river in this complicated way. There's no other explanation, it must be an old custom.' "[21] At the moment when this sentence is spoken it corresponds to nothing in the outside world; no distinguished people or inexplicable phenomenon is in sight. But no sooner is the sentence uttered than its content materializes, and the narrator who has uttered it sees it transformed into fact: "From the thicket on the opposite bank four naked men strode vigorously forth, carrying on their shoulders a wooden litter. On this sat, Oriental fashion, a monstrously fat man. Although carried through the thicket on an untrodden path, he did not push the thorny branches apart but simply let his motionless body thrust through them."[22] Born of a simple grammatical proposition, the new story revolves around a new symbol for the impossibility of living: the Fat Man, a creature whose contours, dilated by fat, extend positively to the infinite, but who, thanks precisely to this singular failing, has also been favored with the purely verbal gift of reducing solid objects to a liquid blur. He admits that he has no other function in the story than to speak, to devise words and phrases that will convince the things of this world of their utter lack of cohesion and hence of the imposture they commit in setting themselves up as reality; indeed, he boasts of it and thus surrenders irrevocably to the immanent justice that punishes most of Kafka's creatures: his power to deprive them of their "lovely outline" turns against himself, and no sooner does he stop talking than he loses his own contours by drowning in the river that is only too impatient to engulf him.

The Narrator, the Fat Man, the Supplicant, the Drunkard, and all those barely differentiated "I's," which are animated verbal entities rather than creatures of flesh and blood, have in common a lack of being which enables the outside world to invade them from all sides as if they had no bodily resistance, no weight of their own to oppose to it. What a young girl says to one of them—"The entire length of you is cut out of tissue paper, yellow tissue paper, like a silhouette, and when you walk one ought to hear you rustle"[23]—could be said to any of them, and all might add that the material they are made of is not exactly yellow tissue paper but, rather, the printed page. And yet, with all their gaps and essential incompleteness, these two-dimensional creatures do not bow before the supposed superiority of the outside world, for though the outside world may loom high above them, it, too, is fissured from end to end, and for all its massive appearance is nothing more than a jerry-built façade, an optical illusion in danger of disintegrating at any moment.

This is the terrifying feeling that makes the Supplicant behave so outrageously; as he himself says, it is not for the pleasure of it that he makes a spectacle of himself in the church, but primarily to obtain a body and then "to learn . . . how things really are, why it is that around me things sink away like fallen snow, whereas for other people even a little liqueur glass stands on the table as steady as a statue."[24] Is it because he suffers from chronic dizziness that he constantly sees the world fading away? Does he alone suffer from perpetual earth-sickness, or is the precariousness of the world a fact, a painful experience shared by others? This is the point on which he wants to be enlightened when he tells the Fat Man about the memorable scene in the Garden ("What are you doing, my dear?" "Oh nothing, I'm having my tea on the lawn"), a direct repetition of the scene that Kafka has just described to Brod[25] as an illustration of the bewilderment induced in him by the real day-to-day world. Although the scene evoked in the letter related to an incident of the day before and not, as in the story, to a memory from distant childhood, here again the author and the Supplicant are one, experiencing the same painful horror in the face of the self-evident, the natural, the familiar—in short, of everything that others accept unknowingly, everything they experience with their eyes closed, not able and not even wishing to think about it. They struggle together, or, rather, they talk together about the need to struggle against the monstrous resemblance that creates a fateful complicity between the nonexistent individual and the imposture that is reality.

Essentially theatrical by nature, the Supplicant undertakes to make a visible cataclysm out of what for Kafka was
only a feeling of intense dizziness, a feeling of fundamental instability in which every object in the environment seems to
participate. He suppresses the affective "as if," with the result
that he immediately sees the world in which he is placed as a
conglomeration of random elements, so poorly put together
that a breeze from anywhere would suffice to knock them
over. In his view, "tall buildings collapse every now and then
for no apparent reason," but when he asks the passers-by,
" 'How could this have happened? In our town—a new building—how many does that make today? Just think of it!' "[26] no
one can give him an answer. Under his eyes people fall down
dead in the streets, whereupon "all the shopkeepers open their
doors laden with wares, hurry busily out, cart the dead into a
house, come out again all smiles, then the chatter begins:
'Good morning—it's a dull day—I've been selling any amount
of kerchiefs—ah yes, the war!' "[27] Just as the inexplicable fall
of buildings goes unnoticed in this tottering, seemingly so solid
universe, so death is spirited away; it is a scandal that no one
wants to talk about. Only the Supplicant gives it a thought, and
when he asks for information—" 'Good morning,' I say, 'I understand a dead man was brought in here just now. Would you
be kind enough to let me see him?' "[28]—he is treated as a suspect. The local population—shopkeepers—cast the same cloak
of indifference over the catastrophes that befall people and the
catastrophe that is making the city tremble on its foundation:
"The spire of the Town Hall is moving in little circles. All the
windowpanes are rattling and the lampposts are bending like
bamboos. The Virgin Mary's cloak is coiling around her pillar
and the wind is tugging at it. Doesn't anyone notice this?"[29]
No, no one does; the people in the shops talk about war or they
talk about the bad weather, but no one notices that the city has
already been undermined and is swaying over a gaping void.

Between this universe, crumbling though indubitably
real in the eyes of people at large, and the figures cut out in the
shapes of human beings who move about without rhyme or
reason, the struggle announced in the title can obviously not

take place. The adversaries are too much alike in their precariousness, and, indeed, the story describes no actual struggle, but merely tells what makes a struggle impossible and how the struggle is constantly averted. It shows adversaries in no condition to confront each other, partly because of their common weakness and partly because of the heterogeneous nature of their respective powers, which permits each to triumph continually in his own sphere but to be continually defeated on the enemy's ground.

The world has the advantage of being there, and even if its being there is only a shared illusion, this gives the world an enormous advantage. Yet the individual is not so disarmed that he must automatically accept defeat, for as the master of language he has a no less certain power over mute things, which like it or not they must submit to. The world as it is retains its superiority only insofar as the speaking individual consents to leave it alone; otherwise, it is irrevocably lost; the mere power of the creative word instantly wrecks its consummate order and makes it fall apart. Even the individual with the strongest reasons for doubting his own existence—the Supplicant, who is obliged to look in the eyes of others for proof of his own material reality—even this furtive, unfinished apparition triumphs over heaven and earth as soon as he starts talking.

The Supplicant cannot cross the threshold of a house without being "assaulted from the sky by moon and stars and a great vaulted expanse, and from the *Ringplatz* by the Town Hall, the Virgin's pillar, the church."[30] But, far from succumbing to this combined assault of human forces and the cosmos, he in his turn attacks with the magic weapon of poetry, which can destroy, reconstruct, and redistribute visible things as it pleases merely by giving them new names, such as inspired poets are privileged to create. Menacing as the moon may look in its inaccessible height, it is nevertheless defeated by the virtuoso of speech, whose art consists precisely in naming and un-naming: "Thank God, moon, you are no longer moon, but perhaps it's negligent of me to go on calling you so-called moon. And why are you less haughty when I call you 'forgotten, strangely-colored lantern?' As for you, pillar of the Virgin Mary, I hardly recognize your threatening attitude when I call you 'moon shedding yellow light.' It really seems to me that thinking about you doesn't do you any good; you lose courage and health.' "[31] Thus literature, though it does not participate in the general struggle for life—there is no conflict of any kind between the different "I's" of the story, they and their challenges merely subsist side by side—finds in its art of naming the surest guarantee of its sovereignty: it need only confuse or destroy the semantic relationship between things and words to assure its supremacy over all things, animate or inanimate, outside the realm of the inspired word.

Marked as it is by defects due to haste and the naïveté of youth—defects encouraged, of course, by the literary fashion of the day[32]—*Description of a Struggle* is remarkable for the fact that, though anticipating the major themes of the novels, it exemplifies everything Kafka had to get rid of before becoming the author of *The Judgment* or *The Trial*, the writer who compelled poetry—in the wider sense that the German language gives to the word *Dichtung*—to abandon lyrical effusion and become a chronicle, an administrative report, a record of experience. A direct product of the Romantic he had within him and whom he would soon be citing before his own tribunal, this story was the warning he would have to heed as soon as, taking cognizance of the real situation in the real world where he was forced to live, he discovered the enormous amount of deception and childish illusion at the bottom of his belief in the magical action of language. At a time when his personal struggle was entering an acute phase—resulting, we recall, from his discovery of Judaism and the crisis in his engagement—it was no longer possible for him to solve the problems connected with his human relations in the shameless manner of a character in his story, by triumphantly declaring himself "engaged," when there was no woman by his side. Nor could he content himself with claiming to have "confounded" people—that is, at once confusing them and convicting them of imposture—by the sole means of a well-turned sentence or of a new baptism as poetic as it was incongruous. That would have been adding a deception to the imposture he wished to unmask, so depriving his personal misfortune and the sufferings of mankind of all dignity.

For in spite of his uncertain and fragmented existence, in spite even of his feeling of not being really born, Kafka was not for one moment an artistically cut-out silhouette, but a man forced to struggle to find air he could breathe, a corner to lodge in, concrete ground to set foot on. And that struggle was too urgent to be dodged by arranging sentences or entrenching himself in his sense of unreality, all the less so since the reality of Prague was not the crumbling façade which the young rebel thought he could topple by force of his inspiration; frail as it might look to the distrustful observer, it had no intention of falling to pieces, but, on the contrary, stood amazingly firm. Indeed, it was more than anything else this stability maintained in spite of everything that made it fantastic.[33]

To describe the real struggle he now proposed to carry on, Kafka had to deny himself the easy solution to which he resorted in his early writings. Now in each contestant he had to respect the mixture of strength and weakness characteristic of all living beings. In particular, he would have to dissociate himself from this self-assertive hero, always ready to display the wounds and gaps in his existence and nevertheless imbued with superiority, this hero who, with his verbose Romanticism and ill-concealed arrogance, ends by doing as much harm to literature as to reality. Since this hero is the direct product of a particular ideological attitude—faith in the "no sooner said than done" of infantile narcissism, to which the Expressionism of the time added the attraction of modernism—Kafka could not break with it without first ridding himself of the semiconscious received ideas that then encumbered his literary thinking. And before he could effect this break in a severely chastened work—a work in which the Romantic that he basically remained, and the incorruptible realist that he was in equal measure, would collaborate—he would have to reinvent his whole idea of his work, or, rather, of literature itself.

* * *

In deciding to remain neutral vis-à-vis his own inveterate tendency to complain, to console himself, to avenge himself for being ill-born, and consequently to seek salvation in
escape, Kafka was led to take an extreme measure—a measure
quite unprecedented in the realm of modern fiction—which
gave a maximum of objectivity to his extremely "self-
centered" work. To avoid contaminating his narrative with the
products of his inner uncertainty and confusion, he radically
disjoined the man and the writer and brought about an apparent break between experience and the written word. (This
deliberate hiatus accounts in part for the attitude of his first
critics, who, knowing little of his biography, or not seeing what
use to make of what they did know, most often interpreted his
writings in terms of ontology.) From this point on, writing
takes precedence over life, if only in the sense that during the
time allotted to it, writing imposes its law upon life. Not that
Kafka from then on spoke of subject matter other than himself—on the contrary, he was his only subject; but Kafka the
man did not come into his text until he had been reduced to a
schema, living in an abstract space from which all his physical
and moral particularities, his social situation, and the facts of
his life had been painstakingly excluded (with a few exceptions which, as we shall see later, are without deeper significance. In this he went directly counter to common opinion,
which regards life as the first requisite of the fictitious hero.
Instead of reaching out to the living man, either to paint his
lifelike portrait or to give him an enhanced existence in a styl-
ized world, he took hold of him only to obliterate him as an
individual and drown him in the multitude—in other words,
to kill him.[34]

This cutting off of writing from life, which amounts to destroying life for the benefit of literature, is justified by the
need to protect the writer from the temptations, the failings,
and the infinite fallibility of the human being. And it is true
that Kafka the man was in no way superior to his fellows in purity of intentions, rightness of conduct, or sureness of judgment. His thinking, like that of all men, was infiltrated with

desires and emotions, which sometimes, most often unbeknownst to him, dictated strange ideas, tendentious attitudes,
unconscionable obstinacy, and unwarranted conclusions. Like
any other man, he sometimes pronounced a categorical yes or
no without being able to enunciate rational motives; like other
men, he had his superstitious beliefs and prejudices, and, despite a lucidity in many respects almost prophetic, his bigoted
and inhuman opinions on the problems of the day. In the preceding chapters we have noted his obstinate refusal, based on
his hatred of official medicine, to undergo proper treatment,
and the ups and downs of his feeling of Jewishness, which led
him sometimes to change his convictions radically and sometimes to cling irrevocably to an extreme judgment—in particular, underestimation of Western Jewry. But if his work was to
be worthy of the sacralized literature to which he aspired; if,
as he wished, it was to become a miraculous fulcrum, by which
to "raise the world into the pure, the true, and the immutable,"[35] he could not let it be infected by contact with what he,
as a limited creature, condemned by his human condition to
impurity, transience, and falsehood, was, with what he had, or
with what he thought and desired. He would have to raise an
insuperable barrier between himself and himself, to break his
earthly bonds and to dwell, for the time it took him to write a
story, in the no man's land of creation, where thought is privileged to manifest itself in positive opposition to logical statement and rational ideas.

In view of all this, we must not expect to find in the author
of *The Trial* the tormented, irresolute man, strangled by anguish and contradictions, with whom we have become acquainted in the first part of this book; he is not present, and
the work itself relates neither the events of his life nor what he
thought about them. Engagements, breaks, Judaism, conflicts,
illness—all this seems absent from the novel, yet plays a decisive role in it, thanks, it is true, to a twofold transposition: the
first reduces real experience to its essential core and so con-
verts it to images, themes, and situations devised for the

express purpose of bringing out its meaning; the second derives not moral but technical lessons from experiences and
applies them exclusively to the formal apparatus of the compo-
sition. Kafka could not relate the detailed circumstances of his
inability to live, and this for the simple reason that he did not
know them all and could not without cheating describe those
that were known to him. He could, however, bear witness to
this inability to live or give the reasons for it by showing, in his
very means of expression, what restrictive measures he was
forced to adopt if he was to be faithful to his true condition. In
other words, he directly transformed substance into form, a
procedure that gave the least of his unfinished stories the
firmest unity known to prose.

If we recall the conditions of life in Prague, described at
length in the preceding chapters, we shall understand without
difficulty why Kafka refused (a strange refusal for a novelist,
but was he really a novelist? In view of this refusal, perhaps
not) to put his personal self into his work. Ever since he had
been old enough to think, he had felt unhappy about the irresponsible way in which most of the Jews he knew formed their
opinions and determined their conduct. Yet, irritating as it
might seem, and unacceptable to a critical mind, the social and
political opportunism of the Prague Jews was not a simple de-
fect of character but, rather, a reaction to the absurdity of
their partitioned society, and one should not condemn it without taking into account the complex historical factors that fostered it. Thus to Kafka's mind the irresponsibility arising from
the overall situation of his fellows was not the kind of failing
that could be satirized or portrayed with indignation, because,
conscious as he was of the small margin of freedom that education and environment left to the individual, he could hardly
claim to be exempt from this same irresponsibility. On the
other hand, he could not pass over in silence the particularity
of the current manner of speaking, for in spite of everything
he found it intolerable, not only in itself but still more because
of its vague threat to his own thinking.

Of course, so commonplace a state of affairs—irresponsible judgment was not the exclusive privilege of the Prague Jews—would have been no problem for most novelists; many, in fact, would have taken it as a windfall for their art and simply represented it by peopling their narratives with characterless individuals, with loquacious cynics and bores offering a striking contrast to the intelligent author and above all avenging him for his many sufferings at the hands of their living models. Some writers have done just this with happy results, in situations that, at least in some respects, suggest Kafka's relations with "little mother" Prague (Musil, for instance, vis-à-vis Vienna, or Gogol vis-à-vis Russia). But Kafka had to refuse this path that novelists found, as it were, ready laid out for them (which does not mean that he condemned it in others), because in his personal struggle the enemy hardest to overcome was not in the outside world, but situated inside him, at a depth from which only a pitiless light could dislodge him.

In view of the general task he assigned to his writing—to reveal to him what was beyond appearances and to strip the world of its false pretenses—Kafka was not free to take the curse of Prague as his subject matter; he could speak of it neither to denounce it, nor to make his readers laugh at its expense, nor even just to record it. He merely derived a lesson from it, a lesson from which he never ceased to profit: instead of painting an imaginary society of characterless people, expressing opinions about anything and everything, he himself abstained from *judging*. To this end he totally eliminated from his stories the narrator brimful of ideas, who interprets the conduct of his characters and comments on events; then even from the words of his heroes he removed every assertion, every general idea, every speculation that did not spring directly from the concrete action itself (K., it is true, meditates endlessly on the nature of the Castle, but neither he nor anyone else mentions an event in the outside world or proffers the slightest idea about world history or the fate of mankind).

Disciplined by his principle of nonintervention, Kafka did not even allow himself to give the character of his heroes any suggestion of his own tastes, phobias, or of his eccentrici-

ties resulting from nostalgia for the lost law. Not one is a vegetarian, not one acts in accordance with Kafka's convictions or
prejudices with regard to medicine, hygiene, education, the
benefits of living in the country, or the dangers of city life; and
though several of them are confronted with occupational
problems, it goes without saying that none knows the happiness or misery of the writer, or shows a passion for writing that
would have given Kafka away.

Kafka's rare breaches of this rule merely confirm his general respect for it; they consist in episodic notations and in details so insignificant at first sight, but at the same time inserted
so logically into the texture of his narrative, that to discern
hidden meanings one requires exceptional familiarity with the
author's life. In rare instances, Kafka takes the liberty of putting himself into an obscure corner of his story, where the un-
enlightened reader has little reason to look for him, since
nothing of importance is happening there. For example: On
Gregor Samsa's wall he hangs an engraving of a woman
swathed in furs, a reminder of his own very special feelings
about furs;[36] he has the Surveyor steal and sample Klamm's
cognac, a beverage which at first strikes him as divine but soon
becomes a vulgar "coachman's brew"—a clear enough reference to his own abstinence and to the disgust and shameful
desire associated with it; in connection with Frau Grubach and
the extraordinary dexterity of "a woman's hands," he attributes to Joseph K. a remark that might well figure in his *Diaries*
alongside the passage where he waxes ecstatic about his
mother's courage because, coming home in the evening dead
tired, she still has the strength to "start her day all over again";
to this same Joseph K. he imputes the decision to perfect his
Italian—a decision that he himself had made continually since
his travels in Italy with Brod—and which, according to him,
he never carried very far (this detail is not without its importance because, when K. wishes to guide an Italian client
through the cathedral, it is his taking advantage of being in
that place to brush up on his vocabulary that puts him at the
mercy of the priest). Such are the few personal elements that

Kafka introduces, surreptitiously as it were, into the impersonality of the whole—in addition, of course, to those that are incorporated into his most constant and at the same time most compromising themes, and are far too skillfully denatured to be identified at this late date. But whether he submitted to fantastic metamorphoses to be sure of not intervening in the affairs of his hero, or allowed himself in a pinch to make a furtive, ironic appearance in his narrative, in any case his intrusion of himself was never accompanied by a value judgment; he never inserted the positive or negative sign that would incline the reader to enter into his views and share his personal scale of values. Whatever he may say about himself when he is hiding in some obscure corner of his fictional world, it is impossible to know what he thinks of that world, whether he finds it pleasant or unpleasant, harmonious, grotesque, reasonable, or preposterous, and equally impossible to know how he wishes to be understood and judged (and this refusal to *orient* his narrative is obviously at the source of the interpretive frenzy that so often seizes his critics, and in their train his readers). It is impossible because the narrator, being really someone other than himself, has not the slightest head start, not the slightest advantage over the uninformed reader: Kafka did not write to communicate a fixed conception of the world, but in order to learn from his heroes, who, though as ignorant as he, show by their way of responding to the experimental situation designed to test them how high and low, true and false, right and wrong, health and sickness are placed in himself and in the world.[37]

The narrator sees only what happens under his eyes and sees it only while it is happening; moreover, he sees it according to his own circumstances, *taking no account whatever of what Kafka may possibly say elsewhere on the same subject.* Thus he is unaware of the ideas about country life and the peasantry that Kafka expressed in his *Diaries* while living at his sister's house in Zürau: "General impression made on me by peasants: noblemen who have escaped into agriculture, where they have arranged their work so wisely and humbly that it fits perfectly into everything and they are protected against all insecurity and worry until their blissful death. True citizens of the earth."[38] Far from reflecting this "general impression," the narrator of K.'s adventure contradicts it; in his eyes the "noblemen who have escaped into agriculture" are scarcely human brutes, who stood gaping at him (K.) "with their open mouths, coarse lips, and literally tortured faces—their hands looked as if they had been beaten flat on top, and their features as if the pain of the beatings had twisted them into their present shape";[39] and throughout the narrative, he remarks on their narrow-mindedness, the servility with which they bear the yoke of the Castle, their supine obedience to the caprices of the Gentlemen, and finally their utter inhospitality to K., merely because he is a foreigner. And here again he does not pass judgment, but confines himself to recording events as they happen, a method that enables him to refute by observation the idyllic picture Kafka himself had formed, on the basis of his prejudices against Prague and big cities in general.

Of course, what made this principle of nonintervention (by which Kafka, tacitly as it were, expressed his reaction to a phenomenon typical of Prague, first frankly acknowledging its existence, then dissociating himself from it) especially binding on Kafka was his ambiguous linguistic situation—typically Jewish and also typical of Prague, but especially painful because it weighed heavily on his work and because he had long believed he could ignore it. At the time when he sent out his hero to conquer the world with no other arms than an all-powerful gift of poetic eloquence, it was language, speech in general, not *the* language that he thought problematic. He wrote and spoke German because it was what he had been taught, because he had no other means of expression and had not yet begun to worry about his right to make use of it. He was convinced that the uneasiness, the doubts, the paralysis of which he complained bitterly in the very first pages of his *Diaries* were the consequence of his unfortunate disposition, and not of the instrument with which he was obliged to create. Apart from snatches of stories in which we still recognize the direct influence of *Description of a Struggle*, his notations for 1910 consist chiefly of sighs and moans over what he then regarded as a monstrous incapacity: "Almost every word I write jars against the next, I hear the consonants rub leadenly against one another and the vowels sing in accompaniment like Negroes in a minstrel show. My doubts stand in a circle around every word, I see them before I see the word, but what then! I do not see the word at all, I invent it. . . . When I sit down at my desk, I feel no better than someone who falls and breaks both legs in the middle of the traffic on the Place de l'Opéra."[40] Indeed, it was in an attempt to get at the causes of this pathological helplessness that he started his *Diaries*. He wanted every day to train at least one line on himself, "as they now train telescopes on comets,"[41] to make every sentence a tribunal before which he would be cited. It is true that every sentence judges him, and that is why he concluded his notes for the year with an admission of defeat: "My strength no longer suffices for another sentence. Oh, if it were a question of words, if it sufficed to set down a word and one could then turn away in the tranquil consciousness of having filled this word entirely with oneself."[42] But in the midst of these unforeseeable highs and lows—for in spite of everything there were highs, his trouble was only intermittent—he had no thought of questioning his possession of the German language; for some time to come, it was the only possession he felt no need to justify.

As we have seen, the question of language did not begin to preoccupy him until 1911, when he discovered Yiddish, a mere dialect, a jargon unworthy to be termed a language, but whose spontaneity and emotional impact suddenly made him feel the coldness, aridity, and utter artificiality of his German—the German of an educated Jew. When he noted, "It is as if I were made of stone, as if I were my own tombstone,"[43] this deadly coldness, he had thought, came only from himself. Now he attributed it to his belief that the word *Mutter*, applied to his Jewish mother, who after all had taught it to him, had stifled all true feeling and affection in him.[44] The day Kafka realized that he had not always loved his mother as he was capable of loving her and as she deserved (because the German language had prevented him) he lost forever his tranquil assurance about the most important tool of his literary activity: at that moment the German language ceased to be the native land where he felt unquestioningly at home and became a foreign country, where he wished to be nothing more than a tolerated guest. And this was true of the form as well as the substance—here again the two could not be dissociated, and the entire orientation of his work was changed.

The profoundly significant detachment that Kafka had assumed toward his own language was not motivated by fear of infringing the rules of vocabulary and grammar; it had many causes—historical, ethnic, and psychological—far more deepseated than any purist's uncertainty about vocabulary and syntax. For a Jew to write in German, whether badly or well, was "appropriation of someone else's property, something not earned but stolen by means of a relatively casual gesture. Yet it remains someone else's property, even though there is no evidence of a single solecism. That does not matter, for in this realm the whispering voice of conscience confesses the whole crime in a penitent hour."[45] Naturally a flawed language did not help matters for Kafka; it merely intensified his inevitable remorse. In this respect Kafka was not wholly innocent. Though his language is almost free from the dialect phrases and impurities that Prague German acquired so easily under the influence of Czech and Yiddish, he was sometimes unsure of a word or a construction (one of these mistakes was the occasion of a quarrel between him and Felice, in which she was undeniably right); he even doubted as a matter of principle, for he was always on the alert, always ready to suspect "the sort of German we have learned from the lips of our unGerman mothers."[46] Be that as it may, the essential here was not a question of grammar; a German Jew could always convince himself even of nonexistent mistakes, because between him and his language there could be no true intimacy but only the dubious relationship of the thief with what he has stolen.

Thus, honest and gifted as they might be in other respects, the German Jewish writers, among whom Kafka could not help counting himself, drew no advantage from the theft to which they were led by their desire to break with their Jewishness. They had begun to write in German for no other purpose than to forswear their origins, but their liberation stopped halfway. "Their hind legs were still mired in their fathers' Jewishness and their thrashing fore legs could find no new ground." All their efforts to escape their "canine" condition served only to bring them back to it, they were torn creatures, doomed to helplessness and despair, with no other source of inspiration than the misfortune into which they had flung themselves. "An inspiration as honorable as any other," says Kafka, continuing his indictment, "but on closer scrutiny showing certain sad peculiarities. First of all, the product of their despair could not be German literature, though outwardly it seemed to be. They existed among three impossibilities, which I at random call linguistic impossibilities. It is simplest to call them that. But they might also be called something entirely different. These are: The impossibility of not writing, the impossibility of writing German, the impossibility of writing differently. One might also add a fourth impossibility, the impossibility of writing (since the despair could not be assuaged by writing and was hostile to both life and writing, writing is only an expedient, as for someone who writes his will shortly before hanging himself—an expedient that may well last a whole lifetime). Thus what resulted was a literature impossible in every respect, a gypsy literature which had stolen the German child out of its cradle and in great haste put it through some kind of training, for someone has to dance on the tightrope. (But it wasn't even a German child, it was nothing; people merely said that someone was dancing)."[47]

To judge by the harshness of tone, unusual in Kafka, the despair of which he paints so dark a picture was far more his own than that of the Jewish writers of his generation who, unaware of the catastrophe that was to descend on them—who could then, in 1921, have foreseen or even suspected it in all

its horror?—were all in all quite content to produce a literature "impossible in every respect," and quite a few of them
achieved fame in the process. Through his Jewish colleagues
who were unaware of their misfortune, Kafka was obviously
implicating himself in this shady family affair, the seamy side
of which was only too well known to him, and if his seemingly
relentless verdict seems unjust in the light of history—which
it was not from Kafka's absolute point of view—he was entitled to uphold it, because he was first to suffer its severity and
also because he was convinced that German Jewish writing, as
a direct emanation of the "as if" that he so abominated, embodied the falsehood and illusory security that his work would
be called upon to combat.

There would seem to be something rather distasteful in
this categorical condemnation of a phenomenon so varied and
so important, especially if we consider to what ideology it
brings fuel and what intellectual and political circles might
have approved it. On the other hand, Kafka never published it
(actually, he never published anything remotely polemical in
character); he was merely imparting his private thoughts on a
subject of the utmost importance to him to an intimate friend
who could not have mistaken his motives. But whatever one
may think of his attitude, it was inseparable from what he was
and what he did, from every last word and image that he set
down on paper. In a writer conscious of being deprived of the
essential possession that every man receives as his birthright, it
reflects a need of which he did not try to make a virtue, but
which he called upon his work to translate, or rather to *be*, as
faithfully as possible.

The only way Kafka could envisage of making his in
every respect impossible writing possible was to demarcate the
area of impossibility by creating a language without particular
color, without local tone, without qualities, as it were. In his
indictment of his Jewish colleagues, he freely admitted that
the *Mauscheln* [speaking German with a Jewish accent] of
which Karl Kraus was the uncontested master—"an organic
compound of bookish German and pantomime," as Kafka

himself defined it[48]—derived a certain justification from the fact that in German "only the dialects are really alive, and except for them, only the most individual High German, while all the rest, the linguistic middle ground, is nothing but embers, which can only be brought to a semblance of life when stirred by overactive Jewish hands."[49] Of these three strata that make up modern German only the third was within his reach, for the dialects and "the most individual High German" were precisely what he was least able to appropriate; and the "middle ground" of language was indeed dead—Kafka, with his excessively sharpened linguistic sensibility, saw more clearly in this matter than other Jewish writers of his time, and he refused to stir up the ashes to revive it. Obliged to forgo the German of the provinces and that of the high literary aristocracy, but unable to content himself with the "linguistic middle ground," whose death agony was being exploited by Jewish writers, he could look for his instrument only in a domain anterior to the written and spoken language, outside of space and time, where German, as a pure system, was still very close to its roots and its truth. To provide himself with a style in keeping with his aims, but faithfully connoting the expropriation of which he felt himself to be at once the agent and the victim, Kafka, in brief, detoured around *the* language and attained directly to *language as such*, outside of history and society. He worked at the zero point of time, at a level where the language, still free from all it owes to its dialects and to its great literature, has nothing to offer but its immediacy and the infinite resources of its combinations.

Because of the detachment he was determined to maintain toward his borrowed language, Kafka refrained from introducing any of the neologisms, archaisms, sophisticated idioms, and syntactic revolutions to which modern writers, especially Germans, feel entitled. He confined himself to a linguistic sector where words, stripped of all signs indicating their age, social and literary usage, or land of origin, preserve their full ambiguity. Hence the at once limpid and unfathomable quality of his prose: freed from the slag in which the usage of centuries has enclosed them, words, bared to the very core, reveal spontaneously the obscure implications of their primary meaning.

Such indeed are the key words—trial, castle, gentlemen, dog, burrow, etc.—that give Kafka's narrative the dynamic needed to launch and maintain its movement. Always used in their absolute grammatical sense, without complement or determinative, these usually ambiguous words start the action in two simultaneous directions, the one manifest, the other more or less dissimulated, between which the words play unceasingly (taken at this level, the *play on words* is the true motive force of the narrative and all the more powerful because one never sees it functioning). The novel *The Trial* has its immediate source in the word *Prozess,* which in German denotes both a judicial action and a morbid process, two meanings that do not ordinarily make for confusion, but that here develop together with so strict a logic that no one would think of dissociating them. Thus Joseph K.'s *Prozess** pertains to the spheres of both the judicial and the pathological (" 'You're involved in a *Prozess,* aren't you?' " one of the characters asks K., "tapping him on the chest with one finger," in other words, with the typical gesture of a doctor auscultating a patient); and since, moreover, neither of the two senses applies to any definite object, there is no way of knowing whether K. is guilty or sick—in the first case, of what crime or misdemeanor; in the second, the physical or moral nature of his illness. Guilty because sick in some corner of his body or mind, or sick as punishment for some inexpiable fault? Guilty of sickness or sick of guilt? Throughout the adventures of Joseph K. this is the grave question asked of the word *Prozess,* an ambiguous yet absolute word in which the old belief in an immanent justice, exempt from all scrutiny or science, makes a law of one of our most terrifying prejudices.

The fundamental ambiguity of Kafka's narratives follows naturally from his key words' aptitude for condensation and

---

* *Prozess* can be translated into English not only by "trial," but also by "lawsuit" or "case." —TRANS.

from the duplicity thus concealed beneath their simple appearance.[50] What, for example, looks more innocent than the word "castle"? Yet what is in reality more tendentious when we consider the fabric of images—wealth, antiquity, power, nobility, privilege—that has been woven around it since the remotest times? To this prestigious edifice, in which beauty and luxury are associated with the memory of absolute power and archaic customs, the German *Schloss* adds one more important characteristic that is not perceptible in the English castle (or the French *château*), since it evokes not only the building but also its enclosed character (*Schloss* also means "lock" and is related to several verbs expressing the idea of closure), so that all the moral, social, spiritual, and aesthetic qualities implicit in the image appear automatically as values defended from within, literally "walled around."[51] In view of all these meanings bearing witness to the power of superannuated things over our dreams and hopes, Kafka had no need to do violence to the word to make a whole novel out of it; the novel is contained potentially in the word, and the word determines the course of its events even when they seem to be absurd, improbable, and incongruous. He discovers that the dwelling place called "Castle" is enclosed for all—and first of all, it goes without saying, for him—in a system of implicit values which no longer correspond to anything in the world of today and which are all the more tyrannical because their obsoleteness relieves them of the need to prove themselves. Hence the task he assigns to his Surveyor—whose profession is indeed well chosen, although, as it turns out, he is unable to practice it—which consists quite simply in learning what "castle" means when the childish dreams, bookish memories, and temptations attached to the word are suddenly projected upon life. He also learns at his own expense what *Herren* ("gentlemen") means, for the *Herren* he has to deal with are at once what is meant by the word today: VIPs, potentates of the administration; "lords" in the archaic sense to the villagers; and to the women, domineering males, who reduce them to sexual slavery. In this test of strength which leads him to attack not only the Castle and its bureaucracy, but beyond it all the social, intellectual, and affective structures of our society, one does not see how K., regardless of his courage and tenacity, could possibly win out. But throughout his unfortunate expedition, he never ceases to dismantle the linguistic apparatus that enables the Castle to consolidate and perpetuate its domination; he forces words and things to confess their complicity in the enslavement of thought, and despite his passing spells of blindness and the terrible fatigue which overwhelms him at the end, he would be justified in boasting—he comes close to doing so—that he has carried out the essential part of his mission.

Though imposed upon him by extreme conscientious scruple, the discretion Kafka showed in his relations with his own language is not only a product of his refusal to appropriate alien property. To an at least equal degree, it is the response of a singularly alert mind, determined to remain on the alert, to the imposture of the world in secret alliance with language. Though emulating the discretion of this conspiracy whose workings are never visible, it nevertheless amounts to a violent attack on the frontiers of the world as it is, the war of one man alone, implacable though without bluster or commotion, against all those who use words as a means of domination. For it is true that Kafka denied himself the right to appropriate the German language and to exploit its riches to the full. But how did he manage to build his work on so radical a restriction, at the risk of paralyzing it and dooming it to aridity? How could he possibly think himself guilty of a serious linguistic crime—kidnapping the German child in its cradle—in a field that was after all his own and where, moreover, the criminal, even if recognized, is never subject to punishment? Whatever neurotic motives may have driven Kafka to mutilate himself—to the great good fortune of his work, it is true, but at the cost of what torments, of what a terrible sense of failure—they would not have had such power over him if they had not received constant confirmation from outside and thereby been charged with an undeniable force of reality.

Of course no law, written or unwritten, forbade him to

speak his adoptive language; he was merely made to feel that his claim to speak it with the naturalness and freedom that a native German possessed from birth was shocking, provocative, out of place, pretentious—in fact, the most flagrant proof of the difference he was trying to efface. German sounded right in the mouths of all those who, having by and large the same history and the same interests, needed no special accommodation of their words or silences to communicate among themselves. In his mouth it would always be false, however perfect, because his true interests were elsewhere, and because all his efforts to pretend this was not so succeeded only in making him a little more suspect. Not only did "the others" give him no real voice in social and national affairs; he did not even have access to the deeper strata of the language, where by his own admission the first words stammered by the child, even "father" and "mother," were only a ludicrous approximation for his Jewish feeling. Thus it would be best for all concerned if he adhered strictly to the tacitly established rule and took from German only what was condescendingly granted him in the sole field of public usage (the Surveyor, who speaks the same language as the people of the Village, but who neither understands them nor makes himself understood by them, clearly states the demands that motivate his constant efforts; what he wants of the Castle is not a favor but his right, and that is the last thing the "administration" is willing and able to grant him).[52]

One reason Kafka could not rebel against the rule—he rebelled only against the hypocritical silence that surrounded him, the "vagueness"—was that he knew very well wherein his German was fundamentally dubious, even when he made no demonstrable mistakes. Transmitted by a mother who was not a *Mutter* and who herself was far from mastering it,[53] German, well as he knew it, remained for him an instrument lacking in sureness; moreover, the flaws in his German were hard to localize. Kafka intuitively recognized the mistakes made by Brod in his translation of the libretto of Janáček's opera *Jenufa*, but confined himself to saying, "Isn't that the sort of German we learned from the lips of our un-German mothers?" because basically that was his only argument. In Prague, no doubt, this uncertainty was imperceptible because all shared it, but for a writer profoundly attached to the living word and intent on authenticity, Prague was evil incarnate, because there was no popular German from which the literary language of the élite could renew and enrich itself. The common people spoke Czech or Yiddish, and if they influenced the German language as spoken in Prague, it was obviously more to corrupt it than to give it health and strength. No popular German, no German people, no peasants or workers—Kafka certainly never met such proletarians as existed in the industrial cities of the Reich; he could have no more than an abstract idea of them, gleaned from books and newspapers (actually, he knew little more about the workers in the asbestos factory he owned in partnership with his brother-in-law).[54] As for the peasants among whom he lived for some time in Zürau, and who as a matter of fact were not Germans but *Deutsch-Böhmen* (Germans of Bohemia), he viewed them with a kind of terrified admiration, from an unbridgeable distance due to the lack of a common language. From this terror, amply attested by the *Diaries*, were born the peasants of *The Castle*, creatures hardly gifted with human speech and totally undifferentiated: in K.'s eyes they are all alike, just as formerly blacks or Chinese all looked alike in the eyes of the sedentary European. Thus the sufferings inflicted on him by language had motives more concrete than intellectual sensibility or an excess of conscientious scruple, for his classless, asocial German actually did banish him to an abstract ghetto, where human relations could only be monotonous and threadbare. It was true that he could have no contact of any kind with a worker or peasant; he could barely make himself understood by children,[55] and for one who placed the common people so high in his conception of humanity there could surely have been no greater curse.

Reduced by his uprootedness to a formal, bookish usage, his language, without breadth or warmth, opened only a narrow margin to communication; it, too, was lacking in "soil, air and law," bloodless, and there was no remedy for its anemia, since he could not possibly gain access to the language of the people, the only source from which it might draw vigor. That is why Kafka, accepting in silence the rule of discretion decreed by "the others," sought freedom only where it was open to him, in the strictly private realm of dream and in the neutral sector of the official language, where his legal status unquestionably authorized him to speak. Things, it is true, were not so simple, as the Surveyor learns to his cost when he discovers that the strict differentiation between the *private* and the *official* is merely one more deception, designed to mislead him a little more, for in reality the official is constantly encroaching on the private and vice versa, with the result that no corner of his life is so private as to escape the encroachment and tyranny of the Castle.

Legally, it is true, Kafka enjoyed equal rights with his fellow citizens of the Austrian empire, whether they belonged to the German majority or to the various ethnic minorities that the two-headed eagle had gathered together; like them he had at his disposal the official language—so-called *Kanzleideutsch,* or chancellery German—which for centuries served to hold the dual monarchy together. While in his daily life his sense of guilt, enhanced by the mute disapproval of "the others," prevented him from treating the German language as his property, in public life no one could deny him the administrative language of the empire, first because it was universal and second because here at least his otherwise doubtful identity was strongly attested. An Austrian citizen on paper, Kafka, neither more nor less than any other subject of his country, possessed the German of his civil status, and since this impersonal instrument of the bureaucracy was the only one wholly at his disposal, he was entitled to appropriate it and with it to fashion an impersonal and anonymous literary work—it, too, in the image of the expropriation to which he was obliged to accommodate himself.

Thus chancellery German became the salvation of his genius, for it enabled him not to overcome but to bypass the threefold impossibility that weighed on him: instead of trying to make himself believe that his talent authorized him to walk in the footsteps of Goethe and Schiller, Kafka simply wrote—a "simply" sustained, it is true, by intense resentment and rasping irony—in the manner of the petty functionary who handed him his papers (the petty functionary that he himself was, in part and very much against his will). Far from the poetic depths of the language from which in his boyhood he had thought he could gather great riches, he composed judiciary chronicles, reports, affidavits with the same glacial indifference, the same inhumanity, but it goes without saying with infinitely more humor, than the world bureaucracy displays to its clients.

From then on it was to the functionary, armed with his neutrality and his logic, that Kafka entrusted the task of organizing the verbal images that sprang directly from his own dream life. But the dreamer did not renounce his privileges; on the contrary, the image, forced to accommodate itself to an official style by no means calculated to heighten it, gained force and truth from its apparent subordination. Indeed, it gained an intensity bordering on enchantment; even in its moments of wildest fantasy, it takes on all the weight that is otherwise confined to reality. In the narrative that Kafka wrests from his "impossibility of writing" by fusing two elements so heterogeneous that they would appear to be quite incompatible, administrative argumentation is allied with subjective enchantment.[56] We see a dream, encoded with mathematical precision, come into the world to throw it off balance, and Medusa's head pitilessly refuted, while at the same time the dullest reality becomes a scene of metamorphoses and enchantments. Hence the strange beauty of this paradoxical art, which, making logic the argument of the fantastic and the fantastic a simple accident of normality, blends all the categories so harmoniously that it is no longer possible to say which is dominant, the cruelty of the realistic observer or the charm of magic.

7 · Fiction and Reality

The technical measures that Kafka took to transpose the anomalies of his situation into the very texture of his work—separating the real man from the writer, employing verbal images in senses remote from all historical and social usage, raising administrative language to the level of a universal language—gave him the great advantage of being able to emulate the traditional storyteller, who makes it his rule never to intervene in his hero's adventures and, unlike the modern novelist, is an insignificant person, of no interest whatsoever in himself, hence laying no claim to originality. Whether he is the author of epic poems, fables, memoirs, parables, or chronicles, the traditional storyteller speaks for the community, the public at large, and must therefore keep out of his narrative; the mere fact of speaking for all forbids him to speak of himself, so that, far from taking the stage, he does his best to make himself inconspicuous by adopting the style and sometimes even the name of traditionally revered masters. From his perspective, which is also that of the public, the slightest allusion to his personal life, the least idea of his own, the smallest fact identified with his period would only detract from the universality of his message; he deliberately refuses to be original so as to merge with the perennial community of geniuses, who in the eyes of his contemporaries are the sole repositories of authority.

Kafka partook of this tradition, which demands that the author efface himself behind the tradition, not so much out of humility as to prevent anything personal, anything temporal, from contradicting the eternal character of the fictitious events related. Thus, with full legitimacy, though in his own way and for reasons that his models could not even have imagined, he wrote fables—obviously all his stories of talking animals are fables, fairy tales—such as *The Metamorphosis*, which is also in a sense a *Märchen*, or the episode in *Amerika* where the hero, like Cinderella, incurs the taboo of midnight; legends—"Before the Law," a legend related in *The Trial* and accompanied by a commentary in the form of a *midrash*; parables dispersed throughout his writings and eminently represented in a text, *Of Parables*, dealing expressly with this genre as such; chronicles—*The Great Wall of China, Josephine the Singer*, and other fragments recording collective happenings; myths—*Prometheus, Poseidon, The Silence of the Sirens*, the story about the Great Nature Theater of Oklahoma in *Amerika*; and finally, an epic novel, *The Castle*, which in keeping with the immemorial tradition surrounding this edifice, tells the story of travails and a quest. Usually, it is true, the story results from a combination of several genres that, from a classical point of view, should not be mixed (though between myth, legend, fable, and tale the dividing lines are never so strict as to be impassable). For Kafka, conscious of his historical place and time, was intent on having this mixture of traditions show the confusion that had come over all human institutions, and literature as well, since the days of classical art.

Thus, as far as the talking animal is concerned, the story of Gregor Samsa is a fable, but one of its central themes—Beauty and the Beast—puts it into the fairy-tale category. The talking mice make *Josephine* a fable, but as a record of memorable events it has something of the chronicle. *Amerika* is an adventure novel containing an element of fairy tale—the punishment of the hero at the twelfth stroke of midnight; a myth—paradise lost and the Great Nature Theater of Oklahoma, which represents paradise regained—and on top of all this a sort of Robinson Crusoe, with the desert island replaced by an overpopulated America. In *The Castle* we find at different levels not only the story of the Grail and a new Odyssey, but also a serial thriller and a *Bildungsroman* in the Goethean sense, examples of the degenerated epic forms with which modern literature is obliged to content itself. For Kafka, as a late imitator, draws not only on the noble forms of the past, but also on the more or less ephemeral products of yesterday and the day before. But since, here again, he does not distinguish between high and low, noble and base, true and false, he provisionally endows the new, prematurely frozen convention with the same dignity as the ancient rendered eternal by tradition.

Thus the detective story (*The Trial*, *A Fratricide*, the murder of the advocate Monderry[1]); the serial thriller (the entire Amalia episode, which forms a large part of *The Castle*); the legal report (again *The Trial*, *The Assistant Attorney*,[2] *In the Penal Colony*); the children's story (the stories of Indians and pioneers, numerous examples of which are to be found in the *Diaries* and the notebooks)—all are treated with the same seriousness as the most revered classical genres. But while Kafka asks universal mythology to give his writings some reflection of the eternity lacking in modern literature, at the same time he exploits this form of degraded mythology (and in the last analysis, all imaginative literature is just that) in order to test the truth of myths, and above all of the ideas that literature itself purveys concerning the relations between books and reality.[3]

Though he imitates the ancients, Kafka lays no claim to participating in their order and their blissful security; on the contrary, he bases his right to imitate them on his own social and spiritual disorder, by constantly pointing to the nowhere to which his disjointed existence relegated him. He imitates for the paradoxical reason that he has nothing, strictly nothing, that seems to authorize him to do so. The traditional genres were obliged to proscribe the "I" because, responding to the needs of a community of individuals conscious of their place in a coherent universe, they addressed themselves not to the individual and his contingencies, but directly to the community. Kafka, on the other hand, far from speaking in the name of anything whatever, does not even represent a fully rounded individuality. What he has to say concerns only himself and the "Who am I?" of his evasive identity. While the ancients had their proper place in an unchanging and perfectly intelligible cosmos, he hovers without ties and without responsibilities on the periphery of an agitated, opaque, hopelessly disoriented world. To their absolute certainties concerning man's relations with the universe and knowledge of how on all occasions to remain in harmony with nature and the gods, he can only counter his absolute doubts and the innumerable questions that his ignorance of the law obliges him to leave in suspense. No one could have been less justified than this man at the far end of time in basing his work on such models, and yet, by a logical reversal carried to the extreme, this was the best possible justification for his imitation: precisely because he was disoriented in a human space that was itself disoriented, he was as far below all individuality as his models were above it, so that, absent from his work as a separate person and anonymous as the tradition prescribed, he achieved a kind of universality which, though negative, brought him infinitely closer to the ancients than to the subjectivism of his contemporaries.

Of course, Kafka's purpose in drawing inspiration from the ancients was not to benefit at small expense from the themes that won them eternal fame; nor, it goes without saying, was he one of those who find subjects for parody in the ancient themes, or who try to rejuvenate them by decking them out in modern dress and ideas. He used his models as a means of expressing his own transience and insignificance—all the flaws that prevented him from resembling them. An imitator, as befits a latecomer to a world where everything has already been done, said, and written, he appropriated the harmony of the ancients in order to show the discord of his own being and the imposture of what was offered him under the name of established order. Veiling his sick, irresolute self with the eternal youth of the epic, he anchored the transient and fortuitous in the millennia, the present in the timeless literature of the past, and his own instability in the permanence of a sacrosanct tradition. But his purpose in borrowing the mask of a Greek armed with unshaking confidence in his heroes and his gods[4] was certainly not to proclaim his attachment to the purported humanism of the "average cultivated European"[5] but, by contrast, to expose the wandering Jew that he himself was in the infinite misery of his lawlessness.

As an average cultivated European—or what, in his case, came to the same thing, as an assimilated Jew—Kafka was well acquainted with the Greeks; he had read them abundantly in secondary school[6] and their world, like everything that came to him from "the other side," was profoundly alien to him. He knew their myths and their legends as well as and perhaps even better than anyone else in his intellectual class; but for him they were mere intellectual ornaments, which, once again, were only lent to him, and whose wisdom, if he recognized it, was of no use to him whatsoever in the conduct of his life. Hence the equivocal nature of all his versions of ancient themes: dictated by the respect due such venerable tales, they start on a note of ingenuousness that goes with uncontested belief; then, little by little, they raise insidious logical questions which are totally out of keeping with the original themes and which end by undermining the legendary edifice. That, for example, is how Kafka relates the legend of Prometheus—or, rather, demolishes it by surreptitiously introducing suspicion in the very heart of his veneration, and sacrilegious questions in the very tone of his belief.

Like the author of the myth and the generations of man after him, Kafka assumes that Prometheus was punished by Zeus for a terrible crime (so well known that he does not think it necessary to mention it). The hero has been chained ever since to a rock in the Caucasus, where an eternal vulture keeps devouring his eternally renewed liver. Up to this point, the legend is clear and its teaching evident: the inexpiable nature of the original offense calls for eternal punishment, and in accordance with the immemorial law exacting corporal punishment for crime, the endless punishment of Prometheus produces an organic wound that remains forever open. But from this point—and this is where the story really begins, though what goes before is implicit in the tone and the choice of subject—matters take an unforeseen turn. For, says Kafka: "There are four legends about Prometheus"[7]—four instead of one, four variants instead of one authoritative version,[8] four interpretations dating from four epochs, which introduce the accidents of time into the eternity of the event. Merely by stating that he does not know the legend in its first and authentic form, the narrator admits that he is not contemporary with his story; he is living not even in a later day when people still took it as one exclusive truth, but in an age where all truth has four aspects, where simple truth no longer has currency and must give way to reasoned commentary. Thus Kafka needs only one sentence to remind the reader of the millennia that separate him from his hero and to distance himself from a traditional truth—original sin, his lifetime obsession and the central theme of his work—which, precisely because it concerned him very intimately, was in urgent need of being reexamined.

Thus, without ceasing to subscribe to the myth, Kafka suggests a doubt, not as to the facts—the reality of original sin cannot be undone by a simple negation—but as to the various interpretations that can be given. Of all the versions of the Promethean drama, which should be regarded as authentic, or as the least adulterated? The first (though not the oldest) does not conform to the original text; it is already a variant, which mentions neither the fire of heaven, nor Zeus, nor the vulture, but a betrayal, eagles, and gods. What it says of the offense is very general, and its author seems to have had no precise knowledge of it; moreover, it replaces what makes for the unity of the drama—a single offending hero, a single god-judge, a single vulture serving as executioner—with an indeterminate multiplicity. And, given its multitude of partly anonymous protagonists in place of the original three, all it has to pass on to the following version is a confused situation in which the point of the drama seems definitely submerged.

In the second variant, which no doubt marks a long historical interval, "Prometheus in his agony, as the beaks hacked into him, pressed deeper and deeper into the rock until he became one with it."[9] Here we have an element that is quite secondary from the traditional standpoint but which in Kafka's legend becomes the center of the enigma: the rock, that block of inert matter which, though a total stranger to crime and punishment alike, suddenly opens to receive the body of the tortured criminal. More merciful than the gods who decreed the punishment or than mankind which has allowed it to be carried out, the rock effects a monstrous fusion between a living being and inert matter, so marking the ultimate end of Prometheus's suffering at a time when it is no longer clear to anyone from what supernatural or natural law that suffering derived its necessity.

Petrified, Prometheus becomes identified with the outside world, of which the rock is the coldest and deadest part, whereas the rock itself takes on life—a life contaminated with guilt, reduced to a mere receptacle of the suffering that engendered it. If one dared, as clearly one should not, belittle this incomparable text with a dated philosophical reference, one might regard the exchange of properties between the suffering man and the stone as a sort of companion piece to or illustration of the young Marx's theory of alienation.[10] In addition to being the only alleviation of his punishment that Prometheus can wrest from fate, his petrifaction has the advantage of reproducing, or more precisely aping, the original unity of the world, the breakdown of which was manifested in the first variant. For although Prometheus re-establishes a semblance of unity between himself and the things of the world by entering the "inexplicable rock," he does not become part of the universal harmony, but merely loses the last vestiges of his humanity, without being able to communicate to the stone affected by his suffering anything but his own absurd oscillation between life and death.

These two versions bring the Promethean drama not to a conclusion—there is none, for it is precisely a drama of perpetual new beginning—but to the kind of end in which a process that has not been completed somehow manages to lose itself. True, Prometheus's torments are not alleviated by decree, but "his betrayal was forgotten over the millennia, the gods forgot, the eagles forgot, he himself forgot." And finally: "Everyone grew weary of what had become meaningless. The gods grew weary, the eagles grew weary, the wound closed wearily." The truth that had justified the punishment was forgotten and lost its efficacy; its feebleness and remoteness undermined the determination of the judges, the victim's spirit of revolt, and the cruel zeal of the eagles. The wound closes but is not healed, everything continues, or, rather, vegetates in the name of an old habit, which, in the mists of universal amnesia, revolves vainly around the tatters of its past. But in this perpetual repetition that is only an aping of lost eternity, the accent of the drama is irrevocably displaced: now it is on the rock, the "inexplicable rock," half-man, half-stone, which becomes the great enigma of this world beset by anarchy, because in this aggregate of suffering, weariness, and forgetfulness, it is not even possible to die.

In a few lines, in a few spare yet inexhaustible words, Kafka projects the untimely questions of the modern world into the world of the ancients, and his commentary, woven inextricably into the text, calls both the past and the present into question—the past, of whose heroism Prometheus is the supreme incarnation, and the present, in which the author himself is painfully implicated. Based on an idea of conquest and power, Promethean civilization contains in germ the transgression, the betrayal, the crime; it engenders the troublemaker, and punishes him so severely precisely because he has done nothing but carry its own principles to their logical conclusion. In the eyes of Kafka, who came from an entirely different cultural horizon, the myth presupposes an equality between the transgressor and his judges that makes it incomprehensible. After all, the Titan was of the race of the gods (that is why Kafka does not speak of the theft of fire, but only of *betrayal*); in the last analysis he is punished by a sort of family council and not by an inaccessible, transcendent god. To judge by their behavior in this episode, the gods are merely the deified expression of the human will to power, and Prometheus, whose actions are perfectly in keeping with their designs, has merely made the mistake of being too impatient and of being the loser in a conflict of interests similar in every way to those among human beings. Thus there is no common measure between the eternity of his punishment and the temporality in which the whole affair remains immersed. From the standpoint of the Jewish law, which, though dim and blurred in his mind, still guided his thinking, Kafka could not feel personally concerned about the legend: Prometheus was nothing to him, representing only a cultural datum at once known and alien, in the presence of which he retained his full freedom.

Clearly it is this incompatibility between the Greek and the Jewish faiths that Kafka mirrored in the incongruities of his pseudo legends,[11] but unlike many Jews of his generation who rejected assimilation or were unsuccessful at it, he saw in this incompatibility not so much an opposition implying a choice—Hellenism versus Judaism—as a subject for meditation on two equally powerful and equally obsolete methods of "national education." On this he expressed himself in a letter replying to Max Brod's polemical essay on the respective merits of paganism and the two monotheisms that came after it:[12] "The Greeks, for instance, were well acquainted with a certain dualism. . . . Only they happened to be unusually humble people—in regard to religion—a sort of Lutheran sect. They could not put the determining divine principle at sufficient distance from themselves; the whole pantheon was only a means by which the determining forces could be kept at a distance from man's physical being, so that human lungs could have air. A great national educational institution, which captured and held man's gaze. It was less profound than the Law of the Jews, but perhaps more democratic (scarcely any religious leaders or founders of religions among the Greeks), perhaps freer (it kept its hold, but I don't know how), perhaps more humble (for the sight of the gods merely made men aware of this: so we are not even, not even gods, and if we were gods, what would we be?)."[13] Thus these Olympians, invented expressly to remove the threat of the transcendent from the Greeks, were distinguished from humans by little else than their disproportionate size, and the threat they suspended over Prometheus was only the sentence of a disproportionately enlarged human tribunal, in other words, from the standpoint of that other "great national educational institution," Judaism, the most inconceivable of mockeries.[14]

But once he had disposed of the "determining divine principle," from which according to Kafka the Greeks sought to defend themselves by inventing the gods, Kafka understood Prometheus only too well, and this for a host of reasons all more or less connected with his own indestructible feeling of guilt. The hero, originally a Titan, a demigod, has betrayed the gods to become the benefactor of mankind; for this he is sentenced to a perpetual punishment, which itself engenders the organ on which it is inflicted (the perpetually renewed liver). Thus, like Kafka, he bears in his own flesh the wound resulting from his betrayal, and this for all time, despite the weariness of all concerned and the oblivion into which the transgression itself has fallen. (Concerning his own "wound," which he undoubtedly foresaw—he gave it to a character in *A Country Doctor* several months before his tuberculosis had been diagnosed—he wrote in his *Diaries*: "It is the age of a wound rather than its depth and degree of infection that makes it painful. To have it repeatedly ripped open in the same spot, though it has been operated on countless times, to have to see it taken under treatment again—that's what is bad."[15]) Afflicted with an incurable wound that is constantly reopened in the same spot, Prometheus has something else in common with Kafka, or, rather, with Joseph K.—namely, that his case is based on a forgotten accusation, so that, since he is being punished for a transgression that can no longer be known, no one is able to defend him or even to state his case. Everything, including his fatigue, a modern phenomenon par excellence and one of the most terrible consequences of his "wound," points to the true object of his meditation on gods and heroes: after traversing thousands of years of culture and thought, Kafka little by little put himself in the Greek's place, and in the end Prometheus Bound served only to reopen his own case.

Though striking in its admirable conciseness and the internal logic of its development, *Prometheus* is by no means the only example of what Kafka achieved by combining extreme subjectivity of content with the neutral expression offered by tradition (or convention, when he imitates degenerate epic forms). Indeed, there is all too much to choose from, for even in the shortest and most fragmentary story the same technique produces the same effects, and his entire work might be cited in support of this contention. In this sense one might say that from *The Judgment* on Kafka's art was no longer open to development; immutable in form, it allowed only its *themes* to be influenced by the fluctuations in Kafka's inner world; its task was to register these fluctuations.

The themes of this impersonal literature, as variable, as sensitive to external events as their formal structure was unchanging, follow the reality of Kafka's biography closely; sometimes they even anticipate it. In 1916, for instance, a year before he spat blood for the first time, he described the wound that his Country Doctor was supposed to treat and attributed to the spool Odradek the laugh "with no lungs behind it" that would not be his own until his tuberculosis settled in for good. *Amerika*, on the other hand, under the guise of a marvelous yet preposterous utopia, recapitulates the past. In it he embodies the old dream of emigration which filled his adolescence and which never really left him. *The Judgment*, written immediately after his first meeting with Felice, plays out the consequences of an engagement which in reality never took place. *The Metamorphosis* was a response to Kafka's violent altercation with his father, who had just made those unkind remarks about Löwy. *The Trial*, following the first breach of his engagement, deals with the consequences of guilt feelings, which he rightly regarded as the principal cause of the break. Finally, *The Castle*, written after his break with Milena, relates in a parodistic style well suited to the subject the "eternal" story of assimilation to which his love for a Christian woman suddenly lent new timeliness. Indeed, everything of any importance that he wrote had its point of departure in the crassest reality, but since his entire work is veiled, as it were, in a generic impersonality, since the anecdotes and accidents of Kafka's real life were strictly excluded from it, every line of it seems to convey a "universal" message.

We are now in a position to understand why many tend to outfit Kafka's themes—solitude, dissociation, grace, justice, exile—with a capital letter, which raises them to the sphere of metaphysics. Kafka himself seems to encourage this tendency as much by what he displays, which is never himself, as by what he is very careful to conceal. The fact of the matter is that if we regard these abstractions as the actual content of his work and fail to realize that they merely provide the framework of a romanced autobiography, we would be justified in attributing a purely symbolic function to Kafka's images, and accordingly in deciphering them with the help of an appropriate key. Such symbolic decoding seems especially necessary because the text puts up no resistance to it, but on the contrary lends itself to all the meanings one chooses to give it, which is not at all surprising, since Kafka actually inserts such meanings in order to test them and in the end to reject them as deceptively easy answers, as so many screens between himself and the truth. In sum, he offers his exegetes all the false keys that his hero tries out in his attempt to save himself, and if they are naïve enough to take them up, he lets them lose themselves on their too well laid-out paths, on which they have no chance of meeting him. Indeed, he misleads his critics and readers in the same way that K. is misled by the complicity between his own unconscious and that impostor the world.

Misplaced, more likely to lead the reader astray than to guide him, the metaphysical or religious interpretation has the additional drawback that, fascinated by the unchanging character of Kafka's models, its proponents totally disregard the inner development that undoubtedly influenced his choice of themes. From *Description of a Struggle* and *Amerika* to *The Trial* and *The Castle*, the themes are, to be sure, so interwoven and unchanging that one might regard them as timeless; yet they reflect conspicuous changes in the hero's inner life and attitude toward the world; they show how, in spite of his inevitable failure in practical matters, he gradually and with great difficulty achieved such lucidity as to abandon almost entirely both his own illusions and the opinions that the collectivity makes use of in order to rule. Since the heroes of the novels are about the same age as Kafka at the time when he conceived them—except Karl Rossmann, who is only sixteen—the advances in self-knowledge registered from one to the next are also those of age and experience. These advantages, it is true, are largely counterbalanced by the effects of the aging process: Joseph K. still has the vitality of a man of thirty, but the Surveyor, who is going on forty, is very tired before even starting on his campaign against the Castle. Thus Karl Rossmann, a naïve, inexperienced boy, remains the dupe of the parental authorities, uncles, directors, etc., who persist in persecuting him. Georg Bendemann's father's judgment, or verdict, suffices to make him jump in the river; like a son incapable of revolting, he cries out at the last moment, "Dear parents, I've always loved you all the same!" Gregor Samsa undergoes his metamorphosis passively; to the very end he remains dependent on the authorities—incarnated as always as parents and hierarchical superiors—which is precisely one of the causes of his transformation. In this respect, Joseph K. is still more advanced; though subjugated by the tribunal and its corrupt judges, he bravely takes up their challenge and little by little becomes aware of the enormous discrepancy between the *symbols* of justice and what happens in reality. He takes another long step forward—too late, unfortunately—when, realizing that the functioning of justice will escape him until he learns to know himself, he decides to give his case a favorable turn by writing his autobiography (as Kafka dreamed all his life of doing, and actually did under the veil of his novels).

In these two realms, self-knowledge and critical examination of the world, the Surveyor makes further progress, for, weak as he is when confronted by the magic power of the "Gentlemen," he is no longer so dominated by them as to believe blindly in the prevailing legends and superstitious rumors about them; in this respect he shows a remarkable clear-sightedness, and were it not for the enormous fatigue that lays him low in the end, he might, it seems, free himself sufficiently from their domination to cast off his last prejudices. As for the inner liberation that is the other aspect of his task and by far the most difficult, he is actively at work on it, learning to distrust seductive figures—Barnabas, his messenger, and the woman with the baby, who is introduced to him as "the girl from the Castle"—whom his cultural reminiscences and indestructible hopes of salvation lead him to regard as his personal saviors. It is surely no accident that one of these pseudo saviors is linked by his name to Saint Paul's companion and the other, with her infant son on her knees and the veil on her forehead, to the traditional iconography of the Virgin Mary.

True, this salutary distrust is neither strong nor constant enough to exorcise all his demons; on the whole, however, he perseveres in it, and at the end of his hard road he casts a glance so clear and piercing at everything around him that the Gentlemen themselves are obliged to avert their eyes. Utterly exhausted but partly delivered from his worst illusions, he at least has the satisfaction of having dismantled, piece by piece, symbol by symbol, sign by sign, the all-powerful edifice, which remains standing thanks only to the despotism of the masters, duly supported by the mental laziness and credulity of the blinded subjects. Thus, in the light of the hero's slow progress toward the reconquest of his self from the tyranny of the "administrative," Kafka's work was not only the attempt at escape to which he at one time reduced it; it also served in his own life the function of a therapeutic treatment which, though not completed, took him a long way toward a cure.

Since Kafka's account of his "dreamlike inner life" is essentially oriented toward escape, cure, salvation—to his mind the three were one—its aim was clearly not to lead the author and his readers into marvelous realms of dreamy irresponsibility, but, on the contrary, to help the dreamer wake up, teaching him to wrest from the dark and stormy forces within him the profound self-knowledge and active energy without which he would be a living corpse, a ghost. Unlike the surrealists, to whom he has often been likened and who themselves like to quote him, Kafka did not work with a view to snatching himself away from reality into dreams and the unchecked freedom of the irrational. Far from taking the dream world as a goal— he was already in it, in fact it was the only place where he really felt at home—he was constantly in pursuit of reality, which to him was precisely the realm of the impossible and the forbidden. He dreamed of reality as of a goal from which he was barred by some magic obstacle, and what he asked of the dream world (which he regarded not as the land without laws or frontiers in which the romantic soul hoped to lose itself, but as the *exact fantasy*, which Freud analyzed) was to reveal the secret of this monstrous order of banishment and if possible the means of countermanding it.

This gave rise to a flagrant contradiction, which has struck many critics: though Kafka's characters consistently make their home in the upside-down world of dream fantasy, *there are no dreams in the narrative works*, whereas there are swarms of them in the *Diaries* and notebooks. He never transgressed this principle (the few exceptions merely confirm the rule, since they occur only in unpublished texts and in carefully crossed-out passages in the novels). *The Metamorphosis* begins "on waking from an uneasy dream"; the dream that may have sparked it off is finished and there will be no further reference to it. Joseph K. is arrested one morning when he has just woken up, and though what happens to him from then on may be the continuation of a nightmare, he experiences it in a waking state and in broad daylight. The only dream in the original version of *The Trial*—in which Joseph K. sees someone slowly cutting the letters of his name into a tombstone—Kafka removed and published in a separate collection,[16] just as he crossed out the passage in which Joseph K., immersed in a daydream, sees the painter Titorelli, who has become his savior, shed "a blinding stream of light" upon him.[17] And another deleted passage in *The Trial* tells us a good deal about the relationship between dream and reality—too much, no doubt, and this may account in part for its deletion: "As someone said to me—I can't remember who it was—it is really remarkable that when you wake up in the morning you nearly always find everything in exactly the same place as the evening before. For when asleep and dreaming you are, apparently at least, in an essentially different state from that of wakefulness and therefore, as that man truly said, it requires enormous presence of mind, or rather quickness of wit, when opening your eyes to seize hold as it were of everything in the room at exactly the same place where you had let it go on the previous evening. That was why, he said, the moment of waking was the riskiest of the day. Once you had got that over without changing place, you had nothing to worry about for the rest of the day."[18]

The mysterious someone who keeps Joseph K. so well informed about the true circumstances of his arrest—apparently Kafka himself, who, for once making an illicit appearance in one of his narratives, was forced to censor himself—this intruder has at least the advantage of delineating for us the particular time and place that make it so disagreeably easy for the case to get under way: it is the interval between sleeping and waking, the riskiest moment of the day, from which the hero, not fully awakened from his dream and not fully adjusted to either state, tries in vain to free himself (the Country Doctor, jolted awake by the night bell, is also a prisoner of this enchanted interval: his earthly wagon harnessed to unearthly horses makes possible neither a true flight from the world nor a return to reality).

Thus dreams in Kafka, absent from the narrative as such,

yet extremely active because of the way they secretly disarrange facts, are a far cry from the fascinating phantasmagorias commonly associated with them; they make themselves felt only through their special way of functioning, which, superimposed on that of the waking world, provokes constant discords, disorders difficult to localize, incongruous shifts that suddenly throw the action off course. Knowing the phenomenon as only an inveterate dreamer can, and acquainted as he could not help being with his dark zones, Kafka wittingly took from dreams only the psychic mechanisms contributing to their elaboration; these work on the organization of his stories in such a way that even in the wildest literary dream the conventional frontier between dream and reality is always blurred. Thanks to these mechanisms of identification, projection, displacement, and condensation, which he knew not merely as if he had read Freud—and we know that he had read him—but as if he himself had reinvented them,[19] he peopled his books with characters who are never what they seem to be and never say or do what one would expect of them in their situation. It is impossible to know what to think of them, sometimes because Kafka distributes among several figures elements belonging to a single character, but which remain alien to this character because, since they are elements of himself incompatible with his conscious and unconscious desires, he has literally expelled them long since, and sometimes because, on the contrary, he condenses into a single figure heterogeneous elements which, since they are not recognized, confirm the hero in his deceptive sense of his own unity. Imitating the dream technique in its most productive aspect, he separates elements that should form an integral whole, confounds what should be separated, exteriorizes the invisible, and interiorizes the outside world—all this for the sole purpose of seeing more clearly amid the disorder of his psychic life and attempting to set it straight by recovering the enormous amount of energy that his neurosis made him squander. But although what he principally asked of dreams was that they show him how to make better use of his energies, he never ceased to derive from them an incalculable aesthetic advantage for his art; for in following the basic principle of dream syntax, which invariably replaces relations of *causality* and *kinship* with simple relations of contiguity, he was able to dispense with the psychological explanations and interior monologues which authors of "profound" novels find necessary. Instead of making subtle observations on the character and behavior of his hero, he makes him live and act in a zone either inaccessibly remote from, or alarmingly close to, the desires that, since they are situated in his unknowable depths, are materialized for him in the form of alien beings. And thanks to this substitution of image for discourse, which is indeed one of the most striking properties of dreams, he quite naturally saved his stories from either the pedantry or the vulgarity associated with the uninspired use of psychology.

It was not for pleasure but out of necessity that Kafka continually represented his own fragmentation through split or duplicated figures. Not only in his imagination was he fragmented, dissociated, endowed with a pathological aptitude for identifying himself with any object in the outside world,[20] and conversely for projecting upon the outside world the dark forces at work within him; rather, the excessive oneirism that affected his inner life would in itself suffice to prove that for him this dissociation was an immediate reality, the same reality that, while irresistibly impelling him to write, also exposed him to the greatest dangers. He speaks of this in one of the aphorisms usually entitled "He," precisely because in them his tendency to depersonalize himself leads him to speak of himself in the third person: "He lives in the Diaspora. His elements, a horde living in freedom, roam about the world. And it is only because his room is after all part of the world that he sometimes sees them in the distance. How is he to shoulder the responsibility for them? Can that still be called responsibility?"[21] Here Kafka identifies himself not only with dispersed individual Jews, but with the diaspora as a whole; he is at once the Jewish people, outlawed by reason of its historic dispersion, and the inwardly alienated Jew, the "he," powerless to regather, to control, or even to know his dispersed elements. For to his mind the loss of the law has the same effects on the psychological, historical, and social planes: it has transformed the people into a horde and the isolated Jew into a little diaspora of truncated selves, impossible to govern.

Thus the famous doubles with whom Kafka accompanies his heroes are not creatures of fantasy; they correspond in every point to the grave disorder that prevented Kafka from living at peace with himself and from finding his proper place in the collectivity. The two warders—warders, not policemen —who come and arrest Joseph K. in his bedroom seem, it is true, to exist in themselves and to come from outside; but on closer scrutiny they show certain peculiarities that the hero of *The Trial* would have profited by noticing (but of course his nature is such that they escape him). First of all, one is named Franz, for a reason obviously well known to Kafka, though Joseph of course is unaware of it (by a supreme irony, their names taken together add up to Franz Josef, the name of the aged Emperor whom the Jews of the Dual Monarchy revered as their traditional protector and whom in Kafka's day people were beginning to regard as eternal). The two warders—the other bears the Germanic name Willem—immediately adopt an attitude of familiarity toward the arrested man, which is one more indication of their origin: they break into his room, eat his breakfast, and steal his underwear, for which offense he will have them punished severely. Franz and Willem describe themselves as minor functionaries who, though not informed about his case, are inclined to the greatest benevolence toward the suspect. They probably, says Willem, "mean better by you than anyone else in the world." To which Franz adds: " 'That's so, you can believe that' . . . and instead of raising to his lips the coffee cup he was holding in his hand, he gave K. a long, apparently significant, yet to K. quite incomprehensible look."[22] But how can K., indignant at the way the two warders have broken into his room, be expected to believe that they are well disposed toward him? How can he be expected to understand that Franz's long look has a bearing on the very

essence of his case? How can he realize that these crude, grasp-
ing, stupid men, for whom he feels only disgust and contempt,
are representatives of the lower strata of his own psyche, members of the wild horde which he himself is and which he wants
absolutely nothing to do with? The two warders have been expelled, literally repressed, from the personality he has fash-
ioned for himself in the image of his spiritual hierarchy, in
which appetites of every kind, beginning with sexual desire,
are irrevocably condemned. Expelled but not destroyed—in
the unconscious, from which they emerge, nothing ever
dies—they come back to haunt him on his thirtieth birthday
(they are really ghosts, which vanish as they came, in an in-
stant) in an attempt to recover their place within him and so
reconstitute his unity. They are right in saying to K. that what
they are doing is for his own good, just as Frau Grubach is
right in regarding his case not as a curse but as something crucial to his happiness.[23] It is true that K., imprisoned in a psychic organization in which high and low, love and sex are
definitively separated, can only be deaf to this language of
common sense; his case, which the landlady associates with his
happiness, is to him "an absurdity," and what according to his
warders is for his good is to him evil and impure, the worst
possible betrayal of his ideal. Consequently, he rebuffs them,
so depriving himself of the positive assistance his arrest was
supposed to give him. His case is lost from the start; taking the
wrong attitude toward it, he transforms his *Prozess* into the irreversible morbid *process* which little by little will isolate him
from all and in the end will remove him from life.

He is punished for his contemptuous and brutal treatment of the warders—in reporting their thefts to the authorities, he makes himself responsible for having them
whipped—by another pair of "gentlemen," these two totally
silent, "elderly tenth-rate actors," "pale and fat," with disgust-
ingly clean faces, which of course he again fails to recognize as
his own face. They, too, are rudely intrusive, but in a very different way from the warders; they have come, not to show him
the need to make himself whole again by restoring instinct to

his affective life, but to communicate something horrible, of which their crudely theatrical look gives him a presentiment: to Joseph K., the lamentable histrionics which are at the bottom of his nature, and to Kafka himself, a condemnation of his dubious, untruthful, botched art, undermined by the twofold effect of a pathological tendency toward silence and an excess of dramatics. Joseph K., who has come steadily closer to his author since deciding to write his autobiography, is not at all willing to reincorporate the theatricality which Kafka wishes above all to eliminate from his work. But now he is obliged to; the two gentlemen in black make this clear to him by squeezing him so tightly between them that they are one with him: "But just outside the street door they fastened on to him in a way he had never before experienced. They kept their shoulders behind his and instead of crooking elbows wound their arms round him at full length, holding his hands in a methodical, practiced, irresistible grip. K. walked rigidly between them, the three of them were interlocked in a unity which would have brought down all three together had one of them been knocked over. It was a unity such as can hardly be formed except by lifeless matter."[24] Thus because he was unable to let his warders and the tenth-rate actors live freely within him, he recovers nothing more at the last moment than the exclusively material unity of his dead body, and when one of the gentlemen takes out "the long, thin butcher knife" that will be used to kill him, K. is well aware that he should take it and plunge it into his own heart. But he does not; like Kafka, he *suffers* the slow death dealt by his inner fatality, doing nothing to hasten it.

Though the specifically sexual attributes of the two warders are evoked only very allusively in *The Trial*—their intrusion into Fräulein Bürstner's room, where K. is first interrogated—his other stories about duplicated objects or persons manifest the sexual attributes with such comic crassness as to leave little room for interpretation, but in this as in many other points, the obvious in Kafka is precisely what is least no-

ticed. Take Blumfeld—a bachelor and, to judge by his name, a
Jew—who drags himself up his six flights of stairs, grumbling
about the miseries of his solitary life. In his room no one is
waiting for him, no wife, no child, not even a dog. A dog! He
has often thought of acquiring one; what a pleasure it would be
to have a little creature that would make a fuss over him when
he got home from the office. Yes, but dogs make messes, they
always do, and Blumfeld, with his mania for order and cleanliness, could never put up with that. Still climbing, the old bachelor considers one by one the annoyances that a dog would
bring into his well-regulated life, and while he is still climbing
the stairs, his imaginary animal has contracted all sorts of ailments: ". . . one wraps it in a rug, whistles a little tune, offers it
milk—in short, one nurses it in the hope that this, as indeed is
possible, is a passing sickness, while it may be a serious, disgusting, and contagious disease"; time passes, the dog grows
old, "and then comes the moment when one's own age peers
out at one from the dog's oozing eyes. Then one has to cope
with the half-blind, weak-lunged animal all but immobile with
fat, and in this way pay dearly for the pleasure the dog once
had given. Much as Blumfeld would like to have a dog at this
moment, he would rather go on climbing the stairs alone for
another thirty years than be burdened later on by an old dog
that would drag itself up, step by step."[25] Before Blumfeld
even reaches his landing his mind is made up; he will remain
alone, and never again will any living creature disturb him.

Selfish, pedantic, petty, calculating, fainthearted, and incapable of love, Blumfeld has renounced living companion-
ship to protect his apartment from disease, disorder, and dirt.
He has deprived himself of the joys of love and sex merely to
spare himself the confusion and worry that a woman, far more
than the dog he continues to dream of, would inevitably bring
into his life. Like all Kafka's heroes, he is punished by the appearance *beside him* of what should be *inside him*, a source of
harmony and happiness. For the most amazing spectacle awaits
him in his room: ". . . this is magic—two small white celluloid
balls with blue stripes, jumping up and down side by side on

the parquet; when one of them touches the floor, the other is in the air, a game they continue ceaselessly to play."[26] Blumfeld is mystified. He thinks the balls are being held by an invisible thread, but soon cannot help seeing that they are moving all by themselves; their inert matter has taken on life for his benefit, and from then on they never stop harassing him. They adjust to his pace, follow his every movement, turn around when he turns, and to make it clear what place they should, but cannot, occupy, they always stay behind him: only to reveal their presence have they ventured to appear in front of him, and from then on this seems to be forbidden them. After a sleepless night Blumfeld, who after all has good reasons for not wanting to destroy them, finally decides to shut them up in his wardrobe. And so as not to hear the obsessive rhythm of their bouncing, he stops his ears with cotton, which is indeed the best way to keep from knowing what they want and exactly why they have come to torment him.

For fear of inconvenience, dirt, and contagion,[27] Blumfeld has eliminated from his life the women, children, and dogs he might have loved. But if he thinks this will preserve his peace of mind, he is very much mistaken. He has not succeeded in killing his sex drive; on the contrary, projected outside his body and taking on a movement that is a caricature of life, it is more of a nuisance than ever. He certainly won't make it stop bothering him by shutting it up in a wardrobe and plugging his ears; all he has accomplished is to make his predicament ridiculous.

After having put the wretched balls under lock and key, and seemingly freed his mind of what they came to remind him of, Blumfeld goes to his office as if everything were all right, and this "as if" of half-unconscious, half-deliberate forgetfulness exposes him to new trouble. For at the office the two balls have their counterparts in the persons of two young men—lazy, timid, clumsy good-for-nothings, whom the director has given Blumfeld as assistants, supposedly to lighten his excessive workload. As the story suddenly breaks off, we do not know what persecutions and annoyances these two young scamps hold in readiness for Blumfeld, but the characters themselves are quite familiar to us; their laziness, irresponsibility, timidity, and childishness—symptoms of the infantilism of Blumfeld and his kind—we identify them as the twin brothers of the two assistants of *The Castle*, the most prominent and exemplary of the pairs of tormentors that Kafka sends his heroes, to bring them back to earth and cure them of their pedantry.

At the beginning of the novel, K., who claims to have been summoned to the Village as a surveyor, announces the imminent arrival of his assistants and of the instruments with which they have been entrusted. A little later he meets "two young men of medium height, both very slim, in tight-fitting clothes," who amaze him with their resemblance to each other and the extraordinary speed with which they move through deep snow. Himself struggling desperately to get ahead, he wants very much to attach himself to them, in other words, make use of them as assistants, but no sooner has he called out to them than he loses sight of them completely. On entering the inn, he sees the same young men stationed on either side of the door, obviously waiting for him. " 'Who are you?' he asked, looking from one to the other. 'Your assistants,' they answered. 'It's your assistants,' the landlord corroborated in a low voice. 'What?' said K., 'are you my old assistants, whom I told to follow me and whom I am expecting?' "[28] Thus K. does not know his own employees; or, more exactly, he does not recognize them, though in some obscure corner of his mind he knows that these young men belong to him and have long been in his service ("my old assistants"). This, of course, is absurd; in broad daylight, or even in the half-light where this story takes place, there can be no rational explanation for such a mixture of knowing and not knowing unless we assume that K. is insane or deliberately lying; and yet, as we go deeper into his relations with his two strange acolytes, we are forced to recognize that this apparently irreducible absurdity constitutes in itself the logic of the novel.

K. treats the assistants who have come to help him with

his hypothetical surveying (they have not brought their instruments, and, of course, they know nothing whatever of this kind of work) with a brutality that seems quite inexplicable when we consider how he lets them invade his privacy. True, the young men are no better than Blumfeld's assistants; despite their exaggeratedly manly beards, they are infinitely childish, docile and timid, lazy, untruthful, and lecherous, yet (like the two characters in caftans in Lateiner's *Meshumed*, who had so struck Kafka's imagination years before), disarming in their innocence and awkwardness. But though in his relations with them K. conducts himself like a ruthless master, conscious of his rights and of his superiority, he is quite incapable of defending himself against their constant meddling in his most intimate affairs. For in reality their mission has nothing to do with the surveying K. talks so much about; their mission is simply to be with him at all times of the day and night, and from this task their master, who has become their slave, is powerless to deflect them.

When K. wakes up, the morning after his first night of love with Frieda, amid the rubbish and beer puddles of the Herrenhof, the first thing he sees is his two assistants sitting at the bar counter, "a little heavy-eyed for lack of sleep, but cheerful. It was a cheerfulness arising from a sense of duty well done."[29] Considering what has happened that night, the "duty" that the assistants have accomplished to their satisfaction can only relate to the night of love and their own active part in their master's amorous success. From then on, in any event, K. and Frieda never have a moment to themselves, never a second's intimacy without the inseparable pair. It seems, in fact, that K. can possess her only in the presence of the two young men, for the day when one of them, sick of K.'s bad treatment of them, complains at the Castle and asks to be relieved of his mission, Frieda drops K. once and for all.

Here again Kafka places, *beside* his hero, but in a significantly intimate relationship with him, instinctive powers that should properly be active *inside* him, in full accord with his higher, spiritual powers. Just as Joseph K. has only contempt and disgust for his two warders, those crude personifications of instinct, so the Surveyor relegates his assistants, deservedly from his point of view, to the lowest rank of humanity. Though he knows their names perfectly well—everyone in the Village calls them Arthur and Jeremiah, and no one mistakes one for the other—he, on the strength of their resemblance, pretends to be unable to distinguish them and calls them both Arthur, which they justifiably regard as a cruel affront.[30] He fails to understand—or, rather, he understands only too well, as he shows by comparing his two assistants to snakes—that the two rascals have really been sent to help him, and that if he wishes to escape from the state of helplessness to which he has reduced himself, he must not only make his peace with them, but also reintroduce them into his living organism. This half-intentional, half-inevitable incomprehension has grave consequences, especially since he persists in idealizing the figure of Barnabas merely because he supposes the young messenger to be connected with the most powerful of the Gentlemen, who, in spite of all K. gradually finds out about them, retain almost to the end their place at the summit of his personal hierarchy. Thus he is deceived on both sides: in rejecting his true helpers and in seeking salvation in the high place where the "documents" of the bureaucracy are made. His mistake ruins not only his marriage projects but also his chances of assimilation to the world of Count West-West, for which he has abandoned everything.

For in addition to their role as emissaries of deprecated, condemned, repressed instinct, the doubles have a very definite social function, which adds a further touch of incomprehension to K.'s attitude toward them. Already subaltern in the erotic sphere that is profoundly theirs, they also occupy the lowest place in K.'s physical entourage—in *Amerika* they are tramps and parasites, in *The Trial* half-starved warders, and in *The Castle* imbeciles—and though he himself is persecuted by the supreme bourgeois authorities, he treats his assistants with the contempt of an all-powerful master. Only Karl Rossmann is free from this arrogance; true, he is a boy of sixteen, and his doubles take shameful advantage of his youth. Joseph K., forever harping on his rights, reports Franz and Willem for stealing his underwear when they came to arrest him, and, though horrified at the cruel whipping they receive in punishment, he does very little to oppose it and hastily shuts the door of the storeroom where the scene takes place, just as Blumfeld shuts the door of his wardrobe on the two active little balls. Full of the importance conferred by his privileged position, he regards almost all those around him as inferiors, people of no account, to whom he shows no respect whatsoever except when trying to pump them for information about his case. He takes pleasure in women but does not love them; in fact, he is concerned only with himself, a trait that largely discredits his protestations of innocence.

Though the Surveyor is without the bourgeois prejudices of his predecessor—having cast them off along with the rest of his human baggage, possessing neither employment nor home nor property, he is a man without caste or class—he nevertheless treats his assistants, who among other things are guileless young peasants, with unnecessary brutality, never taking the slightest interest in their personal lives or showing any consideration for their dignity. He claims to love Frieda, but not once does he question her about her childhood, her thoughts, or her wishes, and she herself deplores his coldness: " 'You have no tenderness to spare me, you hardly have time for me, you leave me to the assistants, it never occurs to you to be jealous, my only value for you is that I was once Klamm's mistress. . . .' "[31] This is true: for him Frieda is only a weapon, a pledge that he holds against Klamm and that he means to cash in. And just as he never thinks of Frieda for her own sake, he has only indifference for what goes on around him; in his eyes the peasants are an undifferentiated mass, in which all individuals are completely submerged; he knows nothing of their customs, their needs, their way of accommodating themselves to the world to which their birth has attached them; but though they all remain indistinguishably alien to him and he dislikes them all equally, he nevertheless wants to reform them, correct their mistakes, rectify their judgment—in a word, civilize them. He looks upon these people as if they had fallen from another planet, and yet in his fatuousness he wants to teach them to reason like him and resemble him in every way, while at the same time persisting in his belief that what he wants most is to be like them (the "most urgent" step, he keeps telling himself, is to become like Gerstäcker and Lasemann). What is astonishing under these circumstances is not so much the failure that awaits him at the end of his eight-day odyssey, as the mere fact that he has thrown himself into this adventure and hoped, for so much as a moment, to succeed.

Thus upon the instinctual affliction attested by his "doubles" K. superimposes the social affliction that has struck the entire Jewish organism in the historic diaspora. What, against a background of supposed fantasy, he evokes through his assistants, his warders, and all the troublesome pairs with whom he peoples his stories, is at once the psychic impotence of a neurotic individual and the social guilty conscience of the Jew of the diaspora—two elements that he never separates and that occupy an obsessive place in his books, precisely because life permitted him neither to resign himself to them, to cure himself of them, nor to take full responsibility for them.

Along with this splitting of the hero into two or more selves impossible to reunite, Kafka made abundant use of another, contrasting, mechanism characteristic of dream thinking, which enabled him to condense several aspects of himself into a single figure. Here the doubles are no longer detached from the "I," who wishes to ignore them; it is the "I" who unwittingly contains them in himself in the form of two divergent and most often radically opposed natures. In the first case, the loss of unity is figured by the exteriorization of the lost elements; in the second, by their condensation within a monstrous hybrid, the sign and outcome of the ultimate disintegration of the individual. Man and insect in *The Metamorphosis*, man and dog in *Investigations of a Dog*, man and mouse in *Josephine*, man and ape in *A Report to an Academy*, man and rock in *Prometheus* and *The Bridge*, and finally, the living and the dead in *The Guest of the Dead* and *The Hunter Gracchus*—whatever transformation he undergoes, the hero of this type of story partakes of two natures, the one animal or inanimate, the other human, since he retains the faculties of thought and speech. Each of these natures develops according to its own law, without concern for the other and its needs, and the consequence is a logical conflict that leaves the hybrid diminished in his being and sometimes ends in his death. (Gregor Samsa starves to death because, though he continues to think like a man, his metamorphosed body feels only disgust for human food, and it does not occur to his family to give him any other.)

Here again Kafka's supposed fantasy is simply an instrument from which he obtains a maximum of realistic precision: his metamorphoses merely represent *visually* the extreme consequences of a specific psychological process, observed with an extraordinary clinical precision.[32] But although it concretizes a state of inner dissociation, the hybrid is not—any more than the doubles—a mere translation of the author's complaints and phantasms; it lives in a narrative that its solidly constructed formal structure distances both from private anecdote and from psychology of any kind. Here it must be noted that Kafka does not always make the same use of these two techniques that he borrows from dreams: duplication occurs especially in the novels, the hybrids exclusively in the short stories. This is explained by the nature of the two genres, since the short story can easily be assimilated to fable and legend with their affinity for metaphysics, while the novel, more rational and extending over a greater lapse of time, would not easily lend itself to prolonged metamorphoses. Here as everywhere the narrator relates improbable happenings in the tone of a routine report; his attitude toward the events he is relating is the cold indifference of an unconscious observer (which, in its contrast with the horror inherent in the content, produces an effect not of humor but of true comedy). At the most he occasionally lets a shadow of melancholy fall on this neutrality,

as in *Prometheus* or, more markedly, in the story of the nameless animal that a monstrous crossbreeding has set apart from
all the other animals of creation.

This cross between a cat and a lamb belongs to the narrator, who makes it clear from the start that it is a legacy from
his father. It has the head and claws of a cat—that is, its aggressive features—and the size, form, and proverbial docility
of a lamb. "It runs away from cats and tries to attack lambs.
On moonlight nights its favorite promenade is along the eaves.
It cannot meow and it loathes rats. Beside the hen coop it can
lie for hours in ambush, but it has never yet seized an opportunity for murder." The aggressiveness of the cat is paralyzed by
the gentleness of the lamb, and, torn between its two contrary
natures, the animal reacts incongruously, sometimes with
striking fierceness, sometimes with terrified passivity. Quite
absurdly, it attacks one set of its racial half-brothers while
running away from the other. Capable neither of meowing nor
of bleating, it has no language of its own, nor has it any appropriate food, for despite its carnivore's canines, it consumes
nothing but sugared milk. It has the anxiety characteristic of
both races and is doomed to the unparalleled solitude of one
who "though it has countless step-relations in the world, has
not a single companion."[33] Of course it has no name, and for
want of a female to mate with, it cannot have offspring. And
so, considering the fate of this unviable creature, vegetating
miserably between two races and two irreconcilable sets of in-
stincts, its master thinks of giving it release with the help of a
butcher's knife. But though the animal sometimes gazes at him
"with human, intelligent eyes, imploring him to perform an
intelligent act," he cannot sacrifice it, for the sole reason that
it is a legacy from his father, and it is neither permissible nor
possible to kill a legacy.

The narrator insists so strongly on the element of heredity
that this must be regarded not as an accessory detail but,
rather, as the essence of the fable. He mentions it at the very
start, adding for greater clarity that the animal, a part of his
heritage, did not take on its monstrous character until the nar-

rator's day; in his father's time it was "more lamb than kitten," hence closer to a normal, classifiable species. Once the living legacy enters into the son's possession, the two become physically close—"Pressed against me it is the happiest"—so close, in fact, that when the man sees "tears dropping from its huge whiskers," he doesn't know whether the animal or he himself is weeping. In the end, the crossbreed, who, not content to be kitten and lamb, also has something of the *dog*, seems to be endowed not only with a heart but with reason as well: he implores its master to be "reasonable" and kill him. In the end it becomes almost human—so human that in it legacy and legatee become one solid lump of wretchedness, as mysterious and as indestructible as the ineluctable fatality of heredity itself.

No great exegetic wisdom is needed to discover the real tragedy that inspired this fable. It suffices to list the elements on which the story centers: a legacy that deteriorates when passed on from father to son; crossbreeding and sterility; anxiety and loneliness connected with inevitable dual allegiance; and, resulting from all these factors, inability to live. The problem of his Jewish descent, which Kafka owed to his father, which he could neither change nor eradicate, and which even prevented him from killing himself (the "intelligent act" in which the animal saw deliverance never ceased to tempt him, but he never did anything more than write about it); the problem of his false situation between two worlds, two cultures, two moralities, divergent especially in the matters of sex and aggressivity; and lastly the problem of a being who, with "countless step-relations in the world," was nevertheless alone of its kind—such, beyond a doubt, is not the message of the fable (actually the hybrid has only himself and nothing above or beyond it to communicate), but the living material that compelled Kafka to create it, because outside of his writing he had no means of expressing himself.

Half-kitten, half-lamb; half-man, half-rock; half-man, half-animal; half-dead, half-alive—Kafka was indefatigable in inventing the forms in which to clothe his own deep trouble so as to observe it and synthesize its elements, undisturbed by episodic considerations that would falsify or attenuate its truth. Noble and degenerate forms, fable, legend, folk tale, or epic—all served him in his attempts to understand his own case and if possible, if possible in spite of everything, to reshuffle the cards of his destiny. And if, in this perpetual examination of his life through a depersonalized sort of writing, he only half reveals himself, it is much less from reticence than because in this inexpressible case even the frankest elucidation would miss the essential; it would merely refer one to the mystery and irreversibility of birth—in other words, to an inexplicable factor that defies all reason.

There is no ultimate explanation, no last word to be said about this work unique of its kind, unfinished by reason of its very perfection, and consequently as limited as to the space it occupies on our bookshelves as it is unlimited in meaning.[34] There is no last word, but perhaps a last example is worth citing nevertheless, a text particularly revealing in that it draws its truth precisely from its extreme lack of plausibility. More provocative than any other because of the figure it chooses to animate (no other writer has ever taken an old spool of broken thread as a hero), it is also one of those in which Kafka's art, so simple in its complexity, best reveals the perfect adaptation of his means to his ends.

The story begins with linguistic considerations concerning the name "Odradek"—the reader has not yet been told what it designates. "Some say the word Odradek is of Slavonic origin, and try to account for it on that basis. Others believe it to be of German origin, merely influenced by a Slavonic dialect. The uncertainty of these interpretations gives us reason to suppose that neither is accurate, especially as neither provides a plausible meaning for the word."[35] Once again we have a composite formation, a word partaking of two languages, for which reason neither its origin nor its meaning can be established with certainty. Once again duality is a factor of uncertainty and confusion; for insofar as the dual object ceases to be directly knowable, it obliges us to replace *knowledge* with *in-*

terpretation—that is, with a confused activity having little utility outside itself. Though Kafka's remarks about the misleading aspect of interpretation were obviously not addressed to his innumerable commentators, these commentators might with reason feel concerned, for they, too, turn indefatigably around Odradek, trying to fathom its secret, and they, too, provide a multitude of more or less plausible interpretations, none of which, however, can boast of being the right one.

With a humor, born once again of the enormous incongruity between the seriousness, not to say pedantry, of the exposition and the total ignorance in which one is left as to its object, Kafka concedes, "No one, of course, would busy himself with such studies if there were not a creature called Odradek." So there is an Odradek, but what is it? A literally indefinable something, which one can hardly attempt to describe without a conditional or two: "At first glance one would say a flat, star-shaped spool for thread, and indeed it seems to have thread wound around it; true, they would only be old, broken-off bits of thread of the most varied sorts and colors, knotted and tangled together." Nothing is certain about the appearance of this unusual object, but little by little certain features become clear; especially the star, which is definitely Odradek's shape and even the vital center of its organism, since that is what enables it to move about (it walks by supporting itself on one point of the star and on a system of bars affixed to the middle of the star) and to appear to be alive. An object with a name that may be Czech or may be German, affecting the geometric shape in which every Jew recognizes the emblem of his people—how can one help identifying this phantasm with the man who imagined it? How can one help translating Odradek[36] by Kafka or Kavka, a name of equally uncertain origin, on which one can likewise speculate ad infinitum? Indeed, there is every reason to identify Odradek with Kafka, all the more so since Odradek, who is endowed with rudimentary speech—he knows his name and when asked for his address he replies, "No fixed residence"—has in common with his author not only the fact of being at once German, Czech, and Jewish, which accounts for his life of perpetual vagrancy, but also the sort of "laughter with no lungs behind it" that would soon be Kafka's.[37] Indeed, the kinship between the author and his spool seems so close as to suggest total identity.

Yet other details, in particular the question of language that the narrator raises in the very first sentence, before even introducing the subject of the story, make it clear that Odradek cannot simply be identified with Kafka, but that Kafka, by insisting so strongly on the anomalies of the name, is thinking of his own name and of the negative implications of his abnormal linguistic situation for his activity as a writer. With his problematic name, which cuts him off both from grammar and from any definite geographical place, Odradek refers us directly to the fact that for German Jewish writers, writing was "in every respect impossible."[38] But as an object without utility or purpose, it is even more precisely the product of Kafka's own "impossibility of writing," from which every page he wrote had to be painfully wrested.

For by making his spool with "old, broken-off bits of thread of the most varied sorts and colors, knotted and tangled together," Kafka points, not too indirectly, to two striking peculiarities in his creative technique: he crisscrosses his themes from story to story and usually breaks off the threads before they have attained their full development. In April 1917 he had as yet published only a few stories, which would have added up to a very thin volume;[39] he had been obliged to abandon his two novels—*Amerika* and *The Trial*—and any number of novellas and stories, barely sketched or suddenly interrupted, far, or only a few lines, from the end. He was thirty-six years old, and though he did not yet have Odradek's "laughter with no lungs behind it" (or "rather like the rustling of fallen leaves"), he already knew that his illness was far enough advanced to add a new, graver, and perhaps definitive obstacle to his usual difficulty in writing. Hence his "worry" as he meditates on the evasive little creature who has chosen to live in his house, though he has not the power to keep him there.

The story indeed deals with the "worries of a family man" over the inconceivable object that has settled for a while in his house and whose small size leads the narrator to treat it "like a child." The title alone provides a precious indication of the nature of this worried family man, which Kafka himself confirms in connection with another of his stories, *Eleven Sons*. The narrator's "Eleven Sons,"[40] Kafka tells us, represent quite simply eleven stories on which he was working at the same time (this was one of his usual mystifications: he pretends to be dealing with a subject while in reality he is speaking only of his writing and the crushing problems it was always confronting him with).[41] The worried father is Kafka as father of his work, whose bizarre and unpredictable inspiration left him anxious, disappointed, troubled, a prey to the special sort of sadness that comes of failure.

With his grotesque shape, his puny stature, and his fleeting apparitions, Odradek—who has a predilection for the corridors, attics, and stairways of the house—is obviously related to the gnomes and kobolds, the helpful or malignant elves of folklore. One cannot lay hands on him, he appears and disappears without warning, stays away for weeks on end, and though thus far he has always come back, one can never count on it. Actually, no one thinks of trying to hold him, for caprice is his law, which connects him not only with the wicked spirits of folklore, but also with the fugitive, irregular, and irregularly available genius which Kafka, at the mercy of its unforeseen whims, regarded far more often as proof of a malignant destiny than of a friendly one.

Made of bits and pieces—"the whole thing looks senseless enough, but in its own way perfectly finished"—Odradek serves no purpose whatsoever, and this uselessness raises the question of his future: "Can he possibly die? Anything that dies has had some kind of aim in life, some kind of activity, which has worn out; but that does not apply to Odradek. Am I to suppose, then, that he will always be rolling down the stairs, with ends of thread trailing after him, right before the feet of my children and my children's children? He does no harm to

anyone that anyone can see; but I find the idea that he is likely
to survive me almost painful."[42] Thus, thanks to his total lack
of meaning and purpose, Odradek is capable of living on in-
definitely—or, rather, of not dying. He can expect an immortality without hope, as empty and as dismal as the useless life
he has led on the fringe of humanity. Hence the "worry" of
the man who created him, who, far from rejoicing at the idea
of his possible survival, confides that he finds the prospect of
this derisory eternity almost painful. Almost—but not entirely, not seriously, in any case not enough to make him in-
terrupt his own posthumous life by suddenly destroying his
work. For the time being Kafka seems more or less resigned to
leaving behind him the mass of imperfect and unfinished
pages, whose pitiful absurdity is indicated by Odradek. Soon,
however, the idea of passing down to posterity work that he
thought in many ways a failure became a source of true torment. It was then that he asked Max Brod, the only man who,
Kafka was well aware, would never be able to carry out this
wish, to burn the literary works and personal writings he
found among his papers—and, moreover, to refrain from
reading them or communicating them to anyone whomsoever,
even on a strictly private basis. But whatever one might think
of this testament and the reservations that the choice of execu-
tor permits us at least to presume, Kafka continued until the
end to wind the thread of his incomparable stories around
Odradek's star. In spite of everything, he wrote uninterrupt-
edly, and on 2 June 1924, the day before he died, he was still
correcting the proof of his last stories.

Notes

1 • The Censored Name

1. This was one point of resemblance between the Samsas and the Kafkas. Another is the two similarly placed *a*s in the name.

2. *The Trial* was begun in 1914, *The Castle* in 1920. Between the two, Kafka broke off his engagement to Felice Bauer; two years later he renewed his engagement and fell ill; in 1917 he broke it off for good. He then went to the country for his health, became engaged to Julie Wohryzek, had an affair with Milena Jesenska, broke off his second engagement, and finally gave up all thought of marriage. During this time, of course, he experienced the First World War, the collapse of Austria-Hungary, the birth of the Czechoslovakian Republic, and the recrudescence of anti-Semitic agitation in Prague—all of which, though not explicitly mentioned in his novels, nevertheless forms part of the emotional and social substance from which they are drawn.

3. In the twelve lines or so devoted to the story of a certain Herr von Grusenhof (*D*, 27 March 1914, II: 30) Kafka manages to name the five horses in this gentleman's stable: Famos, Grasaffe, Tournemento, Rosina, and Brabant. Six names in twelve lines, all, as Don Quixote would have said, "most high-sounding and full of meaning." This is undeniably a lot, one might even say too much, since the story of the five horses is never told. The fact is that Kafka stops giving names only when dealing with a very definite system of human and social relations; everywhere else, he avails himself of an artistic privilege which, we can be sure, only his special aims would have made him forgo.

4. *D*, 6 August 1914, II: 77. See also the entry for 21 June 1913, I, 288: "The tremendous world I have in my head."

5. The story was written in a single night in a kind of ecstasy, which explains why Kafka did not understand the true motives behind it until afterward.

6. *D*, 11 February 1911, I: 215. Kafka met Felice Bauer at the house of relatives of Max Brod on 12 August 1912. He wrote his first letter on 20 September, and wrote *The Judgment* during the night of the 22nd. At that time he was only unofficially engaged. *The Judgment* does not tell the story of his life; it anticipates its events, carries them to a conclusion, and interprets them before they have taken place.

7. *D*, 12 February 1913, I: 279. Kafka's family seems to have been quite aware of the story's autobiographical content. This would indicate why his father was not exactly delighted with his writings and would help to explain the famous sentence with which he regularly greeted the gift of one of his son's books: "Put it on the bedside table."

8. *D*, 14 August 1913, I: 296.

9. Jan, 32. This book, written and published thirty years after the conversations it records, must be used with a certain caution. Among the statements attributed to Kafka, some are certainly authentic, others were probably not made in the form transmitted, and still others seem doubtful because they reproduce, almost word for word, certain passages in Kafka's journals which, published only posthumously, could not have become known to Janouch until long after he took his notes.

10. *DF*, 138–96, 170.

11. The manuscript of *The Castle* provides material proof that for Kafka "I" and "he" and "K." were interchangeable. A first version with "I" goes roughly as far as the middle of the second chapter. In this version K. does not make his appearance until that moment, when the action is already well under way. But since the two people are in reality one, Kafka required no great effort to unify the two versions. He had only to replace the "I" of the first draft with "K." and to put the verbs in the third person.

12. *O*, 10 February 1921, 107; and Letter to Max Brod, late January 1921, *LF*, 256. The best way of avenging himself on the Czech spinster who kept making anti-Semitic remarks at table, he wrote, might be "to defer my statement [that he was a Jew] until she says something absolutely irreparable." Kafka let a month go by before reporting this incident to his sister, as though giving himself time to calm down. The previous year, at Merano, a similar scene had been described in a letter to Max Brod and to Felix Weltsch: "I had asked

to be served at a little separate table in the dining room. . . . Today
. . . the colonel invited me so cordially to the common board that I
was obliged to accept. From that point on, matters took their course.
With the first words it came out that I was from Prague. The general
(sitting opposite me) and the colonel both knew Prague. Czech? No.
How was I going to explain to these keen-eyed Germans who I really
am. Someone said: *Deutschböhme* [German of Bohemia], another:
Kleinseite [the part of Prague on the left bank of the Moldau]. Then
they calmed down and we went on eating; but the general wasn't satisfied; after the meal he grew suspicious of my German accent, or
possibly it was more his eye than his ears that grew suspicious. Then
I tried to explain it by my being a Jew. Scientifically he was satisfied,
but not humanly. . . . Humanly, it doesn't satisfy me either. Why do I
have to be a thorn in their flesh?" Letter to Max Brod, 10 April 1920,
LF, 233.

13. ". . . I have vigorously absorbed the negative element of the age
in which I live, an age which is of course very close to me, which I
have no right ever to fight against, but as it were a right to represent." Kafka puts down this sentence after having explained his failure "in everything" by "the lack of soil, air and law." "Fourth Octavo Notebook," 24 February (1918), *DF*, 99.

14. *DF*, 171.

15. *DF*, 173.

16. It is indeed surprising that in his early letters we find no allusion
to these disastrous events, which caused a considerable stir not only
in Austria but also in other European countries. The year 1901, for
instance, when Kafka entered the university, reverberated with agitation caused by the famous Hilsner case, a case of alleged ritual
murder which unleashed a wave of anti-Semitic frenzy. See Michael
A. Riff, "Czech Anti-Semitism and the Jewish Response Before
1914," *Wiener Library Bulletin*, new series vol. XXIX, nos. 39–40,
and Christoph Stölzl, *Kafkas böses Böhmen: Zur Sozialgeschichte
eines Prager Juden* (Munich, 1975); also note 3 to chapter 3. Yet neither at the time nor later did Kafka mention this frenzy, which he
must have witnessed, since in Prague the anti-Semitic disorders—for
the most part attacks on German Jews by Czech nationalists—always
occurred in the Old City, at his doorstep so to speak. Stölzl's explanation for this silence, that Kafka had no reason to mention these
events in letters to his friends since they were all Jews, does not seem

quite credible, for his friends were no less Jewish later on, and yet at a certain point Jewish themes began to occupy an important place in his correspondence. (I shall have more to say in chapter 2 about this inadvertence and the role it may have played in Kafka's inner life before it became the central theme of his writings.)

17. Since by then Kafka was a socialist, a Darwinist, and an atheist, it naturally never entered his head to join the Bar-Kochba fraternity of Jewish students, which, comprising both Zionists and Orthodox Jews, was regarded by the progressive students as grotesquely backward. The Lese- und Redehalle der deutschen Studenten, to which Kafka belonged and where he met Max Brod, was open to Jews, so much so that the leaders engaged in all sorts of intrigues to prevent them from becoming a voting majority. Concerning Bar-Kochba, Max Brod wrote: "Throughout my student years I was unaware that there existed in Prague a fraternity of Jewish students who did not deny their Judaism; or, rather, I knew it only from their occasional jibes at the assimilated Jews and secret anti-Semites. . . ." (*Streitbares Leben* [Munich, 1960], p. 224.) On Kafka's convictions at this time, see *D*, 30 December 1911, I: 205–06, and Hugo Bergmann, "Erinnerungen an Franz Kafka," *Universitas* 7 (27 July 1972).

18. "Investigations of a Dog," *Stories*, 278–316. The dog theme plays a considerable part in Kafka's work. He seems to have been fond of dogs, or at least of metaphors connected with them, and often uses the adjective *hündisch* (like a dog) in connection with his own life.

19. On 11 September 1922 Kafka wrote to Max Brod: ". . . I will evidently have to drop the Castle story for good, I have been unable to pick it up again since the 'breakdown' that began a week before my trip to Prague, even though the part written at Planá is not quite as bad as the part you know." *LF*, 357.

20. "Fragments" in *DF*, 350. For the chronology of Kafka's works, see *Symp* and Chris Bezzel, *Chronik Kafka* (Munich and Vienna, 1975).

21. *D*, 3 November 1911, I: 131. "Löwy. My father about him: 'He who lies down with dogs gets up with fleas.' I could not control myself and said words I shouldn't have."

22. In a variant of *In the Penal Colony*, the Explorer cries out: "I'm a dog if I allow that to happen," and a moment later he is running on all fours. *D*, 7 August 1917, II: 178.

23. Apropos of Samsa's parasitism, see *DF*, 195: "I admit that we fight with each other, but there are two kinds of combat. The chivalrous combat . . . and the combat of vermin, which not only sting, but at the same time suck blood to sustain their own life. . . . If I am not very much mistaken, you are sponging on me even with this letter." Here Kafka is expressing the thoughts he attributes to his father.

24. *Stories*, 278.

25. An example of the absurd conclusions to which this generalization leads (cited in Hartmut Binder, *Kafka-Kommentar zu sämtlichen Erzählungen* [Munich, 1975]): when this story appeared in Hebrew, Hugo Bergmann, who had known Kafka in secondary school and remained his friend, interpreted the story with reference to Zionism, whereupon three Israeli writers wrote to him saying how shocked they were that Kafka should have chosen the pejorative image of the dog to prove his point. It is hard to see how a serious author could find any direct or indirect reference to Zionism when what is stressed in the story as a whole, as in every detail, is the "unhappy disposition" which prevents the Dog, a "withdrawn, solitary creature, preoccupied with his hopeless little investigations," from joining his fellow dogs and merging with their community. For Bergmann is undoubtedly a serious author; he merely made the mistake of translating "dog" as "Jew," instead of leaving the word "Jew" implicit and himself free to play with all the shadings and possibilities of the word "dog." Knowing from personal connections that Kafka at the end of his life spoke and acted as a convinced Zionist, he inferred that for the Jewish question as raised in the tale the only appropriate solution could be Zionism. But that is precisely the point: Kafka's Zionist convictions toward the end of his life are established beyond a doubt, but he wrote *Investigations* in the same period, and this character who continually stresses his coldness and isolation brings a decisive corrective to Kafka's public choice. In what way we shall see later in this essay.

26. *Stories*, 279.

27. It has long been observed that this canine people is totally unaware of the existence of human masters, and some commentators have taken this as an allusion to the death of God in a modern secularized society (see Marthe Robert, *Livre de lectures* [Paris, 1977], pp. 23–30). Be that as it may, it is true that these dogs have no human masters and that there are no foreign peoples living alongside them;

they have many rites and superstitious beliefs, chiefly concerned
with the origin of food, but, oddly enough, no real religion.

28. *Stories*, 279.

29. *Stories*, 280.

30. The Dog says: "... yet in my distant isolation I have not lost
sight of my people, news of them reaches me, and from time to time I
even give them reports of myself." *Stories*, 278. These "reports" are
obviously Kafka's stories, which do indeed "from time to time"
reach the Jewish people, as distant reports from one of their sons.
Here we recognize Kafka's usual method, which consists in mingling
the theme of art with all his other motifs, either by speaking of literature in general or by mentioning his own work of the moment in a
particular story. Thus, by his own admission, his "Eleven Sons" were
nothing other than the eleven stories on which he was working at the
same time. See Marthe Robert, *Livre de lectures*, pp. 16–54; and
chapter 7, "Fiction and Reality," of the present book.

2 • The Identity Crisis

1. *F*, 7 October 1916, 630/517.

2. *Die neue Rundschau* 2 (1916): 1421 ff. Reproduced in *Symp*,
147–48.

3. "Unsere Literaten und die Gemeinschaft," *Der Jude* I (October
1916): 457 ff. Quoted in *Symp*, 148.

4. The passage is constructed like one of Kafka's short stories: it
begins with an exposé of the situation and of the arguments put
forward by the two sides; then abruptly the discussion shifts to the
realm of parable, where it turns out that it cannot go on, because
there is either no solution to the problem or infinitely many solutions. We also note the theme of the circus, which Kafka uses with
predilection as an absurd yet moving setting for art in general and in
particular for his own production.

5. The notion of an "Old German" Kafka suggested by *The Metamorphosis* is indeed preposterous; it would be much less so if Müller
had referred to Kafka's earliest writings, which must have been
known to him. During the entire period preceding *The Judgment*
(1919) Kafka was very much subject to the influence of *Der Kunst-
wart*, a journal operated by aesthetes who went in for a manneristic,

archaistic sort of writing. Evident in the fragments of *Description of a Struggle* and especially in the early letters, this mannerism disappeared completely only with *The Judgment*, which for that reason German critics have characterized as a breakthrough.

6. To the extent that we can form an idea of Felice from Kafka's letters alone—he evidently did not keep hers—we see her as a largely emancipated young woman (beginning in 1912 she worked for a large business concern, which was not common before the First World War); accustomed to the free life of Berlin, she seems to have shared the tastes, pleasures, and prejudices of the German petits bourgeois who were taken as models by the Jews of her milieu. One of her most serious quarrels with Kafka was about choosing an apartment and its furnishings, to which she wanted to give a "personal note." It was no doubt to cure her of this borrowed bad taste that Kafka tried to move her closer to the Eastern Jews, who alone, he believed, were possessed of an authentic and living Judaism.

7. "Not a bent for writing, my dearest Felice, not a bent but my entire self." *F*, 24 August 1913, 434/309.

8. *DF*, 171.

9. He had already written in a letter to Felice, "These were the rehearsals staged by hell for my future office life." *F*, 16 September 1916, 620/502.

10. *DF*, 171–72.

11. *DF*, 173. In this whole passage we see at how early a date Kafka was to reject all half measures and compromise solutions. Nor did he ever waver in his belief that his upbringing had been responsible for his break with religion. In a letter to Felice in which he suggested a way of answering the children at the Home if they asked questions on the subject, he wrote: "While I should have to tell the children . . . that owing to my origin, my education, disposition, and environment I have nothing tangible in common with their faith (keeping the Commandments is not an outward thing; on the contrary, it is the very essence of the Jewish faith)—thus, while I would somehow hope to admit it to them (and I would do so candidly, for without candor everything would be quite pointless in this case), you on the other hand may not be altogether lacking in tangible connections with the faith. . . ." *F*, 16 September 1916, 620/502–03. I shall have more to say on this subject.

12. See *D,* 31 December 1911, I: 205. The same fact is recorded by Hugo Bergmann: "Franz was living at the time in an atheistic or pantheistic atmosphere. It was springtime; Kafka tried by every possible means to take my faith away and involved me in innumerable discussions. I was really afraid of losing my faith—and of so being deprived of the beauty of Passover Eve, which I very much loved. I thought: if only I can hold out until Pesach. And I did. For once Franz did not defeat me." A little later their ideas really came between the two boys: "In our last years at secondary school the new world burst into our Latin class. Franz became a socialist, I a Zionist in 1898. At the time a Socialist-Zionist synthesis had not yet been devised. In 1899, when the Prague Zionists called their first public meeting, it was broken up by the Socialists (who were all Jews) and the assimilated Czech Jews." (Hugo Bergmann, "Erinnerungen an Franz Kafka," *Universitas* 7 [27 July 1972], 742–44).

13. "This view of your Judaism was in some degree confirmed by your attitude in recent years when it seemed to you that I was taking more interest in Jewish matters." *DF,* 175.

14. A psychological episode like this is attested twice, in a letter to Brod, where it is reported as such and dated as happening some days before, and in *Description of a Struggle,* in which the narrator placed it in his childhood: "When I opened my eyes after a brief afternoon nap, still not quite sure I was alive, I heard my mother up on the balcony asking in a natural tone of voice: 'What are you doing?' From the garden a woman answered: 'Oh nothing. I'm having my tea on the lawn.' I was amazed at how staunchly people can support life." August 1904, *LF,* 17. The passage is repeated almost word for word in "Description of a Struggle," *Stories,* 34.

15. On the relations of the Jews with Emperor Franz Josef, their legal protector during the Dual Monarchy, see Joachim Remak, "The Healthy Invalid: How Doomed Was the Hapsburg Empire?," *Journal of Modern History* (June 1969). Hermann Kafka demonstrated his loyalty by calling his son Franz. And, not without irony, the son embodied himself in heroes named Joseph (or "Josephine"), which enabled him to give himself both parts of the Emperor's name.

16. Christoph Stölzl, *Kafkas böses Böhmen: Zur Sozialgeschichte eines Prager Juden* (Munich, 1975), p. 23. The same author quotes the following passage. "A Jew of that sort, who speaks only Czech with his customers all year long, thinks himself superior when he can read Schiller in German. Knowing German is tantamount to belong-

ing to some order of nobility." Quoted in E. Rychnowsky (ed.), *Masaryk und das Judentum* (Prague, 1931), p. 117. Incidentally, it is this use of two languages that muddles the statistics of the period; on their census forms, Jews often listed Czech as their usual language (*Umgangssprache*), though they spoke German at home and sent their children to German school. See Michael A. Riff, "Czech Anti-Semitism and the Jewish Response Before 1914," *Wiener Library Bulletin*, n. s. vol. XXIX, nos. 39–40, p. 17.

17. In this there was an element of superstition: among the "dialects" Czech, for example, was by no means an impediment to success. The Czech bourgeoisie was much more deserving of the name than the Jewish bourgeoisie, which, though comfortably well off and sometimes exceedingly wealthy, did not attain the social level of a true bourgeoisie. See Hannah Arendt, *Die verborgene Tradition: Acht Essays* (Frankfurt a/M, 1976), in which the situation of the Jews is analyzed from the point of view of this discrepancy between their prosperity and the utter unreality of their social life—or, as the author says, between the Jew as pariah and as *parvenu*.

18. *Weiber* is a disparaging term for "women."

19. *Wiener Jahrbuch für Israeliten*, 1863–64, p. 99. Quoted by Stölzl, *Kafkas böses Böhmen*, 24.

20. Once Kafka took up with Eastern Jews, he developed an interest in the Czech and Yiddish languages, for which his fellow Jews, with their craving for respectability and social prestige, professed equal contempt. In his *Introductory Talk on the Yiddish Language*, delivered on 18 February 1912 at the Jewish Community House in Prague (*DF*, 381–86), he took up the defense of the Yiddish language in a provocative tone which, coming from a cultivated Jew, must have left his audience flabbergasted if not scandalized. Kafka, who must have suspected that such a public statement would seriously exasperate his father, noted sadly in his *Diaries*, "My parents were not there" (*D*, 25 February 1912, I: 235). Concerning this lecture, see pp. 56–60. Kafka's attitude toward Yiddish can be related to his rehabilitation of the "minor literatures" in a passage in his *Diaries* (*D*, 25 December 1911, I: 191 ff.). It should be noted that Max Brod, himself a Germanized Jew, was a pioneer in the movement for solidarity with the despised languages. Nothing made him happier than discovering Czech talents, not only in literature but in the plastic arts and music as well.

21. Letter of June 1921, *LF*, 289.

22. On this letter to Brod, see pp. 152–154.

23. See p. 59.

24. See note 12 to chapter 1, the letter about the colonel and the general. Convinced by experience of the impossibility of a true assimilation *from above*, the Surveyor in *The Castle* (written in the same period as this letter) makes a last attempt to become assimilated *from below*, by merging completely with the indigenous population of the village: ". . . the village folk, who were now so suspicious of him, would begin to talk to him once he was their fellow citizen, if not exactly their friend; and if he were to become indistinguishable from Gerstäcker or Lasemann—and that must happen as soon as possible, everything depended on that—then all kinds of paths would be thrown open to him, which would remain not only forever closed to him but quite invisible were he to depend on the favor of the gentlemen in the Castle." *Cas*, 32. We know how the Surveyor's attempts turned out, though he spoke the same language as those whose fellow citizen he wished to become. Concerning the illusion based on a common language, see note 29 to chapter 3.

25. "In my class there were only two conscious Jews: they both killed themselves before the end of the year. . . ." And: "Jewish schoolboys in our country often tend to be odd; among them one finds the most unlikely things; but never anywhere . . . have I found anything like my cold indifference. . . ." *DF*, 178.

26. The Bar-Kochba Zionist Association was founded in 1899.

27. Letter to Oskar Pollak, 24 August 1902, *LF*, 4.

28. Letter to Max Brod, mid-August 1907, *LF*, 25.

29. Letter to Hedwig W., early October 1907, *LF*, 35.

30. Letter to Oskar Pollak, 20 December 1902, *LF*, 5–6.

31. The topography of the anonymous city in *The Trial* is described with such precision that there can be no doubt of its being Prague. Many devoted readers have taken pleasure in tracking down the itinerary followed by Joseph K. in his peregrinations. To this day one need only leave the city to find the swarming tenement where the hero on his own initiative goes looking for his tribunal; one can even reconstitute his "Calvary" and approximately situate the empty lot where he is stabbed "like a dog." Some years before *The Trial*, in the fragments of *Description of a Struggle* (1909)—Prague, already anonymous, is nevertheless present in its scenes and monuments, but

even at that time the author expresses his resentment by turning all the buildings of the Old Town upside down. In *The Trial* his revenge is more cruel; apart from the cathedral, which is not named, none of its monuments or buildings are mentioned; having failed to set fire to the city in his childhood, Kafka now relegated it to literary immolation.

32. See chapter 6, "Escape."

33. Letter to Oskar Pollak, 6 September (1903?), *LF*, 8.

34. Letter to Oskar Pollak, 9 November 1903, *LF*, 10.

35. "Yesterday it occurred to me that I have not always loved my mother as she deserved and as I could have, and this because the German language prevented me. A Jewish mother is not a *'Mutter,'* to call her *'Mutter'* makes her a little ridiculous (the word *'Mutter'* is in itself not ridiculous, because we are in Germany). We give a Jewish woman the name of a German mother, but forget the contradiction, which affects our feeling all the more deeply; *'Mutter'* is peculiarly German for the Jew, it unconsciously contains Christian coldness along with Christian splendor; the Jewish woman who is called *'Mutter'* thus becomes not only ridiculous but strange as well. *'Mama'* would be preferable if only one didn't imagine *'Mutter'* behind it. I believe that the Jewish family is preserved only by memories of the ghetto, for the word *'Vater'* is also far from signifying a Jewish father." *D*, 24 October 1911, I: 111. This passage, indispensable for an understanding of the development of Kafka's attitude toward the German language, occurs in a significant context, among notations almost all devoted to Löwy's theatrical productions, stories, and memories. Among the expressions used by the actors, Kafka gives special attention to those relating to family life: *Tateleben, yiddische Kinderlach.* This last, he wrote on 5 October, "made his cheeks tremble." See p. 48 of the present work. Thus there is good reason to suppose that his doubts about German were born of this first shattering contact with Yiddish, a language for him as true as German was false, because in Yiddish words coincided fully with their emotional content.

36. Kafka knew what most of his critics prefer to ignore, either because what they mostly see in his work is the violence of masochism, or because they systematically attenuate his thinking. He himself made no mistake. One day, contemplating the radically destructive character of his art, he wrote: "Sometimes in his pride he is more

afraid for the world than for himself." "The Series of Aphorisms Called 'He,' " in *The Great Wall of China*, 14 January 1920.

37. Letter to Oskar Pollak, 6 September (1903?), *LF*, 9.

38. See Chris Bezzel, *Chronik Kafka* (Munich and Vienna, 1975), p. 26.

39. It is interesting to note that all the problems the mature Kafka related to his *language* were in his youth attributed to speech as such. In *Description of a Struggle*, there is no question about language, whereas speech is treated as suspect; the hero accuses it of lending objects an illusory solidity and thus of being the accomplice of society in maintaining falsehood. See *Stories*, 41. When speech ceases to mask language for him, Kafka's technique changes completely; instead of *making phrases* denouncing words as agents of universal imposture ("Thank God, moon, you are no longer moon, but perhaps it's negligent of me to go on calling you so-called moon, moon . . ."), he denounces words from within by simply taking them as words. See chapter 6, "Escape."

3 ● The Road Back

1. See note 16 to chapter 1.

2. See Michael A. Riff, "Czech Anti-Semitism and the Jewish Response Before 1914," *Wiener Library Bulletin*, new series vol. XXIX, nos. 39–40. For everything concerning Czech anti-Semitism I have drawn on this remarkable study and, to a lesser extent, on Christoph Stölzl's previously mentioned essay. What lends special interest to the facts recorded in these two works is that most of them seem to have been forgotten—for reasons, it is true, that might be explained by the history of the period between the two world wars.

3. Leopold Hilsner, a vagabond Jew of ill repute, was accused of the ritual murder of a Czech seamstress, based on the fact that the investigating physician had found only a tiny quantity of blood in and around her body. He was tried twice, and twice condemned to death. His sentence was commuted to life imprisonment. Subsequent efforts to renew the trial were unsuccessful, but Hilsner was pardoned, in 1916, on the accession of Emperor Charles I of Austria.

4. Leo Hermann, a high official in the Zionist organization, wrote to Martin Buber on 14 November 1908, asking him to address the stu-

dents of the Bar-Kochba Association: "For we in Prague are living
under very special conditions. A large and old Jewish community—
which has spent the greater part of its existence dissolving itself into
the German cultural sphere and what it believes to be German ways.
During this time the entire Aryan population has gone in for Czechization, and as a matter of fact a good many Jews have been affected.
Only Jews think themselves obliged to defend Germanism. But since
they have no contact with the German nation, they remain largely
Jewish in character. No Jew notices this. And nearly every one of
them is on his guard against his conscious Judaism." (Martin Buber,
Briefwechsel, vol. I, 1897–1918 [Heidelberg, 1972], pp. 268–69.)
This remarkable document goes straight to the core of the young
Kafka's personal Jewish question and of the depressing situation
confronting him. The Zionists and Czech nationalists were not alone
in condemning the Jews for their obstinate Germanism; the Czech
Jews took the same attitude. In 1960 a Czech-speaking Communist
notable gave me proof that on this point at least there has been little
change. Wishing to justify the persistent ostracism of Kafka and his
work in Prague, the Communist explained that the Czechs were not,
as one might naïvely suppose, opposed to Kafka on Marxist grounds,
but quite simply because, having chosen to remain German in language and spirit, he had written nothing in which the Czech people
could take an interest. Thus the language was still at issue: anyone
writing in German, after 1919 even more than before, thereby demonstrated his indifference or hostility to Czechoslovakia. As if for an
artist as profound as Kafka language had been a superficial trapping,
which he could cast off at will! Obviously he could not change his
language any more than he could have changed the disposition of his
vital organs or nervous system. But, as it happened, his conception of
a language organically bound up with the personality led him to respect the languages of others, especially Czech, which he sincerely
regretted not knowing more thoroughly than he did. See *Letters to
Ottla*, in which he often expresses his fear of offending against that
admired language, and also his previously cited essay on the
"minor," i.e., Czech and Yiddish, literatures.

5. *DF*, 174.

6. *DF*, 160–62.

7. It is interesting to note that Hermann Kafka's premises were always spared in the anti-Semitic riots. One day, it seems, rioters were

about to pillage the shop, but were stopped by some passers-by who said, "Leave Kafka alone, he's a Czech" (W, 19). Kafka's "Czechism," however, was not very convincing; though Czech was his first language, he never changed the spelling of his name, which in Czech would have been Kavka (the word means "jackdaw"). He gave German names to all his children and had no qualms about sending his son to German schools. It is true that in official censuses he called himself a Czech, doubtless in the hope of political advantage. In the census of 1910 he even tried to force Franz to list himself as a Czech, and this was the occasion of one more conflict between them.

8. This early trauma may account in part for other prominent character traits: his predilection for the humble, his idealization of manual work, his asceticism and condemnation of luxury, and finally his rejection for himself of any sort of power, including the form of sovereignty he exerted in spite of himself through his charm, his talent, and his intellectual ascendancy.

9. See Chapter 6, "Escape," for the influence this attitude would later exert on his style.

10. Theodor Herzl, *Die entschwundenen Zeiten* (Vienna, 1897), quoted in W, 69.

11. DF, 156.

12. DF, 145.

13. *D*, 5 October 1911, I: 80–81.

14. D, 3 October 1911, I: 79–80.

15. Evelyn Torton Beck, "Kafkas Durchbruch: Der Einfluss des jiddischen Theaters auf sein Schaffen," *Basis*, vol. I, *Jahrbuch für deutsche Gegenwartsliteratur* (Frankfurt a/M, 1970).

16. I cite the titles of the plays in German, as Kafka does in his *Diaries*; I have likewise kept his spelling of Yiddish names, such as Lateiner, Scharkansky, and Feimann, which is very much influenced by German.

17. Löwy himself was aware of this decline. One day he read Kafka a letter from a young Jew in Warsaw, complaining of the decadence of the Jewish theater and saying he preferred going to the Novosti, "the Polish operetta theater, rather than to the Jewish one, where the wretched equipment, the indecencies, the hackneyed couplets, etc., are unbearable. Just imagine the big scene of a Jewish operetta, in

which the prima donna with a train of small children behind her, marches through the audience to the stage. Each is carrying a small scroll of the Torah and singing: *Toireh iz die beste skhoire*—the Torah is the best merchandise." *D*, 8 December 1911, I: 170. Among the reasons for the degeneration must be included the contempt for Yiddish among the great Jewish poets who had gone over to Zionism and the Hebrew language; and above all the taboo on all theater, Jewish or not, within strict Hasidic circles. Löwy told Kafka about the scandal he had created in his youth by violating this prohibition: "My father kept walking up and down the room; with his hand on his little black beard, he spoke not to me but only to my mother: 'You must be told; he's going from bad to worse. Yesterday he was seen in the Jewish theater.' " "Concerning the Yiddish Theater," *DF*, 133.

18. In his *Histoire de la littérature judéo-allemande* (Paris, 1911), Pines devotes a whole chapter to the Yiddish theater and its most prominent authors. Concerning the mediocrity of the works produced and their playing down to the public, he quotes a note by Gordin, the most famous of the Jewish writers at the end of the century and apparently the most critical of his own production: "I want to state publicly that the Judeo-German theater will never be able to develop normally as long as the main body of Jewish intellectuals continue to ignore a problem so important for the people at large as the development of a serious literary theater. In spite of the hundreds of thousands of people making up its audience, the Judeo-German theater cannot hope for the coming of a talented author, as long as most of the playwrights are men like me, who have only become dramatic authors by chance, who write plays only because the circumstances of their lives oblige them to and who like me remain isolated, seeing around them only ignorance, envy, hostility, and rancor." Preface to a collection of plays titled *The Yiddish Theater* (New York, 1897), quoted in Pines, p. 506.

19. *D*, 10 October 1911, I: 91.

20. Madame Tschissik figures in Isaac Bashevis Singer's story *A Friend of Kafka.*

21. *Geschichte der Juden von den Ältesten Zeiten*, 11 vols. (Leipzig, 1853 ff).

22. *D*, 1 November 1911, I: 125.

23. *D*, 24 January 1912, I: 223. Kafka read Pines's book in the French edition, the only one then published. By "Judeo-German" Yiddish is meant.

24. These extracts do not figure in the German edition of the *Diaries*, but only in the English translation, which also contains other extracts from books, and an entry (about Werfel) that Brod omitted from the original. Kafka took various passages from Pines's book, translating some, leaving some in Yiddish, and quoting still others in French. Thus we find in these pages four lines in German taken from two soldiers' songs, two lines in Yiddish, a note on the Haskalah ("Its members call themselves Maskilim, they are hostile to popular Yiddish, and oriented toward Hebrew and the European sciences. Before the pogroms of 1881 the movement was not nationalist, then it became strictly Zionist. Principle formulated by Gordon: 'Be a man in the street and a Jew at home.' To disseminate its ideas the Haskalah must employ Yiddish, and intensely as it hates that language make it the foundation of its literature"); a note on the Badchan (or strolling poets), another on the popular novel; a quotation from the Talmud in German ("He who interrupts his study to say: 'How beautiful that tree is!' is deserving of death"); a summary of a poem, "The Shammes's Daughter"; several entries on the great Yiddish writers, a mention of the Baal Shem, and, finally, a passage on the Yiddish Theater, which ends with the quotation from Jacob Gordin that we have quoted in our text. *D*, I: 224–25.

25. *D*, 4 February 1912, I: 228.

26. *D*, 13 February 1912, I: 233.

27. *D*, 25 February 1912, I: 222–23, 234–35.

28. "Introductory Talk on the Yiddish Language," *DF*, 381–86.

29. "Introductory Talk," *DF*, 382. Later, Kafka repeated this statement about linguistic illusion almost word for word in an unfinished and untitled text dating probably from 1920. A great swimmer returns to his home town after breaking the Olympic record. His compatriots give him a triumphant reception, and in the course of a banquet in his honor a fat gentleman makes a speech that plunges the hero into perplexity. When he in turn takes the floor, he says: "First I must observe that I am here in my own country and that in spite of all my efforts I do not understand one word of what you are saying. One would be tempted of course to think of a case of mistaken identity, but there is no mistaken identity. I have established the record, I am in my native country, my name is the one you call me by, up to that point we are in agreement, but from there on we are not in agreement at all, I am not in my native country, I do not know you

and do not understand you. Actually there is something else which disproves, if not completely then at least in a certain degree, the possibility of mistaken identity, to wit: the fact of not understanding you does not greatly trouble me, nor do you seem greatly troubled at not understanding my words." *DF*, 288.

30. *DF*, 382–86.

31. *DF*, 386.

32. According to Max Brod, he went so far as to say that a Western Jew had no right to marry.

33. In this respect he attached no importance to race, nationality, or religion; one was as good as another, provided the individual experienced it with his whole being, his flesh and blood and mind. Thus, when his sister Ottla became engaged to a Christian Czech he wrote to her: ". . . he enjoys his work, he lives in the midst of his people, is cheerful and healthy, in the main (and we are not concerned with nonessentials) he is rightfully pleased with himself and his large circle of friends, rightfully (there is no other way of putting it, as rightfully as a tree grows in its own ground) and in certain respects displeased with others. . . ." *O*, 1 May 1920, 82. David's dissatisfaction "in certain respects" is no doubt a reference to the anti-Semitism from which as a fanatical nationalist he was certainly not exempt.

34. See pp. 34–35 of the present work. Brod suggests that Kafka's letter on Judeo-German literature should not be taken literally. I believe, on the contrary, that it should be, and this regardless of his judgment of any particular author. In Kafka's view, a German Jewish author could write masterpieces without ceasing to be an impostor— he even says a gypsy, who has kidnapped the German child in its cradle—simply because in him the unity between language and being is broken. I shall have more to say of this intransigence, which had a great deal to do with the particularities of Kafka's style and his attitude toward his own works.

35. On this subject he wrote to Milena: "We both know, after all, enough typical examples of Western Jews, I am as far as I know the most typical Western Jew among them. This means, expressed with exaggeration, that not one calm second is granted me, nothing is granted me, everything has to be earned, not only the present and the future, but my past too—something after all which perhaps every human being has inherited, this too must be earned, it is perhaps the hardest work." *M*, 219.

4 ● The Thornbush

1. *D*, 6 January 1912, I, 215. Kafka was noting his disappointment at Feimann's *Vice-König* (Viceroy), but to judge from the context, the preceding plays had already disillusioned him.

2. This esteem for faith over and above the content of doctrines was not exactly a product of intellectual syncretism. Of course Kafka did not make a system of it, but with him it was definitely an emotional constant, which explains his strange attraction to the most varied sects. See chapter 5, "Before the Law."

3. *F*, 12 September 1916, 617/500–01.

4. *F*, 11 September 1916, 614/498.

5. Felice had evidently asked him in what way the Home was related to Zionism. Kafka replied: "The connection between all this and Zionism (valid for me, not necessarily for you) lies in the fact that the work in the Home derives from Zionism a youthful, vigorous method, youthful vigor generally, and that where other means might fail it kindles national aspirations by invoking the ancient prodigious past—admittedly with the limitations without which Zionism would not exist." *F*, 12 September 1916, 617–18/500–01. Here again we see that Kafka took more interest in people than in ideas.

6. In this respect Dora was in roughly the same situation as Löwy: having fled at an early age—she was not yet eighteen when Kafka met her at Müritz—from the stifling rigorism of her family, she, too, had "turned out badly," and her people regarded her as lost. Nevertheless, in London, where I knew her after the Second World War, she was no more "assimilated" than she had ever been in the course of her troubled life. Though she had long ceased to practice Judaism, she felt at home only among the Polish Jews of Whitechapel, and remained the same daughter of the *shtetl*, humble, proud, and full of humor, to whose songs and stories Kafka had listened with delight. In general the Eastern Jews with whom Kafka made friends were far from Orthodox. On the contrary, they had had the courage to break with what they could no longer be or do in all sincerity, but were not tempted to join the other camp. Believers or not, they were authentic, without desire or curiosity for what would have falsified them, and it was just this that made Kafka think them exemplary.

7. *D*, 24 December 1911, I: 190–91.

8. *D*, 14 September 1915, II: 128–29.

9. Whatever may be the religious implications of this association of physical uncleanliness and spiritual purity, Kafka could find its image in his real father, who had a "not at all disgusting" way of picking his nose at the table. In general—and this was certainly related to his father's bad manners—Kafka had a marked predilection for the unsavory little habits of exceptional people who, in the general estimation or sometimes only in his own, were endowed with high authority. See *D*, 28 March 1911, I: 57–59, the story of his visit to the theosophist Rudolf Steiner, which also concludes with a mention of nose-picking.

10. This comparison was suggested by an article in the American magazine *Present Tense* (Summer 1977) devoted to the republication of a work by Jiri Langer. Published under the title *Nine Gates to the Chassidic Mysteries* (New York, 1976), it contains a number of Hasidic tales collected by Langer and a preface by his older brother Frantisek Langer, a poet, who also associated with Kafka in Prague. Jiri Langer did not remain in Galicia for long. In 1914 he followed the rabbi of Belz into exile. After escaping the Nazis in 1939, he lived in Palestine until his death, in 1943.

11. *D*, April 1916, II: 152–53. Following the word "bitter"—that is the taste that the rabbi's faithful followers find in his lump of clay— Kafka abruptly steps out of his story and cries out, "Bitter, bitter, that is the important word. How can I hope to weld fragments together into a story that will sweep me along?"

12. Letter to Max Brod, mid-July 1916, *LF*, 119–23. Before starting his story, Kafka is careful to put aside Langer's explanations: "I don't intend to report on what he told me but only on what I myself saw."

13. *LF*, 120–23.

14. *LF*, 121–22. According to friends of mine versed in Hasidism, this letter dating from 1916 shows more than any other document how unfamiliar Kafka was with the symbolic world that he saw the rabbi traversing. He was indeed unfamiliar with it, but the fact does not seem to have troubled him. In any event, he gladly abandoned the "deeper meaning" to specialists and concentrated on the "human meaning," which, as he tells us here, he thought quite sufficient. In a letter to Felice (*F*, 18 July 1916, 598/475), he introduces the rabbi of Belz as "the most distinguished visitor to Marienbad." By "most distinguished" he means "a man in whom so many place their trust"; about God and the rabbi's religious vocation he says absolutely noth-

ing: the man alone interests him as a sovereign father capable of inspiring his people with "a happy and serene confidence" (letter to Brod), a confidence, he says, that he could "sense," though unfortunately he could not share it. It should also be noted that the persons of the rabbi and his father were so confused in his mind that in his more benign moments he applied the same image to them. For instance, when Hermann Kafka was taking the waters at Franzensbad, he, too, had the air of a "king on his travels" (*DF*, 169).

15. *D*, 16 September 1915, II: 130.

16. See note 35 to chapter 3.

17. *M*, 196. The letters to Milena are undated and it is not always easy to date them. This one was probably written on 6 September 1920. See Chris Bezzel, *Chronik Kafka* (Munich and Vienna, 1975), p. 160. *One* is underlined by Kafka.

18. Heinz Politzer, *Das Kafka-Buch* (Frankfurt, 1965), p. 53.

19. *Die Selbstwehr* (9 September 1910). Quoted by Christoph Stölzl, *Kafkas böses Böhmen: Zur Sozialgeschichte eines Prager Juden* (Munich, 1975), pp. 111–12. On Kafka's relations with the Zionist organ of Bohemia, which was directed by his friend Felix Weltsch, see Hartmut Binder, "Franz Kafka und die Wochenschrift *Selbstwehr*," in *Deutsche Vierteljahresschrift für Literaturwissenschaft und Geistesgeschichte* 41, no. 2 (1967): 283–304.

20. Arthur Schnitzler, *Der Weg ins Freie* (Berlin, 1908). Quoted by Stölzl, p. 109, from Schnitzler's *Gesammelte Werke: Die erzählenden Schriften* (Frankfurt, 1961), p. 755.

21. *O*, 19 April 1917, 33.

22. There were no limits to Kafka's power to invent these figures hovering between two realms, two states of being, two worlds, on which his reputation as a writer of fantasy is based—quite mistakenly, since they represent nothing other than his own reality. Straddling two realms like Gregor Samsa and the ape-man in *A Report to an Academy*, this world and the beyond, like the Hunter Gracchus, whom a mysterious transgression prevents from either living or dying; straddling two animal species like the cross between a kitten and a lamb, who nowhere has his like and to whom death by the butcher's knife is denied, because he is a *legacy*; finally, straddling two cultures and two languages like the spool called Odradek, upon which the very absurdity of its existence confers a kind of eternity— Kafka's hero is always in some way a dual creature, a sport of nature,

a chimera in the biological sense. We shall see in chapter 7, "Fiction and Reality," how all his work is organized around this theme of heterogeneity, which to his mind was the direct cause of his curse.

23. *F*, 16 September 1916, 620/502.

24. *D*, 2 July 1913, I: 289. He also sobbed when reading Arnold Zweig's *Ritual Murder in Hungary*. "At one point I had to stop reading, sit down on the sofa, and weep. I hadn't wept for years." *F*, 28 October 1916, 640/530.

25. Letter to Brod, 6 February 1919, *LF*, 213.

26. Julie Wohryzek was the daughter of a shoemaker who served as *shammes* at the synagogue of Prague-Weinberg; in other words, she occupied just about the lowest rank in the social hierarchy of her time and place. When his son's engagement to a girl of such humble station was announced, Hermann Kafka flew into a violent rage ("I suppose she put on some carefully chosen blouse, as Prague Jewesses know how to do, so then you naturally decided to marry her"), which was what led Franz Kafka to write his *Letter to His Father*. In general, Hermann Kafka detested the excessive humility that led his son to seek contact with the lower classes—housemaids, Eastern Jews, etc. He saw it as a mark of contemptible pusillanimity, and even more, no doubt, as a condemnation of his own ambition.

27. *O*, 24 February 1919, 70. This was not his real ground for complaint, as Ottla was well aware; more pertinently, Kafka feared that in marrying she would abandon him.

28. *O*, 20 February 1919, 68–69.

29. *D*, 15 October 1913, I: 301. "The stay in Riva was very important to me. For the first time I understood a Christian girl and lived almost entirely within the sphere of her influence." And *D*, 22 October 1913, I: 305: "Too late. The sweetness of sorrow and of love. To be smiled at by her in the boat. That was most beautiful of all. Always only the desire to die and the not-yet-yielding; this alone is love."

30. *D*, 6 July 1916, II: 159: "I have never yet been intimate with a woman apart from that time in Zuckmantel. And then again with the Swiss girl in Riva. The first was a woman, and I was ignorant; the second a child, and I was utterly confused."

31. *D*, 22 January 1922, II: 207–08. His break with Milena had become inevitable and it left him no hope of "returning one day to Canaan after all." His entries for 1922—he died in 1924—all add up

to a meditation on his long "wandering in the desert" and on the causes of what he regarded as his spiritual degeneration. It was in this context that his story *Bachelor's Ill Luck* and his uncle Rudolf came to mind. The day before he had written: "Without forebears, without marriage, without heirs, with a fierce longing for forebears, marriage and heirs. They all of them stretch out their hands to me: forebears, marriage and heirs, but too far away for me." *D*, II: 207.

32. "Travel Notes," 14 July 1912, *D*, II: 307.

33. *F*, 18 November 1912, 154/49.

34. Letter to Max Brod and Felix Weltsch, Merano, 10 April 1920, *LF*, 232. It is in this letter that Kafka tells his friends about the incident at table with the colonel and the general. He begins by describing the society at the first pension at which he stayed: "The guests consisted of some distinguished Italians, then a few other interlopers, while most of the rest were Jews, some of them baptized (but what horrid Jewish energies live on close to the bursting point inside a baptized Jew, only to be modulated in the Christian children of a Christian mother)."

35. *D*, 11 March 1915, II: 117.

36. *D*, 17 December 1913, I: 324.

37. *D*, 17 December 1913, I: 324.

38. *D*, 8 January 1914, II: 11.

39. *M*, 59. Kafka wrote this abominable sentence in 1920. Obviously he could not know how others, twenty years later, would undertake to carry out his wish—a wish uttered half in provocation and half in jest, which can be understood only in the following context: Milena never ceased to protest about the importance Kafka attached to Judaism in their relations. For her, differences of race and religion did not count. She had married a Jew, she admired the Jews in general, etc. To which Kafka replied that she was very much mistaken and that he for his part would gladly have the Jews killed if only to prevent them from coming between him and the woman he loved.

40. *D*, 12 September 1912, I: 272.

41. See note 33 to chapter 3.

42. *D*, 1 July 1913, I: 288.

43. *D*, 24 November 1914, II: 97. This remark was inspired by a certain Chaim Nagel, who directed an agency that distributed clothing

to Galician refugees, and who showed his perfection in the tact and intelligence with which he performed this modest task.

44. In thus giving people pre-eminence over ideas, Kafka undoubtedly put himself in the ranks of the great masters of Jewish thought; though he studied them very little, he definitely belonged to their spiritual family.

45. *F*, 12 September 1916, 618/501.

46. Concerning Kafka's relations with the Prague anarchists, and especially with Michal Mares, see W, 150–51 and 213. According to the recollections of Michal Mares, Kafka took part in a demonstration against the execution of Francesco Ferrer, the founder of the Free School movement (October 1909), and attended lectures on Malthus, on the Free Union, etc. In 1912 he was said to have taken part in a demonstration against the execution of the Parisian anarchist Liabeuf. See also Janouch.

47. *F*, 12 September 1916, 618/501.

48. See letters to Elli Hermann, autumn 1921, *LF*, 290–97. Kafka attached enormous importance to education and was passionately interested in everything that seemed new in this field. In 1921 he wished to send his nephew to the Dalcroze School at Hellerau. He knew Dalcroze personally and did everything in his power to win his sister over. First he cited Swift, then a school textbook poem about a traveler's return to his native village—he had been gone so long that no one recognized him except his mother. But, says Kafka, "if her son had stayed at home, she would never have recognized him, their everyday life together would have made her son unrecognizable in her eyes. . . ." This mother was assuredly not "eager to take responsibility or to share the joys and, what can be worse, the sorrows of her child (he will have nothing entirely!) . . ." Moreover, with her the son might not have incurred such great dangers because, as Kafka adds in parentheses to make his point absolutely clear, "she was no Jewish woman of Prague but some pious Catholic from Styria" (*LF*, 297). These four letters addressed to his elder sister are indirectly a terrible indictment of his own Jewish mother and the "mean, sordid, niggling spirit" which had permanently deformed him. It seems all the more unusual that his mother plays an extremely minor role in his work, quite out of proportion with that of the all-powerful father.

49. *Diaries of Theodor Herzl (1895–1904)* (Magnolia, Maine). See W, 238. For the list of works comprising Kafka's personal library, see W, 232–44.

50. *F*, 10 September 1913. [These notes are not included in the published English translation. I have translated them here from Marthe Robert's French version, *Lettres à Felice* (Paris, 1972), II: 530. —TRANS.] Kafka had left for Vienna in a poor state of health. The Zionist congress was certainly not the only reason for his bad humor, but his notes are nonetheless significant.

51. Letter to Brod, 16 September 1913, *LF*, 100: "I would wish to tear those days in Vienna out of my life, tear them out by the roots. It was all a useless business. It is hard to imagine anything more useless than such a congress."

52. *F*, 12 September 1916, 618/501.

53. This was Puah Ben-Torim, his third Hebrew teacher, with whom he was on terms of close friendship for a time. I am indebted to the kindness of Yoram Bar-David for showing me a letter in Hebrew that Kafka wrote him and that is not included in his correspondence: "I well understand the fear that comes over one when one is waiting for a letter that keeps wandering about. How many times in my life have I been consumed by a fear of this sort. What a miracle that fear does not transform one who waits to ashes, before it even becomes real." (Translated into French by Mr. Bar-David. No date or source given.)

54. Letter to Brod, 1 February 1921, *LF*, 260.

55. Most such interpretations are based on a passage in the *Diaries*: "All such writing is an assault on the frontiers; if Zionism had not intervened, it might easily have developed into a new secret doctrine, a cabala." *D*, 16 January 1922, II: 202, 203. It is clear, however, that in this passage Kafka employs the word "cabala" as a common noun and not as a proper noun associated exclusively with the tradition. He uses "cabala" for "secret language, demanding a certain initiation of the reader," which is far from implying a desire to go back to the historic Cabala. The mere fact that he wished to create a new cabala all by himself, without teacher or previous initiation, indicates, rather, how alien the spirit of the Cabala, or Tradition, remained to him. More interesting is the allusion to Zionism, which, according to him, prevented him from dropping out of the world and living in the indefinite elsewhere that the hero of *The Castle* calls his country.

But this influence of Zionism in his work is not so clearly defined as he seemed to think; from 1917 on, it is true, we note the appearance of more specifically Jewish themes—in *In Our Synagogue, Jackals and Arabs*, etc.—but otherwise his storytelling technique did not change at all.

56. Letter to Robert Klopstock, 19 December 1923, *LF*, 373–74.

57. *M*, 236.

58. Letter to Else Bergmann, July 1923, *LF*, 373–74.

59. *D*, 23 January 1922, II: 209.

5 • Before the Law

1. To eat indiscriminately struck him, however, as preferable for anyone who could do so without thinking, hence without guilt, which occurs either in extreme poverty, as in the case of the Jewish refugees, or at a higher level of wisdom, as in the case of people "who are good vegetarians in their hearts but for reasons of health, from indifference, or simply because they underrate the importance of food as such, they eat meat or whatever happens to be on the table" (*F*, 24 November 1912, 167/60). Kafka does not claim credit for being obliged to calculate in this situation where true health resides precisely in a total absence of calculation; from his point of view, his calculation is actually a weakness which deflects him from his ideal.

2. "Investigations of a Dog," *Stories*, 306.

3. *Stories*, 308–09.

4. The pathos of this end, which was already atrocious in itself, was increased by the fact that at the very last moment Kafka wanted to live and seemed to become aware of his madness. Prevented by tuberculosis of the larynx from eating, drinking, or speaking, he was sometimes almost delirious with hunger and thirst. On one of the little slips of paper he used for communicating with those around him, he wrote to Robert Klopstock: "The time you came when I was kept in bed, how easy it was, and yet I didn't even have my beer, just preserves, fruit, fruit juice, water, fruit juice, fruit, preserves, water, fruit juice, fruit, preserves, water, lemonade, cider, fruit, water." "Conversation slips" in *LF*, 422. To add to the horror, it was just then that he received proof of *The Hunger Artist*. He was able to

correct no more than the first galley, and the story did not appear until after his death.

5. *Stories*, 309–10.

6. *Stories*, 310.

7. *Stories*, 310.

8. When the Dog thinks he is dying he says: "It seemed to me as if I were separated from all my fellows, not by a quite short stretch but by an infinite distance, and as if I would die less of hunger than of neglect. For it was clear that nobody troubled about me. . . . Perhaps the truth was not so very far off, and I was not so forsaken therefore as I thought; or I may have been forsaken less by my fellows than by myself, in yielding and consenting to die." *Stories*, 311–12. And in his *Diaries* for 29 January 1922 (II: 215), Kafka wrote: ". . . forsaken, moreover, not only here but in general, even in Prague, my 'home,' and what is more, forsaken not by people . . . but rather by myself vis-à-vis people, by my strength vis-à-vis people . . ." And a little farther on: "I get my principal nourishment from other roots in other climes. . . ." *D*, II: 215.

9. "For months on end, until he got used to it, my father had to hide his face behind the newspaper while I ate my supper." *F*, 7 November 1912, 131/30–31.

10. *D*, 24 November 1911, I: 162.

11. Actually, the subject is treated in the two oldest stories to have been preserved, *Description of a Struggle* and *Wedding Preparations in the Country*, but in both of these, celibacy is not yet a curse; the hero fears it only vaguely and disposes of it simply by saying he is engaged.

12. *D*, 14 November 1911, I: 150.

13. *D*, 3 December 1911, I: 168–69.

14. "When I arrived at Brod's on August 13th, she was sitting at the table, and I nevertheless took her for a housemaid. I was not at all curious who she was, but rather took her for granted at once." And further: "As I was taking my seat, I looked at her closely for the first time; by the time I was seated I already had an unshakable opinion." *D*, 20 August 1912, I: 268–69.

15. *D*, 3 July 1913, I: 289.

16. This *midrash*, taken from a lecture by Emmanuel Levinas, was communicated to me by Rachel Goitein-Galperin, whom I hereby thank.

17. *F*, 7 November 1912, 131/31.

18. *F*, 11 November 1912, 139/37.

19. *F*, 24 November 1912, 166–67/59–60. Kafka found this poem in Hans Heilmann's collection *Chinesische Lyrik vom 12. Jahrhundert v. Chr. bis zur Gegenwart* (Munich, 1905). He had a great predilection not just for this anthology but for Chinese literature in general, as he knew it in translation. In his notebooks for 1920 we find, without indication of source or author, another poem and two extracts drawn from *Ghost Stories*, a book of Chinese legends. The poem ends with the sentence "I have spent my life resisting the desire to end it." "Fragments," *DF*, 303, and *M*, 212. Kafka's affinity for Chinese wisdom is of course also shown in the fragments that made up *The Great Wall of China*.

20. *F*, 14–15 January 1913, 271/155–56.

21. *F*, 14–15 January 1913, 272/156. The emphasis is Kafka's.

22. F, 19 January 1913, 277/161.

23. *F*, 21–22 January 1913, 282/165.

24. *F*, 21–22 January 1913, 282/165.

25. *F*, 21–22 January 1913, 283/165–66.

26. *D*, 14 August 1913, I: 296.

27. *M*, 137.

28. *M*, 137. See the love scene between Frieda and the Surveyor in *The Castle*. During their embrace K. "was haunted by the feeling that he was losing himself or wandering into a strange country, farther than ever man had ever wandered before, a country so strange that not even the air had anything in common with his native air, where one might die of strangeness, and yet whose enchantment was such that one could only go on and lose oneself further." *Cas*, 54. K. was in so painful a state that he was almost relieved to be interrupted by Klamm's voice calling Frieda from the next room.

29. *D*, 29 January 1922, II: 216.

30. Letter to Julie Wohryzek's sister (Wagenbach in *Symp*, 45–53), written shortly after the break between Kafka and Julie. Julie was

thirty and Kafka thirty-six, and, so he says, she "no longer felt the primitive urge to have children." This of course fell in with his intentions.

31. *D*, 21 July 1913, I: 292. Kierkegaard, Flaubert, and Grillparzer were the great examples of unmarried writers most often invoked by Kafka to justify his own retreat from marriage. But in his eyes Kleist was the only writer to have found the right solution (double suicide never ceased to tempt Kafka, who twice even suggested it to Felice).

32. *F*, 1 April 1913, 349–50/233.

33. Letter to Max Brod, mid-April 1921, *LF*, 273.

34. In this Kafka was no different from other young men in Prague who, after their long sessions at the literary cafés, liked to stop at a brothel. The first years of his *Diaries* show traces of his visits to these establishments, which he often dreamed about. Later on, to be sure, he stopped frequenting them, for reasons no doubt connected with the crisis created by his marriage plans and the ascetic discipline to which he was increasingly subjecting himself. But the role played by prostitution in his novels is all the more significant: the enormous Brunelda, who in *Amerika* is represented as a singer, ends her career in a mysterious building which, with its closed doors and big numbers, can only be a brothel; if one considers only its most evident function and the role it plays in bringing the sexes together, the Herrenhof Hotel in *The Castle* is nothing but a common brothel. Women seldom appear in Kafka except in the role of prostitute or of "the little maid"—Else and Leni in *The Trial*, Frieda and Pepi in *The Castle*—whose favors the hero gains as in a dream, without even asking for them.

35. *M*, probably end of November 1920, 217, 218. "You say, Milena, that you do not understand it. Try to understand it by calling it illness. It is one of the many manifestations of illness which psychoanalysis believes it has uncovered. I do not call it illness, and I regard the therapeutic part of psychoanalysis as a hopeless error. All these so-called illnesses, sad as they may appear, are matters of faith, efforts of souls in distress to find moorings in some maternal soil. . . . And it's this they hope to cure." See "Fragments," *DF*, 300–01, where this passage from the letter to Milena is reproduced almost word for word.

36. Letter to Brod, mid-April 1921, *LF*, 273. "In itself it's nothing special, one of your earliest stories deals with it, sympathetically moreover. It's an illness of instinct, a product of the times. . . ."

37. *LF*, 273.

38. When he was beginning to torment himself about his future, his mother, as he tells us, spoke to him with the common sense typical of a middle-class mother. "There are thousands of possible solutions. The most probable is that I shall suddenly fall in love with a girl and will never again want to be without her. . . . But if I remain a bachelor like my uncle in Madrid, that too will be no misfortune because with my intelligence I shall know how to make adjustments." *D*, 19 December 1911, I: 184–95. But Kafka observes on this occasion "how untrue and childish is my mother's conception of me."

39. In *The Castle*, however, Saint Paul does make a curious appearance—indirectly, to be sure, and under the half-serious, half-ironical cover of an onomastic allusion. One of the leading characters in *The Castle* is named Barnabas, like the indefatigable missionary who in The Acts of the Apostles is represented as Saint Paul's closest friend and collaborator. Kafka's Barnabas is also a missionary, since it is supposedly his function as the envoy from the Castle to bring K. messages from the Gentlemen, and as the ensuing events make clear, he is only too indefatigable. At first K. builds his highest hopes on this liaison agent who, he believes, will finally put him in touch with the high spheres of the Castle, but he is soon forced to change his mind. Seen at close quarters and divested of his shining silk garment, Barnabas turns out to be nothing more than a vulgar groom without "official" position or uniform, and he has never been given a message to transmit. K. is defeated largely by his unwarranted confidence in this deceptive, weak-minded creature, this "will-o'-the-wisp" who in reality is just as helpless as he is and even more infantile.

40. It is nevertheless remarkable that one of the culminating scenes of *The Trial* takes place in a cathedral and that Joseph K., who has supposedly gone there to guide an Italian visitor, is stopped by the prison chaplain, apparently a Catholic priest, who speaks to him of his trial more seriously and with more real interest than anyone else thus far; it is true that the famous "Legend" that the chaplain bids him meditate fits in with no known theology; moreover, Joseph K. does not understand it and it does not avert his doom. In one of the unfinished chapters of *The Trial*, titled "K.'s Visit to His Mother,"

we read that the hero's mother, whom he has not seen for three years and who has gone almost blind in the meantime, has been displaying a surprising bigotry in her old age; though hardly able to walk, she has been dragging herself to church every Sunday, which inspires K. with "something like repugnance." To judge by this remark, K. belongs to a Catholic family but, if his mother's piety repels him, is not religious. However, since K.'s religion is mentioned only in this one passage of an unfinished chapter, it would be incautious to draw any inferences from it. K.'s visit to the cathedral and the help he seems to expect from the chaplain remind us that less than two years before starting work on *The Trial*, Kafka had wished to seize upon his "one chance of salvation" by writing to the adept of the "Christian Community." See pp. 78–79 of the present book.

41. As soon as Kafka knew he was ill, he interpreted his tuberculosis as a consequence of the psychological conflict connected with the long crisis in his engagement: "Sometimes it seems to me as if my brain and my lungs had come to an agreement without my knowledge. 'Things can't go on like this,' said the brain, and five years later the lungs agreed to help." Letter to Brod, mid-September 1917, *LF*, 138.

42. Kafka met this apostle, a manufacturer at Warnsdorf in northern Bohemia, in 1911. Having determined that all Kafka's ailments came from poisons lodged in his spinal marrow, Schnitzer prescribed an excessively strict regime, which Kafka observed. It was definitely under Schnitzer's influence that he became a vegetarian and began to develop his "system." When he fell ill in 1917, he wrote to Schnitzer, asking if a total fast might not be advisable (for tuberculosis!); but the apostle, seeing no doubt that things were going badly, was careful not to reply. Concerning this individual, whom Kafka himself thought stupid but whose precepts he nevertheless followed, Kafka wrote in reply to his friend Felix Weltsch's skepticism: "You are right in what you say about Schnitzer, but it is easy to underestimate people of that kind. He is totally artless and therefore magnificently sincere; therefore when he is out of his depth, as a speaker, writer, or even thinker, he is not only uncomplicated as you say, but downright stupid. But sit down opposite him, study him, try to analyze him, especially his effectiveness, try for just a little to approach his point of view—he cannot be so easily dismissed." Letter to Felix Weltsch, middle or end of October 1917, *LF*, 159–60.

43. *D*, 26 and 28 March 1911, I: 59–60.

6 • Escape

1. B, 24.

2. See p. 34 of the present book (the letter to Max Brod about Karl Kraus) and pp. 152–53.

3. Letter of 12 February 1907, *LF*, 23. "This name will have to be forgotten," he wrote to Brod, in reference to an article in which Brod—perhaps in an excess of enthusiasm, since at that time Kafka had published nothing—had spoken of him as an important writer.

4. *D*, 11 February 1913, I: 278.

5. *D*, 23 September 1912, I: 275–76. *"In this way"* was underscored by Kafka. It is also worth noting that, contrary to his habit, Kafka gives the exact date of the story and describes the circumstances surrounding its genesis, as though wishing to preserve—for himself—the memory of the event.

6. Though the letter from the "cellar-dweller" strongly suggests one of the hymns of Saint John of the Cross, we have no indication that Kafka was especially interested in the Spanish mystics. He was undoubtedly more familiar with the German mystics, at least with Meister Eckhart, whom he quotes at some length in a letter to Oskar Pollak. Letter of 9 November 1903, *LF*, 10–11.

7. We shall see later why and how Kafka excluded from his stories everything that might suggest the state in which they were written. In his work we find neither dreamers, nor visionaries, nor persons gifted with second sight; no mention is made of supernatural happenings or of those ineffable experiences for which the Romantics and tellers of fantastic tales had such a marked predilection. The reason for this is simple: in Kafka the man and the writer were strictly separate. The man experienced the happenings of his life; the writer observed them from a distance and noted his reactions; since each performed a well-defined function in his field, the observer never took the place of the observed, and the observed—the character in the story—had no way of participating in the writer's illumination at the time of creating him. Thus, by a stroke of humor the blackness of which there is no need to stress, the author of *The Judgment* "walked on water," whereas the hero of the story jumped in the river and sank to the bottom.

8. This refusal to make practical use of his works, a further indication of the extent to which writing and the sacred were associated in his mind, definitely placed Kafka in the current of traditional Jewish

thought, which held that a scholar should practice a manual trade so as not to draw profit from his teaching of the Torah. A real trade, like that of the rabbis or of Spinoza, would indeed have delighted Kafka; he dreamed of this as much as he detested his profession of jurist, which he regarded as artificial and parasitical, an occupation in which the living energies of the body and mind could not really employ themselves but could only be worn down. Hence his various attempts at gardening and carpentry, and later his plan to set himself up as a bookbinder in Palestine.

9. Contrary to what he may have led some people to believe, Kafka was by no means an idle pen-pusher, paid to dream and yawn. His position at the Arbeiter-Unfall-Versicherungs-Anstalt für das Königsreich Böhmen und Mähren—a seminationalized insurance company that specialized in work accidents—was one of responsibility. His employers regarded him as an excellent worker, and to judge by the technical articles published by Klaus Wagenbach (W, 279–337), he combined with his qualities as a jurist an astonishing knowledge of machinery (indispensable for judging the danger of certain machines). It was not ordinary boredom that made him hate his job, but the fact that it took a good part of his time and energy away from writing.

10. *D*, 21 August 1913, I: 229–300.

11. *F*, 28 August 1913, 439/313. The version that Kafka finally sent is very much attenuated. "I am nothing but my writing and neither can, nor wish to be, anything else" is replaced by "my whole being is directed toward writing; I have followed this direction unswervingly until my thirtieth year, and the moment I relinquish it I shall cease to live."

12. *D*, 19 February 1911, I: 45.

13. *D*, 3 October 1911, I: 77.

14. "Fragments" in *DF*, 312.

15. *F*, 2 September 1913, 442/315–16.

16. *F*, 22 August 1913, 433/308. The emphasis is Kafka's.

17. *F*, 2 September 1913, 442/315–16.

18. *D*, 19 January 1911, I: 43–44.

19. "A Country Doctor," *Stories*, 225. It is interesting to note the perfect concordance of Kafka's images, whether they occur in a pas-

sage in his *Diaries* or in an imaginative work. The little boy remembered in the *Diaries* knows "the cold space of our world," while the Country Doctor experiences "the cold of this unfortunate age"; he undertakes to search for the fire capable of warming reality, and the author of *The Judgment* has found this "great fire." Unfortunately, however, fire was more than a metaphor for Kafka; he really burned those of his manuscripts that he judged unworthy to endure, as though to punish them for not having purified themselves in the flame of true inspiration.

20. Obviously the story of the two brothers prefigures *Amerika*, the novel which, Kafka said, was keeping him "in the shameful lowlands of literature" and which for that reason remained unfinished. Karl Rossmann has no brother, but has been sent to America by his parents because of an "offense" recalling the one for which the "good brother" was punished in the first sketch.

21. "Description of a Struggle," *Stories*, 25.

22. *Stories*, 25.

23. *Stories*, 37.

24. *Stories*, 34. The Supplicant's histrionics are a transposition of Kafka's own adolescent grimacing and gesturing, which he much later regarded as the beginning of his "spiritual decline": "I deliberately cultivated a facial tic, for instance, or I would walk across the Graben with my arms crossed behind my head. A repulsively childish but successful game. (My writing began in the same way; only later on, unfortunately, its development came to a halt.)" *D*, 24 January 1922, II: 210.

25. See Letter to Brod, 28 August 1904, *LF*, 17. In the letter Kafka concludes the episode thus: "I was amazed at the steadfastness with which people endure life," which does not appear in the tale.

26. *Stories*, 35.

27. *Stories*, 35.

28. *Stories*, 35.

29. *Stories*, 35, 36.

30. *Stories*, 40.

31. *Stories*, 41.

32. The influence of Hofmannsthal (*Lord Chandos's Letter*) on Kafka's story has often been noted. That of German Expressionism is

no less evident, especially in the baroque technique of animation which, taking the metaphoric "as if" literally, makes objects live and move.

33. See the dialogue recorded by Janouch about an Expressionist painting by Kokoschka, entitled, significantly, *Prague*: " 'The big painting with the green dome of St. Nicholas in the middle?'—'Yes, that one.' Kafka bent his head to say: 'In that picture the roofs are flying away. The cupolas are umbrellas in the wind. The whole city is flying in all directions. Yet Prague still stands—despite all internal conflicts. That is the miracle.' " Jan, 84.

34. He kills him in any case, as we have seen in discussing the controversial question of anonymity and impersonality. Endowed with a rudimentary existence, transformed into an animal, an object, a ghost wandering in an infinity of space and time, Kafka's hero retains next to nothing of his earthly nature. He is dead to everything that constitutes his individuality; of the living creature he preserves only as much as is needed to represent the horror and absurdity of his incapacity for existence. This is what seems to situate him entirely in the realm of metaphysics, when actually the chief reason he is dead is that he is *written*, for in the very special perspective that was Kafka's after the revolution of *The Judgment*, writing accomplishes its true purpose only when it truly kills its subject. Kafka might well have drawn this eminently quixotic lesson from his own case; and as a matter of fact he did, as he shows by explicitly identifying himself with the Knight of the Mournful Countenance in one of his aphorisms: "One of the most important quixotic acts, more obtrusive than fighting with windmills, is suicide. The dead Don Quixote wants to kill the dead Don Quixote; in order to kill, however, he needs a place that is alive, and this he searches for with his sword, both ceaselessly and in vain. Engaged in this occupation the two dead men, inextricably interlocked and positively bounding with life, go somersaulting their way down the ages." "The Eight Octavo Notebooks," *DF*, 69–70.

35. "I can still take passing satisfaction in works like *A Country Doctor*, provided I can still write such things at all (most improbably). But happiness only if I can raise the world into the pure, the true, and the immutable." *D*, 25 September 1917, II: 187.

36. On his aversion to fur, see *O*, 21 December 1920, and *F*, Letter to Grete Bloch of 24 May 1914, 545/414. The erotic nature of the

engraving, which is barely suggested in the description, is sufficiently stressed by the place it occupies in Gregor's room. It is directly opposite his bed, and the moment he becomes aware of his metamorphosis his eyes fall on it. From this, one critic has inferred that *The Metamorphosis* is a sort of variation on Sacher-Masoch's *The Venus with the Fur Piece* (Madame M. Jutrin, personal communication). This is deriving quite a lot from a detail that is mentioned only once and has no real bearing on the story. Moreover, Samsa's masochism—or Kafka's, expressed through the mediation of all his self-destructive heroes—has nothing in common with the sexual perversion to which Sacher-Masoch gave his name. Samsa's and Kafka's was manifested not in clearly defined sexual practices but only in the moral sphere, where its effects are much more dangerous.

37. The main difficulty in understanding Kafka resides not, as has often been claimed, in his supposed symbolism, but in the fact that the narrator is really trying to find out what is high and what is low in a given fictitious society, because he cannot content himself with the preconceived ideas on which collective thinking bases its hierarchies. Thus the internal topography of Kafka's narratives is of necessity absolutely indeterminate. Most critics dispose of this obstacle by replacing the indeterminate with a topography in keeping with the traditional symbols: the high is the residence of noble, exalted things, the low is the vulgar and earthly. But in Kafka's perspective this is a grave mistake. We shall see later that *The Castle* has no other meaning, no other message, than a continual rectification of the conventions determining the place of the high and the low in our scale of values. K.—like every reader and ultimately like every cultivated man—spontaneously identifies the Castle with a higher authority and the Village with the most prosaic and deplorable aspect of earthly reality. For this he is severely punished, since the high and the low are mere illusions, due to habits of thought, to received ideas that no one bothers to examine and which it is precisely the narrator's task to reject. In the course of his journey, K. comes to realize how mistaken he has been and what superhuman efforts he would have to make to put the high and the low in their right places. In this respect he takes an enormous step toward the truth, despite his failure.

38. *D*, 8 October 1917, II: 188.

39. *Cas*, 29.

40. *D*, 15 December 1910, I: 33. This reference is to Paris, which Kafka had visited briefly that summer in the company of Brod.

41. *D*, May 1910, I: 12. This entry is not dated exactly, but the following entry is dated 17–18 May, the night of the comet, Kafka tells us.

42. *D*, 27 December 1910, I: 39.

43. *D*, 15 December 1910, I: 33.

44. *D*, 24 October 1911, I: 111.

45. Letter to Brod, June 1921, *LF*, 288.

46. Letter to Brod, early October 1917, *LF*, 152.

47. Letter to Brod, June 1921, *LF*, 289.

48. Letter to Brod, June 1921, *LF*, 288.

49. Letter to Brod, June 1921, *LF*, 288.

50. See S. Freud, "The Antithetical Meanings of Primal Words," *The Complete Psychological Works of Sigmund Freud* (New York, 1964), II: 155. If Kafka had had this marvelous little example of Freudian analysis, he would probably have subscribed to Freud's conclusions. But he did not need it to be aware of the basic ambiguity of primal words; as one who had been flayed by language, he was in the best possible position to know how treacherous the most familiar words can be and what advantage writing can derive from the extreme condensation they are capable of. He himself continually exploits this remarkable property by condensing in his own images a maximum of meanings associated not by a logical tie but by pure contiguity. To judge by a formula recorded by Janouch (Jan, 47), "Creative writing is a condensation . . ." (*Dichtung ist Verdichtung*), he was, on this point at least, in agreement with Freud, who regarded condensation as an essential mechanism in the elaboration of dreams and in all related creative activity.

51. *Schloss* says the same thing as Latin *castellanum*, the primary meaning of which, "enclosed area," is no longer conveyed by the French *château*. [But it is somewhat more by the English "castle," defined in Webster's dictionary as "a large fortified building or set of buildings . . . Originally the medieval castle was a simple tower or keep," whereas the French *"château,"* applying mostly to buildings from the sixteenth century on, no longer has this quality of the closed and forbidding. —TRANS.] This, paradoxically, is one of the

main difficulties in translating Kafka: the simplest words are those surest to be betrayed, because their equivalents have neither the same age, the same degree of condensation, nor the same ambiguity. Though there is no other word to translate the original, our "trial," confined as it is to the juridical sphere, cannot fully perform its function. The same is true of "gentlemen," which does not convey the idea of the tyranny of the archaic over the present implicit in *Herren.*

52. *Cas,* 96: ". . . 'I want no favors from the Castle, only my rights,' says K. to the mayor of the Village. To which the mayor, upset by such incongruous talk, replies by saying to his wife: 'Mizzi, my foot is beginning to throb again, we must renew the compress.' "

53. To judge by the letters from her that were published in *Letters to Felice,* Kafka's mother wrote a German strongly influenced on the one hand by business jargon and on the other by Yiddish (for example, the adjective *lieb* [dear] regularly attached to people's names). As for his father, whose first language was Czech, we know that his German was highly composite. Kafka mentions this in a letter to Ottla, though he adds in reference to a Czechism that has struck him, "As far as a half-German like me can judge" (*O,* 20 January 1919, 67). "A half-German"—that is how the creator of the densest, purest German, a German even now widely regarded as classical, defines himself in speaking to his own sister, or even to himself.

54. This factory, of which he was part owner, was one of the worst causes of friction, first between Kafka and his father and later between him and his fiancée, for Felice insisted on his taking an active part in the operation of the business, whereas he hated the factory and wanted nothing to do with it, regarding it as just one more threat to his literary work. Every time he went there, he came home in despair, and once, when he was obliged to take the place of his brother-in-law, who had been mobilized, he suffered such a collapse that in a letter to Brod he speaks of seriously contemplating suicide. See Letter to Brod, 7 October 1912, *LF,* 88–90.

55. See "Travel Diaries," *D,* II: 310. While on vacation in Germany, in a naturist colony in Thuringia, Kafka made friends with some little girls at a village dance. "Lack of a really common language. I ask if they have had dinner [*genachtmahlt*], complete lack of understanding; Dr. Sch. asks if they have had supper [*Abendbrot*], a glim-

mer of understanding . . . ; but they are able to answer only when the hairdresser asks if they have had their grub [gefuttert]."

56. "There is an enchantment accompanying his argument of the case," writes Kafka in an aphorism in which he identifies himself with Abraham. "The Eight Octavo Notebooks," *DF*, 103.

7 • Fiction and Reality

1. Untitled. The fragment, some two pages long, is written on a loose leaf. "Fragments," *DF*, 374–76.

2. Fragments, *DF*, 330. The fragment bears no title, but Kafka gives it a title in a diary entry, *D*, 31 December 1914, II: 106–07.

3. See Marthe Robert, *L'Ancien et le Nouveau* (Paris, 1963). This book, devoted to Cervantes's *Don Quixote* and *The Castle*, deals precisely with this quixotic imitation which serves to discredit the conventional relationship between books and life by showing both their common interests and the falsehood they foster by their complicity. In this context the personal history of the author is dealt with only in general terms and only insofar as it serves to confirm the analysis. Accordingly, Kafka's Judaism, though continually related to the sum of facts corroborating the analysis, cannot play the same preponderant role as in the present work.

4. See "Le dernier messager" in *L'Ancien et le Nouveau*, 175 ff.

5. Kafka often speaks of this "average cultivated European," a type of which he regards himself as a representative. When applying for work at the Great Nature Theater of Oklahoma, Karl Rossmann, who has neither trade nor papers, claims to be a student at an "average" European school. The ape turned man in *A Report to an Academy* explains his mutation by his desire to acquire the culture of an average European. And the Castle, too, is European, since his very name situates its master, Count West-West, at the peak of Western civilization, a detail that suffices to make the whole novel a sort of last attempt at assimilation.

6. Wagenbach has reconstituted the curriculum in force at the Prague gymnasium in Kafka's time. The amount of time devoted to the humanities was out of all proportion to that devoted to other subjects. One can hardly be surprised that this left a deep mark on Kafka's mind. He read the Greek authors in the original. See W, 36

ff., and Marthe Robert, *From Oedipus to Moses: Freud's Jewish Identity* (New York, 1976), pp. 53 ff.

7. "Prometheus," *DF*, 84.

8. Here Kafka is evidently exploiting the fact that the most important myths occur in different versions reflecting the trends of thought prevailing in the holy places or towns that propagated them. As long as the myth is alive, each local version claims to be the only authentic one, but may conceivably incorporate others. The task of collating these versions falls to the later scholiast; that, of course, is what Kafka was, but with the disadvantage that he no longer knew the legend, only its variants.

9. *DF*, 84.

10. This parallel has often been suggested, especially with the passage in the first book of *Capital* where the wooden table, the product of the worker's toil, suddenly takes on life and stands on its feet. In Kafka, it is true, the stroke of magic is provoked not by the outrageous transformation of human labor into a commodity, but by the inexplicable outrage of human suffering.

11. Especially *Poseidon* and *The Silence of the Sirens*. Kafka's *Poseidon* is still god of the ocean, but he has never seen this ocean; he spends all his time in his offices, bringing his infinite bookkeeping up to date. As for Kafka's Ulysses, he secures himself against the temptation of the Sirens by the traditional means, but it so happens that the Sirens refrain from singing on that day.

12. Max Brod, *Heidentum, Christentum, Judentum* (1920).

13. Letter to Max Brod, 7 August 1920, *LF*, 242.

14. In *The Castle* (begun in 1920), this Olympus where mankind finds so little to envy is represented by two clearly satirical figures: Momus, the Greek god of mockery, who constantly changes his appearance and attributes (many of the villagers believe that this Momus-Proteus is one with Klamm, the all-powerful "Gentleman" on whom K. is dependent not only in his love affairs but also in his efforts to obtain "official" employment); and Bürgel—from the verb *bürgen*, "to vouch for"—whose utterances, despite their crucial importance, so bore K. that he falls asleep while listening to Bürgel and sees him in a dream in the form of a totally naked Greek god. ("But there he is, that Greek god of yours! Get him out of that bed!") In the Surveyor's desperate, last-minute attempt at assimilation, he calls on

Greek culture for help—in vain, of course, because Momus and Bürgel are there only to deflect him a little more from his goal.

15. *D*, 19 September 1917, II: 183. *Prometheus* was written in 1918 (two years before the letter on paganism), at a time when his tuberculosis was driving Kafka more than ever to ponder the question of a causal connection between a very specific physical punishment and an unknown spiritual transgression.

16. "A Dream," *Stories*, 399.

17. *Tr*, "Unfinished Chapters," 249.

18. *Tr*, "Passages Deleted," 257–58.

19. It is not known exactly how much of Freud's work Kafka had read, but he speaks of it often enough to suggest that it was well known to him. At least once—in connection with *The Judgment*, as he notes on the day after the famous night—he mentions "thoughts about Freud of course" among those that had accompanied him in his work—proof that at that point he was clearly aware of a resemblance between his and Freud's ways of interpreting dreams. See *D*, 23 September 1912, I: 276.

20. An excellent example of this identification may be found in a letter to Brod, in which Kafka describes his amusement at watching his puppy chasing a mole. At first he is thinking only of the mole: "But suddenly when the dog again struck it a blow with its paw, it cried out: ks, ks, it cried. And then I felt—no, I didn't feel anything. I merely thought I did, because that day my head started to droop so badly that in the evening I noticed to my astonishment that my chin had grown into my chest." Letter to Brod, 28 August 1904, *LF*, 17. The mole image recurs several times in Kafka, for instance, in a letter to Milena and in the fragment entitled *The Village Schoolmaster*. The subject of this story—a pseudo-scientific report—is a giant mole which is never seen and which, one suspects, no one has ever seen.

21. Here Kafka raises a question that, since it has its source in the discovery of the unconscious, somewhat troubled the first psychoanalysts. To what extent is a dreamer responsible for the unconscious desires—murderous desires, for instance—that analysts brings to light? Is one responsible for dangerous but unknown desires, which only a special technique can bring to light? "Can that still be called responsibility?" says Kafka in "Paralipomena to the Aphorisms

Called 'He,' " *DF*, 378. Freud says yes. Kafka tried to convince himself of the contrary, but the conscious, not to mention the unconscious, guilt from which he suffered all his life proves that he did not succeed.

22. *Tr*, 6. Max Brod tells us that Kafka threw his friends into stitches by reading them the first chapter of *The Trial*. Today this seems quite incomprehensible, because a modern reader's first impression is one of horror at the arbitrary arrest. Kafka's friends seem to have been struck primarily by the comedy of the situation, and the appearance of a warder named Franz must have had something to do with it.

23. "It's a matter of your happiness, and I really have that at heart. . . ." The landlady adds, speaking of K.'s arrest: "It gives me the feeling of something very learned, forgive me if what I say is stupid, it gives me the feeling of something learned, which I don't understand, but which there is no need for me to understand." *Tr*, 19.

24. *Tr*, 221.

25. "Blumfeld, an Elderly Bachelor," *Stories*, 184–85.

26. *Stories*, 185.

27. Undoubtedly the dog is here a substitute for the woman Blumfeld did not wish to be mixed up with. The "serious, disgusting and contagious" disease he fears would then be an allusion to the venereal diseases of which Kafka, like many young men of his generation, had a partly justified, partly exaggerated fear.

28. *Cas*, 24.

29. *Cas*, 55. It is Frieda who draws K.'s attention to the two young men, saying, "Just look how those two are laughing."

30. For the novel this undoubtedly creates a difficulty, for though the assistants whom he likens to *snakes* are for him simply the embodiments of the lowest instinctual temptations, they are not particularly bad in the eyes of the village; they are good, native-born boys; Frieda played with them as a child and everyone is friendly to them. So on the one hand they belong to the realm of the psyche, which K. is trying to discipline, and on the other to the social sphere to which he is seeking access. But in addition to this dual role, which makes them doubly alien to him—as elements of his internal diaspora and as members of a community solidly united against him—they also point to the two cultures to which their names allude: Arthur, which

recalls the legendary King most typical of Western civilization, and Jeremiah the Jewish prophet, the latter of whom the Surveyor, bent on assimilation, does his best to get rid of. Kafka does not always succeed in making these three planes coincide in perfectly coherent images, and quite possibly it was his inability to surmount their incoherence that prevented him, at least in part, from finishing the novel.

31. *Cas*, 203.

32. The clinical precision with which Kafka described the *states* of Gregor Samsa has often been noted: if we disregard the metamorphosis itself, which is quite possible without disrupting the logic of the events, we observe that the story describes the characteristic development of a schizophrenic state with remarkable accuracy. Gregor, who at the start is still intellectually active, presents by degrees all the symptoms of autism, that is, of psychic death, the culmination of which is his real death.

33. "A Crossbreed," *Stories*, 426–27.

34. Of the twelve volumes constituting the complete German edition of Kafka, only five are devoted to works of the imagination, three to the novels, and two to the stories. Further, there is one volume containing a mixture of personal notes and literary fragments. The rest are taken up with the *Diaries* and correspondence.

35. "The Cares [Worries] of a Family Man," *Stories*, 427–28.

36. Understandably, the word has aroused the zeal of countless commentators, yet none of their theories is more solidly founded than those provided by Kafka in the story. To Brod's mind, Odradek suggests a whole series of Slavic words signifying "renegade," renegade in relation to sex (*rod*), renegade in relation to the divine decrees, *rada*. For Wilhelm Emrich the word derives from the Czech verb *odraditi*, which, coupled with the diminutive *-ek*, yields the meaning "the little dissuader," or, according to Heinz Politzer: "Leave me alone! Don't touch me! Don't follow me! Don't try to find out who I am!" According to G. Backenköhler the word breaks down into *rad*—order, regulation—a privative prefix *od-*, and a diminutive *-ek*, and might be translated as "little creature cut off from order." We see that the question cannot be decided on the basis of etymology. As Kafka foresaw, Odradek has kept all his secrets. For the above-cited references, see Hartmut Binder, *Kafka-Kommentar zu sämtlichen Erzählungen* (Munich, 1975), p. 232.

37. *The Worries of a Family Man* was written at the end of April 1917. Kafka had his first hemorrhage in August of the same year.

38. The letter about Karl Kraus from which this quote is taken dates from 1921, but obviously the ideas expressed in it were not improvised. Kafka had had them for a long time: witness, among many other examples, this Odradek straddling two languages, neither of which gave him a complete language and vehicle of existence.

39. These would be *Meditation* (1913); *The Stoker*, first chapter of *Amerika* (1913); *The Metamorphosis* (1916); and *The Judgment* (1916). In all, 249 pages in the German edition, even though the *Meditation* collection is printed in oversized type.

40. "Eleven Sons," *Stories*, 419 ff.

41. See Malcolm Pasley, "Drei literarische Mystifikationen Kafkas," in *Symp*, 26 ff., and "Die Sorge des Hausvaters," in *Akzente* 13 (1966): 303 ff. Mr. Pasley also recognizes that the story of Odradek is literary in content, but in his view it refers not to the peculiarities of Kafka's work in general, but to another story—*The Hunter Gracchus*—which he was writing at the same time and which, like so many others, remained unfinished. There are indeed striking affinities between the spool and the hunter: the hunter—in one variant—is usually standing on a staircase; he is unstable—he flies "like a butterfly"; he appears and disappears for no reason; and like Odradek he has the kind of immortality characteristic of things that cannot wear out because they have never been used. It seems to me, however, that though Gracchus accounts for Kafka's "worry"—because he is unable to finish it—it does not exhaust all the implications suggested by the spool; it is unfinished, but its variants are neither so numerous nor so complicated as to suggest an inextricable tangle of threads. Nor does the fact that Gracchus was born in the Black Forest and bears a Latin name suffice to explain the grave linguistic problem raised by Odradek; and it does not mention the star, which in my opinion is absolutely decisive.

42. "The Cares of a Family Man," *Stories*, 429.

Index